John Saward was formerly Chaplain of Lincoln College, Oxford. He has recently become a Roman Catholic.

PERFECT FOOLS

PERFECT FOOLS

Folly for Christ's Sake in Catholic
and Orthodox Spirituality

༄

JOHN SAWARD

Oxford New York Toronto Melbourne
OXFORD UNIVERSITY PRESS
1980

Oxford University Press, Walton Street, Oxford OX2 6DP

OXFORD LONDON GLASGOW
NEW YORK TORONTO MELBOURNE WELLINGTON
KUALA LUMPUR SINGAPORE HONG KONG TOKYO
DELHI BOMBAY CALCUTTA MADRAS KARACHI
NAIROBI DAR ES SALAAM CAPE TOWN

© *John Saward 1980*

British Library Cataloguing in Publication Data

Saward, John
Perfect fools.
1. Christian life _ History
2. Experience (Religion)
3. Catholics
I. Title
248'.2   BX2350.2   80-40164
ISBN 0-19-213230-X

Typeset by Oxprint Ltd, Oxford
Printed in Hong Kong by Bright Sun Printing Press Co. Ltd.

Contents

Let us contemplate the mirror of all the penitent saints: Jesus Christ in the Praetorium of Pilate and upon the cross. In the Praetorium he appears as an object of abomination before the whole people, in the ludicrous regalia of a mock king. . . . For since an Incarnate God was willing to appear in that state in which Pilate showed him to the people, what point would it have if not to say to men, through his example, what St Ignatius says in his Constitutions, *that 'out of gratitude and love for him, we should desire to be reckoned fools and glory in wearing his livery'.*

From the *Correspondence* of Jean-Joseph Surin

Preface

'If you want to know the truth', so runs the modern Greek proverb, 'ask a child or a fool.' Jesus says that the Father has hidden the mysteries of the Kingdom from the wise and revealed them to babes (Matt. 11: 25), and St Paul, the steward of those mysteries, the guardian of apostolic truth, rejoices to be known as a fool for Christ's sake (1 Cor. 4: 10).

This is the story of those who have taken the Lord and his apostle at their word and have received from God the rare and terrible charism of holy folly. In what follows we shall encounter a wide variety of fools for Christ's sake: the wild men of Byzantium, Russia, and Ireland, whose apparently outrageous and provocative behaviour masks a deeper sanctity; the 'merry men' of the Middle Ages, God's jongleurs, who proclaim the 'Gospel of Good Humour'; and, finally, those who have gone the darker and more perilous way of being written off by the world as mad and contemptible but who 'rejoice and are glad' (Matt. 5: 11f).

It will not be argued that all the saints of God conform to one or other of these categories, nor shall we claim that folly for Christ's sake is itself a homogeneous phenomenon. The Communion of Saints is a mystery of unity-in-diversity, not of regimented uniformity: if there is 'one glory of the sun, and another glory of the moon, and another glory of the stars' (1 Cor. 15: 41) within the created order, how much more so in the firmament of the new creation. The purpose of this book is to isolate and examine one strand in the tapestry of sainthood, a vocation which at times has been the quick of the Church but, at least in the West, has seldom been recognized. Only in the Christian East does the fool for Christ's sake take his place in the martyrology alongside the martyr, doctor, and virgin. And yet the tradition has flourished in the West—in most countries and regions, in many religious orders, and in the lives of ordinary Christian men and women. Moreover, even at times when individual witnesses to the tradition have been absent, the Pauline 'folly texts' have been of constant inspiration.

Two aspects of the book's shape and definition must be explained

at the outset. First, I shall be concerned in what follows only with
the fools for Christ's sake in the Western Catholic and Eastern
Orthodox traditions, and not with those in the Protestant
denominations. Such demarcation is practical rather than
polemical. There are many instances of Protestant folly for Christ's
sake. It can be seen in the radical and spiritual wings of the Reformation in the sixteenth century, in the 'Methodism' (in the full
pejorative, eighteenth-century sense of the term) of the early
followers of Wesley, and in many revivalist groups of the present
day, indeed in all the enthusiastic and hectic religion on the fringe,
and sometimes at the centre, of the Reformed communions. It
would require another book, beyond the competence of the present
author, to do justice to this rich tradition. However, there is also a
theological reason for my exclusive concern with Catholicism and
Orthodoxy. This is a book about charism and institution, about the
relationship between the gifts of the Spirit in their astonishing
diversity and the fixed and given hierarchical structure of the
Church. Folly for Christ's sake raises this question in a particularly
acute and interesting way, because here is the development of an
apparently wild and unrestrained spirituality *firmly and loyally*
within the limits of what to some seem monolithic, authoritarian,
ecclesiastical organizations. This explains the exclusion not only of
the Protestants but also of such figures as Pascal or Madame Guyon,
who were fervently concerned with the folly of the cross but were
associated with movements (Port Royal and Quietism) at odds with
Catholic orthodoxy.

A second aspect of the book's structure that should be explained
is what may seem a disproportionate number of chapters devoted to
a detailed examination of holy folly in a single school of spirituality
in seventeenth-century France. Such imbalance is due simply to the
enormous richness and vitality of French religious thought at that
time. One indication of this is to be found in the most recent revision
of the Roman Calendar. Of the saints commemorated there, seventeen are from the seventeenth century, a number exceeded only by
the fourth century. Similarly, Henri Bremond (1865–1933), in his
voluminous survey of French religion 'from the end of the wars of
religion to our own day', concentrates almost entirely on the seventeenth century. It is truly *le grand siècle,* and folly for Christ's sake
has an important part to play in it.

In telling the story of the holy fools of West and East, my

intention is not to indulge in nostalgia for a quaint and forgotten style of piety but to present the challenge of a living tradition to Christians of the present day. On every side, there are pleas for making the gospel 'relevant' to the world, of adapting the faith to the mind of Modern Man. Here, in contrast, is a tradition that has kept alive Johannine and Pauline non-conformity to 'the world', to 'this present age', and rejects any capitulation to contemporary sensibility. Yet it has not canonized unreason or sullenly ignored secular wisdom; as we shall see, many of our tradition's leading exponents have taught the reasonableness and intellectual integrity of Christianity. The fools protest against any reduction or diminution of the riches of Christ, any attempt to deprive the gospel of its cutting-edge by conforming it to the wisdom of the world. The holy fools proclaim Christian orthodoxy as a creed of insurrection against the oppressive 'mind that is set on the flesh' (Rom. 8: 7). Above all, they witness to the Incarnation, to the foolishness of God incarnate, who, in the Praetorium of Pilate, was stripped naked, clothed in mocking scarlet, and exposed to the cruel laughter of the worldly wise. The fools for Christ's sake are men made mad and merry by their faith in a God 'silly in the crib' and 'foolish on the cross', a God whose sage folly alone can save us from the raving lunacy of the princes of this age. To the fools' prayers I commend myself and this book.

*

I must express my gratitude to the many institutions and individuals who have assisted me in my research: to the Rector and Fellows of Lincoln College for electing me to a research fellowship and for five happy years in their society; to the Rhys Trustees for financial assistance; to Père Brunet at Chantilly and his fellow Jesuit librarians at Heythrop College, London, and Campion Hall, Oxford; to the religious communities with whom I have stayed during my travels—the Jesuits at Les Fontaines, Chantilly, the Dominican Fathers of the Couvent de l'Annonciation, Paris, the Benedictines at Landévennec (especially Abbot Jean de la Croix and An Tad Gregor), the Passionists of Mount Argus, Dublin (especially Father Declan and Father Patrick Rogers), and the Dominicans of Galway; and to the friends and colleagues whose advice, comments and encouragement have been invaluable:

Canon Donald Allchin, Sister Benedicta SLG, Dr Sebastian Brock, Professor James Carney, Fr Hilary Costello OCSO, Professor Sir Idris Foster, Mr Azhar Kalim of Blackwell's (for suggesting the title), Dr Alban Krailsheimer, Dom Jean Leclercq, Fr Andrew Louth, Professor Gearóid MacEoin (especially for allowing me to make use of his translation of *Imthechta na nÓinmhideadh*), Professor Tomás Ó Broin, Dr Geoffrey Rowell, Fr Simon Tugwell OP, Archimandrite Kallistos Ware, Mr Donald Whitton and Dr Rowan Williams. Finally, I must thank the Community of the Sisters of the Love of God and the staff of the University Press for their unfailing charity and patience in helping me to prepare for publication what must sometimes have seemed not so much a study of folly as an active demonstration of it.

1 April 1979   *Lincoln College, Oxford*

1

Folly to Greeks

The holy fool is a commonly encountered figure in the folklore of many cultures and religions.[1] In Jewish-Christian tradition perhaps the earliest example of a religious form of folly is the 'symbolic action' of the prophet, the strange, sometimes quite outrageous form of behaviour imposed upon him by the Lord to shock the people into perceiving the truth of their situation.[2] Isaiah walks naked and barefoot for three years as a warning to the people against placing their trust in an alliance with Egypt, for 'the king of Assyria shall lead away the Egyptians captive and the Ethiopians exiles, both the young and the old, naked and barefoot' (Isa. 20: 2ff). Ezekiel is told to eat excrement, for 'thus shall the people of Israel eat their bread unclean, among the nations whither I will drive them' (Ezek. 4: 12ff). Even when unaccompanied by such eccentric behaviour, the prophets' message was invariably greeted with derision and scorn by the people; madness, as we shall see, is a common charge against those who tell the disturbing truth. As Hosea says:

> The days of punishment have come,
>   the days of recompense have
>   come;
>   Israel shall know it.
> The prophet is a fool,
>   the man of the spirit is mad,
> because of your great iniquity
>   and great hatred (9: 7).

In a world gone mad the guardian of truth is invariably dismissed as a raving lunatic. That is the lot of every prophet. Sometimes, as in Isaiah's case, he is called to go one step further and deliberately act in a foolish way, so that no one is left uncertain about his message. Within modern Judaism the prophetic 'madman' has developed into the 'fool of God', very much like the fool for Christ's sake. 'He is', writes Martin Buber, 'a human being who, because of his undamaged direct relationship with God, has quitted the rules and regulations of the social order, though he continues to participate in the life of his fellow men.'[3]

St Paul, the Fool for Christ's Sake

The specifically Christian tradition of the holy fool begins with the teaching and experience of the apostle Paul (1 Cor. 4: 10).[4] He first used the phrase 'fool for Christ's sake', and constantly alluded to the theme of holy folly, in the midst of his turbulent relationship with the Christians at Corinth.

The Corinthian church seems to have been riddled with religious élitism. Rival factions were loudly asserting their spiritual superiority, their excellence in wisdom, discernment and knowledge. In reply Paul offered himself as a living parable to demonstrate the absurdity of their pride, for God had worked miracles through the weakness and folly of the apostle; Paul had come to Corinth in weakness, fear and trembling, without lofty words or wisdom (2: 1ff). He speaks as a fool and boasts only of the things that show his weakness (2 Cor. 11: 30). In the moving climax to the correspondence he reports the Lord's words to him: 'My grace is sufficient for you, for my power is made perfect in weakness' (2 Cor. 12: 9). Moreover, he shows that such a reversal of human expectations is only an extension of the paradox of the Incarnation, whereby Christ, being rich, for our sakes became poor (2 Cor. 8: 9); being divine, he assumed the condition of a slave (Phil. 2: 7). God's grace subverts the unholy alliance in which the world, the flesh, and the devil conspire to fortify the ego of fallen man. God leaves no room for human pride—except in all that humbles him and brings him to acknowledge his dependence upon God: his infirmity and folly in the eyes of the world. According to St John Chrysostom, this capacity for sharing the sufferings of others, this vulnerability and folly, are what constitute the true greatness of the apostle:

> Paul himself we admire on this account, not for the dead he raised, nor for the lepers he cleansed, but because he said, 'If anyone is weak, do I not share their weakness? If anyone is made to stumble, does my heart not blaze with indignation?' . . . He nowhere boasts of his own achievements where it is not relevant; but if he is forced to, he calls himself a fool. If he ever boasts, it is of weaknesses, wrongs, of greatly sympathizing with those who are injured.[5]

Folly is a relative concept. It only has meaning in distinction from some kind of wisdom. This is an obvious but far from trivial truth, for the New Testament never beatifies wisdom or folly *in general*, but only wisdom or folly under a certain description. We can, therefore, only understand what St Paul means by folly for Christ's sake by examining a pair of oppositions: the wisdom of God and the wisdom of the age; the foolish but humble apostle and the wise but proud Corinthians.

The only true wisdom is divine wisdom, 'Christ the power of God and the wisdom of God' (1 Cor. 1: 24). But Christ-wisdom is Christ-crucified and thus a hidden, secret wisdom (2: 7).[6] When judged by the 'debater of this age' and the 'wisdom of the world' (1: 20), the gospel of Christ crucified looks foolish. But what is the 'wisdom of the world'? It is a fleshly wisdom, the wisdom of *sarx* (2 Cor. 1: 12), a man's trust in his knowledge and experience, 'taking his stand on visions, puffed up without reason by his sensuous mind' (Col. 2: 18).[7] It is a knowledge that 'puffs up' a man in pride and pretentiousness (1 Cor. 8: 1). It is self-obsession and self-sufficiency, a 'glorying in the flesh' (Gal. 6: 13; Phil. 3: 3), a preoccupation with pedigree, with racial or religious superiority. Worldly wisdom is *idolatry,* the substitution of human cleverness for faith, 'relying on ourselves' rather than on 'the God who raises the dead' (2 Cor. 1: 9).

The gospel message of life through self-oblation and sacrificial death cuts clean through the assumptions of the present age. The world lives by the law of the flesh and strives wherever possible to consolidate self. The world believes that power and glory come through calculating self-preservation. The world can make no sense of the word of the cross, of Christ-wisdom-crucified, and so regards it as 'insanity' (*mōria,* 1 Cor. 1: 18ff). The apostle always gives glory to God, so that men might not have their breath taken away by merely human accomplishment but rather put their faith in the power of God (1 Cor. 2: 5).

Paul appeals to the honesty of the Corinthians. It is not only the content of the gospel (the cross) and the manner of its preaching that involve weakness; those to whom it is preached are weak too. God chooses the most unlikely candidates to fulfil his purposes.

For consider your call, brethren; not many of you were wise according to worldly standards, not many were powerful, not many were of noble birth;

but God chose what is foolish in the world to shame the wise, God chose
what is weak in the world to shame the strong, God chose what is low and
despised in the world, even things that are not ['mere nobodies'], to bring to
nothing things that are, so that no human being might boast in the presence
of God (1 Cor. 1: 26ff).

Paul is adamant that this folly is a relative folly—a folly 'in the
world', 'according to worldly standards'. It is the powers that be
('things that are', v. 28b), the rulers of this age, the secular establishment, who write off Christ's gospel as folly. But Paul insists that
the foolishness of God 'is wiser than men, and the weakness of God
is stronger than men' (v. 25); Christ is 'our wisdom, our righteousness and sanctification and redemption' (v. 30).

If the wisdom of the world is folly to God, and God's own
foolishness is the only true wisdom, it follows that the worldly wise,
to become *truly* wise, must become foolish and renounce their
worldly wisdom (3: 18). To attain to true wisdom a man must
abandon the wisdom of the *status quo*, must 'go out' of the mind set
on the flesh (Rom. 8: 7) and have the mind of Christ (1 Cor. 2: 16),
who emptied himself and became obedient unto death, even death
on the cross (Phil. 2: 5ff).

This, then, is the first opposition: the wisdom of God *versus* the
wisdom of the world. The second follows from it. If there is a
necessary distinction between the self-centred wisdom of the world
and the cross-centred wisdom of God, there must also be an opposition among Christians between those seduced by the world into
adjusting the gospel to worldly wisdom, and those who trust in
God's wisdom alone. This is the issue between the apostle and the
Corinthian church. Paul uses biting sarcasm in his effort to humble
the Corinthinans and make them give up the vanity that has
deformed their Christian character:

For it seems to me God has made us apostles the most abject of mankind.
We are like men condemned to death in the arena, a spectacle to the whole
universe—angels as well as men. *We are fools for Christ's sake, while you are
such sensible Christians.* We are weak; you are so powerful. We are in
disgrace; you are honoured. To this day we go hungry and thirsty and in
rags; we are roughly handled; we wander from place to place; we wear
ourselves out working with our own hands. They curse us, and we bless;
they persecute us, and we submit to it; they slander us, and we humbly make
our appeal. We are treated as the scum of the earth, the dregs of humanity,
to this very day (1 Cor. 4: 9ff: NEB).

This is not empty rhetoric. Paul was constantly accused of being mad. His preaching of the resurrection was mocked by the wise men of Athens (Acts 17: 32), and when he made his stirring testimony before King Agrippa, Festus exclaimed 'with a loud voice, "Paul, you are mad; your great learning is turning you mad"' (Acts 26: 24). The word Paul uses to speak of himself as a fool for Christ's sake (*mōros*) is a common one in classical Greek. The verb *mōrainō* can be used of foods becoming insipid or losing their taste, and indeed is so used of salt by Jesus in his parables (e.g. Matt. 5: 13). It can be used, in a physiological context, of the slackness and fatigue of nerves.[8] It is most commonly used, however, with a psychological meaning, to denote not mere eccentricity but that real insanity in which the mind is darkened and the understanding confused. Sophocles uses the word to describe the madness of Antigone. The tragedian, like the apostle, also acknowledges the relativity of insanity and madness; he perceives that what looks like folly to one may be true wisdom to another.

ANT: And if my present deeds are foolish in thy sight, it may be that a foolish judge arraigns my folly.[9]

Mōros does not occur very commonly in the Septuagint, where the more usual word is *aphrōn*. When it does, it is clearly insulting, as for example when Jeremiah says that the house of Jacob is 'foolish and senseless' (LXX Jer. 5: 21). At LXX Isa. 44: 25, there is a usage closely paralleling Paul's. God's intervention in history, when he makes Cyrus his anointed instrument for the deliverance of his people, goes quite contrary to all human expectation, is in defiance of the wisdom of the world, and yet corresponds to the truth of God as the only redeemer and creator. In St Matthew's Gospel the word *mōros* occurs when Jesus is warning against anger.

You have heard that it was said to the men of old, 'You shall not kill; and whoever kills shall be liable to judgement.' But I say to you that every one who is angry with his brother shall be liable to judgement; whoever insults his brother shall be liable to the council, and whoever says, 'You fool!' shall be liable to the hell of fire (Matt. 5: 21ff).

To call a man *mōros* is to place oneself among the 'righteous persons who need no repentance' (Luke 15: 7), who despise others while fearing contempt themselves. But the vocation of the Christian is to be mocked rather than to mock; to be killed rather than to kill. Jesus

warns his disciples that they will be hated by the world (John
15: 18f); they will be delivered up to councils, flogged in syn-
agogues, dragged before governors and kings (Matt. 10: 17f); in
fact, the time is coming when men will regard it as their religious
duty to kill them (John 16: 2). The world does this out of ignorance
because it has known neither the Father nor the Son (cf. John 16: 3).
Jesus tells his followers that their rejection will mean not only
hatred but also contempt, scorn, and reviling: 'Blessed are you
when men revile you and persecute you and utter all kinds of evil
against you falsely on my account' (Matt. 5: 11). Jesus and his
disciples endure not only physical torment but also verbal assault
and mockery, especially the accusation of madness. Jesus was
thought to be 'beside himself' (Mark 3: 21), 'possessed by
Beelzebul' (v. 22); his words about the ruler of the synagogue's
daughter are met with laughter (Mark 5: 40). In his Passion Our
Lord is subjected to mockery and derision. In the Praetorium,
'before the whole battalion', the soldiers stripped him, put a scarlet
robe on him, placed a crown of thorns on his head and a reed in his
hand, and 'mocked him' (Matt. 27: 29; Mark 15: 20). On the cross
he is derided by the people (Matt 27: 39; Mark 15: 29); scoffed at
(Luke 23: 35) and mocked (Mark 15: 31) by the religious authorities,
and here the joke is that the one who saved others will not save
himself.

As we have seen in Paul's teaching, the Gospels show that what
the world finds most absurd and ridiculous is self-oblation, the
renunciation of self-protection. The crucified God-Man is made
game of, a subject for satire (*illuserunt ei*, Vulgate Mark 15: 20). It is
precisely this buffeting of the Lord which was to inspire many saints,
especially those of the Society of Jesus, as we shall see later, to wear
'the purple livery' of Christ's humilation. As the world's rulers
perceive the inevitability of their defeat by Christ, in their anger
they deride the true wisdom of God as sheer nonsense. Obsessed by
the desire for immediate self-gratification ('the lust of the flesh and
the lust of the eyes and the pride of life' (1 John 2: 16)), they see the
Incarnation as dangerous folly and do all they can to mock it. A God
who empties himself and becomes a slave, who endures mockery
and humiliating death, and yet is raised from the dead in glory,
exposes the lie, the real madness, of living only for self; God's
ecstasy-in-Incarnation, his leaping down from heaven, demonstrates once and for all that self-preservation leads to death, while

self-oblation leads to eternal life. The gospel of 'an Incarnate God, a God put to death',[10] disrupts and subverts the worldly mind, shows it up for the madness it is.

Holy Infancy

There is one other gospel text of importance for the tradition of holy folly:

At that time Jesus declared, 'I thank thee, Father, Lord of heaven and earth, that thou hast hidden these things from the wise and understanding and revealed them to babes; yea, Father, for such was thy gracious will. All things have been delivered to me by the Father, and no one knows the Son except the Father, and no one knows the Father except the Son and any one to whom the Son chooses to reveal him.' (Matt. 11: 25ff; Luke 10: 21f).

This passage is of interest for several reasons. First, what Our Lord says here of his relation with the Father closely resembles his teaching in the Fourth Gospel, has no real parallel anywhere else in the Synoptics, and has been called 'a meteor from the Johannine heaven'. Secondly, it contrasts the disciples ('the babes') with the wise and understanding: the simple uneducated fishermen with the learned scribal and pharisaic establishment. This contrast is important for what will be said later of the 'holy idiot', the one unlettered but enlightened. It also contains a criticism of 'worldly wisdom' and implies that the wisdom of wise men and Pharisees blinds them from seeing the truth of God's mysteries. Thirdly, and most importantly, there is the motif of childlikeness. Joachim Jeremias has shown that in the teaching of Jesus 'being a child is *the* characteristic of (God's) kingly rule. . . . The gift of being a child stamps the whole life of Jesus' disciples.'[11] The firm and insistent teaching in the Synoptic Gospels that becoming like a child is *essential* to entry to the kingdom (Matt. 18: 3f; cf. Mark 10: 15; Luke 18: 17), that the mysteries of the kingdom are revealed *only* to babies, complements Jesus' teaching in St John's Gospel that no one can see the kingdom of God unless born anew (John 3: 3): rebirth, becoming a baby, enables the soul to *see*; the adult, unregenerate mind of the worldly wise is blinded and darkened. While St John's Gospel does not contain any parallel to the Synoptic texts about childlikeness, the theme expresses itself in other, more indirect, ways. The word *teknon* or its diminutive, *teknion* ('little child'), are used by Jesus to address the disciples (John 13: 3), and John addresses those to whom he writes his first letter as 'my little children' (*teknia mou*, 1 John 2: 1). The first epistle of St John trenchantly expresses the idea that we are the children of God: 'See what love the Father has given us, that we should be called the children of God; and so we are. . . . Beloved, we are God's children now' (1 John 3: 1f). Paul, of course, develops the theme of our adoptive sonship, our status as God's children, at great length (especially Rom. 8: 16f) and refers to the Galatian Christians as 'my little children' (Gal. 4: 19).

The disciples of Jesus know that it is God's will that none of the little ones should be lost (Matt. 18: 10–14). Consequently, being a child means an uninhibited trust and confidence in God the Father who knows what his children need (Matt. 6: 8); God cares for and protects his little ones and will ensure their safety. 'It is to the smallest that God extends his special protection; in the heavenly world built up in circles round God's throne, the guardian angels of the *mikroi* stand in the innermost circle, immediately before God (Matt. 18: 10)'.[12]

It is above all trust in the Father in the face of suffering and death, the absence of panic and of the desire for self-preservation, which characterizes the little one, the child of God. God has a hand in the death of sparrows, he cares even about them, and the little ones are more than sparrows. Even the hairs on the disciples' heads are counted; God's concern for his children includes the tiniest detail. There is no need to fear (Matt. 10: 29ff).

It has already been mentioned that the text containing the teaching about childlikeness also presents a rich Christology (Matt. 11: 27ff). These two themes are not unconnected. Jesus does not just teach the disciples trust and confidence in the Father and encourage them to remember that they are God's children. Their status as God's children by grace is dependent on their relation to Jesus, who is child of God by nature. Jesus is the Son from whom all childhood in heaven and earth is named. We become God's children, his sons, through incorporation into Christ; we are sons-in-the-Son. Childlikeness is more than just one element among many in Our Lord's teaching; it is a necessary corollary of orthodox belief about his person. Thus the name for God which Jesus encourages his disciples to use when they pray is the intimate, bold and familiar name he himself uses: *abba*, Father.[13] We only 'dare' to call

God our *abba* because Jesus is the Son of his heavenly *abba* and calls us to be sons and children in himself. The Aramaic word *abba* is the children's word for their father and for that reason was never used by the Jews of Jesus' day as a way of addressing God. God was thought of as, but never called, *abba*. And yet we know that this name was used by Jesus (Mark 14: 36), chosen by him as the definitive name for God in prayer (Luke 11: 2), and used by the early Church (Gal. 4: 6; Rom. 8: 15). This radically original religious idea is introduced so spontaneously and unselfconsciously by Jesus that we must conclude that it implies his ontological equality with the Father: he does not seek to justify his use of the term; he just *is* the *abba's* Son. Even at a moment of crisis and anguish, in the agony in the garden, he speaks to the Father as *abba*. He is the only-begotten Son of God, of one substance with the Father.

Christology and childlikeness are connected at an even deeper level. It is not only that *abba* in its childlike boldness proves Our Lord's divinity; what is also striking is that our Divine Lord should have incorporated, freely and without embarrassment, the experience of his childhood, a word from hearth and home, in his teaching and adult ministry. '*Abba* is the term used by someone who has a consciousness like that of other children, but with this difference, that in this case the father is not a human father, but is God.'[14]

How is this excursus into the mingled themes of childlikeness and Christology relevant to the subject of this book? Man fell when he disobeyed God and ate the fruit of the tree of the knowledge of good and evil. For a number of early Fathers, this attempt to be 'wise and prudent' was an act of immodest maturity on the part of Adam, who, according to this school, was created a *child*. Original sin, for these Fathers, is precocity, growing up too quickly. As Theophilus of Antioch, the apologist of the late second century, puts it:

> The tree of knowledge was good and its fruit was good. For the tree did not contain death, as some suppose; this was the result of disobedience. For there was nothing in the fruit but knowledge, and knowledge is good if it is used properly. In his actual age, Adam was as old as an infant; therefore he was not yet able to acquire knowledge properly. For at the present time when a child is born it cannot eat bread at once, but first it is fed with milk and then, with increasing age, it comes to solid food. So it would have been with Adam. Therefore God was not jealous, as some suppose, in ordering him not to eat of knowledge. Furthermore, he wanted to test him, to see

whether he would be obedient to his command. At the same time he wanted the man to remain simple and sincere for a longer time, remaining in infancy. For this is a holy duty not only before God but before men, to obey one's parents in simplicity and without malice. And if children must obey their parents, how much more must they obey the God and Father of the universe. Furthermore, it is shameful for infant children to have thoughts beyond their years; for as one grows in age in an orderly fashion, so one grows in an ability to think. . . . It was not that the tree of knowledge contained anything evil, but that through disobedience man acquired pain, suffering, and sorrow, and finally fell victim to death.[15]

A similar doctrine was maintained by St Irenaeus (*c*.130–*c*.200), who depicted man's redemption and restoration as 'beginning all over again', recapitulation; Christ, the Second Adam, recapitulated the whole experience of the old Adam, from infancy to manhood, suffering and death, so that, being incorporated into him, we may be reborn into a new, spiritual infancy and grow into 'the measure of the stature of the fulness of Christ' (Eph. 4: 13).[16] According to a later Father, this is the significance of Our Lord's infancy: 'in his own he sanctifies the infancy of all little ones and shows that every age is capable of the divine mystery'.[17] Jesus, the divine and perfect child, reveals not simply the childhood we have lost but a new childhood in him, a childhood which is a necessary condition of Christian progress and growth.

The relevance of this to holy folly is clear. The defining mark of the spiritual man, the man regenerate and conformed to Christ, is not worldly wisdom or prudence, but spiritual infancy, the appearance in him of that gift of childhood and sonship bestowed by God in baptism. Christian perfection demands that we *unlearn* the self-important, prematurely adult mind of the flesh and follow the Little Way. Holy folly is but one manifestation of our baptismal non-conformity to the grown-up world in all its 'cleverness'. Holy folly is always, then, childlike and Christocentric, the revelation of that trusting sonship and childhood we have been given in and by Christ, the repudiation of the world's vainglorious knowledge and precocious wisdom.

The holy fools for Christ's sake imitate and proclaim the God-child wiser than the Magi, the boy in the temple more learned than greybeards and doctors, divine wisdom at the pillar mocked and laughed at by men. Folly for Christ's sake as a specific charism in the Church dramatizes the vocation of us all: to be conformed to the

Incarnate Son of God, to renounce self-will and false wisdom, to accept the folly of infancy and the cross, to be God's trusting little ones and so shame the worldly wise.

2

Folly in the Orthodox East

In the Holy Orthodox Churches of the East 'fool for Christ's sake' is a hagiographical category like 'martyr', 'virgin' or 'confessor'. The *salos* or *yurodivy* (the Greek and Russian technical terms for 'holy fool') is regarded as one called by God to obey the words of the apostle: 'if any one among you thinks that he is wise in this age, let him become a fool that he may become wise' (1 Cor. 3: 18). Folly for Christ's sake is an integral part of Orthodox spirituality, consciously celebrated and revered, and the fools are among the most beloved saints of the East. In recognizing holy folly as a true form of sanctity, for whose assessment tradition offers precise criteria, Eastern Orthodoxy provides a theological schema for our study of this phenomenon in the West. In this chapter we shall tell the story of the holy fools of the East, from their first appearance in the deserts of Egypt and Syria to their spiritual invasion of Holy Russia.

Folly and Monasticism

Holy folly is nearly always in close historical relation to monasticism; indeed, it might almost be said that the history of folly for Christ's sake is but the history of monasticism under a certain description. Not all monks have been holy fools, nor have all the fools been monks, but the two forms of following Christ have a common inspiration and may rightly be studied together.

Holy folly first emerges in the East among the founding fathers of Christian monasticism, as a single, brilliant ray of the 'eastern light' which dawned in the early fourth century with Antony, Pachomius and the rest. The literature of early monasticism furnishes us with examples of two distinct, though closely related, kinds of 'holy unwisdom', namely, *holy idiocy* and *folly for Christ's sake*. Both are commended as true expressions of the monastic spirit. The term *idiōtēs* in Greek denotes a private man, with no particular public function or skill. Similarly, the Latin *idiota* means a rustic, one with no science or discipline, an illiterate. The New Testament describes the apostles Peter and John as 'uneducated, common men' (Acts

4: 13), who nonetheless could preach the gospel with lucidity and fervour. In their effort to realize a truly apostolic life in the desert, the fathers of monasticism became acutely aware of the charisms of the simple and uneducated and commend to us the wisdom of the 'idiotic' desert father, who, by the grace of God, humbles the wise and prudent. St Athanasius (c.296–373), in his *Life of St Antony* (251–356), the 'perfect pattern of anchoretic life', gives us an early example of this motif. Antony, he tells us, 'was most prudent; the wonder was that although he was unlettered, he was an astute and wise man'. He was visited on one occasion by two Greek philosophers and conducted the following interview.

'Why, O philosophers, are you bothering to come to a foolish man?' And when they said that he was not a foolish man but in fact very prudent, he said to them, 'If you come to a foolish man, then you're wasting your time. If you think I am prudent, be like me, for we ought to imitate what is good. If I had come to you I would have imitated you; but if you come to me, be like me, for I am a Christian'. But they departed in awe, for they saw that even demons feared Antony.[1]

The sayings of the Desert Fathers often allude to the need for the monk, even if well-educated, to be simple and ignorant of the world's wisdom. John Cassian (c.360–435), whose writings preserve monastic teaching he had received as a monk in Palestine and Egypt, records in his *Conferences* a saying of Abba Moses which commends the ascription of the title *idiota* to monks: 'It is undoubtedly this same faith which has made you despise the love of your parents, the soil of your native land, the delights of the world, and cross so many countries, to seek out the company of people like us, rustic and ignorant men [*rusticos et idiotas*], lost on the desolate horizons of this desert.'[2]

The Greek Alphabetical Collection of the *Apophthegmata Patrum*, which in its present form dates from the end of the sixth century but contains material from the middle and late fourth century, includes many sayings on the subject. Holy idiocy is specially beloved of Abba Arsenius (b. 360), who, before withdrawing into the desert, had received an impeccable education in Rome and served as tutor to the princes Arcadius and Honorius.

One day Abba Arsenius consulted an old Egyptian monk about his own thoughts. Someone noticed this and said to him, 'Abba Arsenius, how is it that you, with such a good Latin and Greek education, ask this peasant

about your thoughts?' He replied, 'I have indeed been taught Latin and
Greek, but I do not know even the alphabet of this peasant'.[3]

Much later on, in the seventeenth century, Armand de Rancé, the
Cistercian reformer of La Trappe, saw the significance of this motif
in the literature of the desert and its permanent relevance for
monastic renewal.[4]

The holy idiot is either an uneducated rustic endowed with great
spiritual gifts, or an educated monk who transcends his learning in
order to arrive at evangelical and divine wisdom. There is, however,
nothing necessarily foolish about his behaviour. The fool for
Christ's sake, by contrast, is one who is recognized not only by the
world but also by his fellow Christians as foolish—a foolishness
which conceals his spirituality, or rather which is a medium for the
foolishness of God, wiser than men. Cassian, in drawing up his
Institutes for cenobitic life, enjoined on every monk the prescrip-
tion, 'be a fool to be wise':

> Become a fool in this world, according to the commandment of the
> Apostle, in order to be wise. Do not criticise or discuss what you are
> commanded. Always show obedience with all simplicity and faith. Regard
> as holy, beneficial and wise only what the law of God and your spiritual
> father's direction thus designate. Once established in these practices, you
> will be able to remain permanently under this discipline, and no temptation
> or device of the enemy will be able to draw you from the monastery.[5]

The giving up of self-will, which is at the heart of monastic and
Christian obedience, is indeed 'folly to the Greeks', because it
strikes at the black heart of the world's sin—egoism and pride. To
such folly all monks are called. Some monks, however, are called to
folly in a more literal sense as a prophetic sign of the universal
requirement. Those called literally to folly are a reminder to the rest
of the monastic family of the challenge presented by the Lord and
his apostle.

It is probable that the desert of fourth-century Egypt was the
birthplace of the tradition that sees folly as a definite vocation and
gift of the Holy Spirit.[6] Palladius (c.365–425), the historian of early
monasticism and friend of St John Chrysostom, in his *Lausiac
History*, tells the story of one Sarapion Sindonites, a vagabond
ascetic, who never wore anything but a loincloth and lived in the
utmost poverty. On one occasion he sold himself to a troupe of
Greek actors, whom he later converted. From Egypt he wandered

to Greece and Rome, and in the latter met a female ascetic. To prove that she is truly dead to the world, Sarapion commands her to undress, place her clothing on her shoulders and follow him, similarly naked, through the streets of the city. The woman replies that this would cause a scandal and people would accuse her of being insane and demon-ridden. 'But what does that matter?', asks Sarapion, and he tells her not to consider herself holier than others, if she is not prepared to walk naked. He then shows that he is more dead to the world than she is and walks about naked.[7]

Palladius also tells of a woman fool for Christ (identified in some calendars as St Isidora), who was considered mad by all the other Sisters in her convent. She never sat at table, never partook even of a piece of bread, but was content to wipe up the crumbs left at table. Abba Pitiroum was led by an angel to the convent, having been told that one of the nuns was a saint. He demanded to see the whole community, but when all had assembled, he insisted that one was missing. They said that only one was missing—the mad one. Pitiroum ordered them to bring her to him, and so the Sisters went off and dragged Isidora in from the kitchen. When she entered, Abba Pitiroum fell at her feet and said, 'Bless me!'

> She also likewise fell at his feet and said, 'Bless me, master'. They were all amazed and said to him, 'Father, do not let her insult you; she is mad'. But Pitiroum said to them all, '*You* are mad. For she is your mother and mine . . . and I pray to be found worthy of her in the day of judgement.'[8]

The word used to describe the nun-fool is the feminine form of *salos*, which becomes the technical term in Greek for the fool for Christ's sake. It probably originates in common slang and should perhaps be translated 'crackpot'. In the *Apophthegmata* Ammonas anticipates the later *saloi* in that he simulates madness for the sake of humility. But the story told of him in this connection suggests the difficulties of this way, and that even the saintly Ammonas could be stung into 'sanity' on hearing a contemptuous remark:

> It was said of him that some people came to be judged, and Abba Ammonas feigned madness. A woman standing near him said to her neighbour, 'The old man is mad'. Abba Ammonas heard it, called her, and said 'How much labour have I given myself in the desert to acquire this folly, and through you I have lost it today.'[9]

Anyone who enters the desert to pray has followed the apostles' footsteps in eschewing the cautious wisdom of the age and embracing the daring folly of the cross. His action inevitably seems foolish to the worldly wise. Moreover, as with Isidora, the secret of a monastic fool's sanctity can remain unrecognized even by fellow-religious, who may treat the fool with scorn. This 'folly-within-folly' is the beginning of the tradition of holy folly as such. Its inspiration is the wisdom of the desert, but it is not confined to that life and may well appear outside it, or within it as an internal challenge. The desert life is intended to lead all men to the folly of the cross, the foolishness of God, although it may need the occasional fool for Christ to remind it of its destiny and to bring it back from compromise or moderation.

Monasticism of the fourth century was an attempt to establish a Christian 'counter-culture'. While it would not be true to say, as is sometimes claimed, that early monasticism was no more than a movement of protest against the settled condition of the Church following the conversion of Constantine, the first monks did, indeed, try to preserve the ideals of martyrdom in their spiritual warfare against the powers of evil, and to maintain that non-conformity to world rulers for which Christians had striven until the Peace of the Church. The anchorites and cenobites were committed to a life of creative protest: renunciation (*apotaxis, apotaxia, apotagē*) has a strongly active sense of 'dropping out of line' and of engaging in a new form of human living. Indeed, 'renunciation' can be used almost as a synonym for monasticism. Renunciation of Satan, sin and self is accompanied by a commitment to a new, spiritually-based polity. St Basil defines renunciation as 'the transference of the human heart to a heavenly mode of life, so that we can say, "But our conversation is in heaven"; what is more, . . . it is the first step towards the likeness of Christ, who being rich became poor for our sake'.[10] Going into the desert expresses a longing to 'unlearn' the sensibility of the age, to be remade in body, mind, and spirit, to become truly and without compromise a new humanity in Christ. Renunciation is not an end in itself but only a step towards greater conformity to Christ and final participation in the heavenly commonwealth. Athanasius, in his *Life of Antony*, sees the monasteries as alternative, Christocentric societies: 'The desert was made a city by the monks who came forth from their own people and enrolled themselves in the polity of heaven.'[11]

What was 'foolish' about monasticism was not any element of irrationality or animality but its shockingly immoderate 'counter-culture'. The fool who emerges *within* that counter-culture becomes a fool twice over; the joke is on him *twice*. His vocation would seem to be to recall his brethren to their vocation to be unconformed to the world's wisdom. The folly of the monastic desert is *not* mental illness: in a famous passage Athanasius is at pains to underline Antony's soundness of body and mind after his long solitary life; his anchoretic life is a way to true, God-given wholeness. On the other hand, that wholeness is not comprehended by the world and is condemned as dangerous nonsense; Antony remains a fool according to the standards of the present age.

We have spoken somewhat loosely of the fool in 'the desert'. In fact, while folly remains a characteristic aspect of the extreme asceticism of the anchorites, it reaches its classical form among cenobites; the holy fool as such is always defined by his relationship to a particular *community*. Indeed, some of the later fools are monks who leave their monastic community to play the fool in the wider community of the city. In either case holy folly is a social manifestation. As Jacques Lacarrière has said: 'There is in it a sort of transferred asceticism, in the sense that by mortifying the body one aims, in fact, at the mortification of one's social being, at cutting oneself off from society *while living in the bosom of society itself.* Obviously, this is something the anchorite could not do.'[12] The apparently mad stance of the anchorite at the extreme margin of society is transferred back into society itself, whether that of the city or of the monastery.

In the cycle of stories associated with Daniel of Skete (sixth century),[13] Mark the Mad is a monk who for fifteen years 'fails' in the desert by sinning against purity but comes to the city of Alexandria to atone for his sins and failure by simulating folly. He sustains himself with bits of food picked up in the market and wins a little cash from time to time at the hippodrome, where he sleeps on the benches. On meeting Abba Daniel, who immediately recognizes sanctity in this madman, he plays his part, screaming and crying out for help. A crowd gathers and tells the old man to leave Mark alone as he is nothing but a madman. 'No,' replies Daniel, 'you are the fools! This is the only reasonable man I have found in this city today.' Daniel and Mark proceed to the Patriarch's palace, where the holy fool reveals his strange ascesis and dies that night in peace. Here, as always, the heart of comedy is the clash and interplay of incompatibles. The holy fool is in a society yet not of it, challenging its most basic assumptions (in the case of the city) or its failure to live the gospel (in the case of the monastery).

Another kind of interplay is found in the life of one who appears to be a lunatic but who secretly, at night and in solitude, is a man of prayer and Christian discipline. The Monophysite historian, John of Ephesus (c.507–586), gives us a dramatic example of this in the lives of Theophilus and Maria, 'children of eminent men of Antioch, who despised the world and all that is in it and lived a holy life in poverty of spirit, wearing an assumed garb'.[14] They were originally betrothed to one another but were converted to celibacy and a life of simulated folly by one Procopius of Rome, whom Theophilus saw clad as a beggar, standing in a pile of dung in his father's stable, yet with arms outstretched to pray and with a ray of light proceeding from his mouth. They dressed themselves in strange and outrageous costume—Theophilus as a mime-actor and Maria as a prostitute—and went to the city of Amida, where 'they used often to perform drolleries and buffooneries, being constantly in the courts of the church like strangers, making fun of the priests and the people, and having their ears boxed by everyone as mime-actors'.[15] The narrator of the story, however, discovered their true identity by following them one day and observing them over the pinnacle of the city wall. 'I saw that both placed themselves standing with their faces towards the east, and stretched out their arms to heaven in prayer in the form of a cross, and after a time they fell upon their faces in prayer, and they stood up and again fell upon their faces in prayer . . . and they went through the same form for a long time.'[16] Until John discovered them at vigil, the sanctity of these two holy fools was known to no one but God, who saw them in secret. To the world about them they were a comedian and a whore.

A story closely parallel to that of Theophilus and Maria is the life of St Alexios, the 'Man of God'. The earliest version is the Syriac legend, composed towards the end of the fifth century and preserved in an early sixth-century manuscript. Thereafter the story was taken up by Byzantine hagiographers and others, who have left us a truly amazing profusion of lives in many languages, including Old French, Old English, and Ethiopian.[17] It appears that Alexios was the only son of a rich Roman senator. He married a rich young lady, but on his wedding night, leaving his bride untouched, he fled to Syria and embraced total poverty, living in a hut next to the Church of the Mother of God in Edessa. For the next seventeen years he lived in obscurity and poverty until one day the image of Our Lady spoke and revealed his sanctity to the people, whereupon he fled back home to his father's house. However, his father, who did not recognize him, received him with charity as a beggar, gave him employment and assigned him a corner under the stairs as his lodging. For another seventeen years he lived thus, unknown in his own home, ill-treated and laughed at by his fellow-servants. Only on his death were his identity and the true nature of his life revealed.

Two Saloi

One of the characteristics of the lives of Theophilus and Maria, and of St Alexios, is the tension between the desert and the city. This appears also in the life of St Simeon Salos, the first saint to be venerated explicitly as a fool for Christ's sake. His life was written by the accomplished hagiographer, Leontius, Bishop of Neapolis in Cyprus (?610–?650).

Simeon (d. ?590) and his companion, Deacon John (with whom he is commemorated in the Byzantine Calendar on 21 July), were originally from Edessa but became monks in Palestine at the monastery of St Gerasimus. Here they lived a rigorous ascetical life, but Simeon was beset by temptations to spiritual pride and doubted whether the solitary life was, for him, the most successful way of winning souls. With his superior's grudging approval, he went off, about the year 551, to the city of Emesa where he at once embarked on the life which earned him his surname:

On a dung-heap outside the city he found a dead dog. He took off the cord belt that he wore and tied it to the dog's foot. Dragging it behind him, he ran through the city gates, close to a boys' school. When they saw this spectacle, the children began to shout, 'the monk's mad!' and ran after him, boxing his ears. The next day, which was a Sunday, Simeon took some nuts and entered the church. At the beginning of the Liturgy, he threw them and extinguished the candles. When they rushed to throw him out, he went up into the ambo and attacked the women with nuts.[18]

Thereafter Simeon simulated the most outrageous lunacy, dressing in strange fashion, exhibiting violent changes of mood, publicly eating sausages on Good Friday, and, on one occasion, running into the baths reserved for women. His eccentric behaviour was explained by him at the end of his life to his faithful friend as the expression of his passionlessness—*apatheia*:

Believe me, my son, as wood is with other pieces of wood, so I was then. I felt neither that I had a body, nor that I had entered a place where there were bodies. My whole soul was taken up with the Lord's work, and I did not desist from it.[19]

It was this quality of *apatheia* which enabled Simeon to continue in his wild life. Christian *apatheia* is not the cold insensibility of the Stoics, but the Holy Spirit's emancipation of the senses, whereby man ceases to be an automaton, a victim of compulsive behaviour, pulled now this way, now that, by his passions and instincts, and attains a sovereign freedom in his relations with others, refusing to regard them as objects of possession, exploitation, and domination. Moreover, by shocking the righteous, Simeon denounces spiritual pride and pharisaism, without, on the other hand, condoning any breach of the moral law.

Simeon's madness is feigned; only his faithful friend, Deacon John, knows his secret. Under the cover of folly, Jews and heretics are converted and the possessed are healed. Such hiddenness is Simeon's final triumph over pride: his ascesis, prayer, and fasting are all *unknown*; his worldly reputation is unreservedly bad; everything has been done in secret, so that the Father who sees in secret will reward him (Matt. 6: 6).

The other major Greek life of a *salos*, and one which has had considerable influence on Orthodox religious tradition, is that of St Andrew the Fool.[20] Andrew was a handsome young man, a Scythian slave of one Theognetus in the city of Constantinople. One night he had a vision in which the Lord commanded him to become a fool. After consultation with Nicephorus, his spiritual father, he set off on a career of simulated folly. His master sent him to the Church of St Anastasia, famous for its cures of the mentally sick, but after four months of confinement, which he spent in unceasing prayer, he was discharged as incurably mad. For the rest of his life Andrew went about naked, winter and summer, often sleeping in the open air or in dirty corners with stray dogs. At all times he behaved like a vagabond and beggar, half-witted and troublesome. His remarkable gift of discerning spirits enabled him, with piercing accuracy, to unmask evil wherever it concealed itself. He made friends with Epiphanius, who became his disciple and later Patriarch of Constantinople. Andrew's death is movingly described. First he and Epiphanius prayed together as 'paupers and pilgrims, in our wretchedness and nakedness . . .'.[21] He kissed his friend good-bye, and then, moving to the outskirts of the city, he spent the night in prayer for the sinful, the needy, and the whole world: Finally, laying down his head on the ground, he died peacefully 'with a smile on his face'. His body was taken up to heaven, leaving behind a fragrance where it had lain.[22]

The authenticity of St Andrew Salos has been questioned, for we have no evidence for his cultus until the end of the twelfth century. Whether or not the figure of Andrew has any historical foundation, Byzantine Christianity was truly fascinated by the figure of the holy madman, the unruly misfit whose repellent aspect conceals a Christ-like beauty. The *Life of St Andrew the Fool* had particular influence on Russian Orthodoxy. According to Nicephorus, St Andrew used to pray at night in the Church of the Blachernae in Constantinople, where the precious relic of Our Lady's Veil was preserved. During one such vigil, the Mother of God appeared to Andrew and Epiphanius, stretched her veil over the assembled company and promised to care perpetually for her city. This is the incident depicted in the famous *Pokrov* icon, the image of 'The Protecting Veil of the Mother of God'. It is significant that, while the story behind the *Pokrov* devotion takes place in Constantinople, no Byzantine but only Russian icons of the incident are known to exist, and the feast was not kept in Greece until the nineteenth century, while the Russians were already observing it in the twelfth century.

Why was the *Pokrov* tradition, and with it perhaps the tradition of the holy fool, so attractive to the Russians? Andrew himself was a Scythian, but nationality alone cannot explain this astonishing hagiographical and liturgical development. John Wortley has recently reminded us that, according to Russian sources, the vision of Andrew and Epiphanius took place in 911, at the time of the treaty between the Byzantine government and Prince Oleg of Kiev who, four years previously, according to the Russian Primary Chronicle, had attacked Constantinople. Following the peace treaty, cultural exchange along with trade and diplomatic contacts increased between Kiev and Byzantium. Wortley suggests that one of the 'goods' taken back to Kiev by the delegates of Oleg was the story of their fellow Slav, Andrew the Holy Fool.[23]

The Russian Fools

The Russian Church maintained the tradition of folly for Christ's sake longer and more enthusiastically than did the Greeks; altogether thirty-six Russian fools have been canonized, but only six Greeks. Wortley's hypothesis is only one plausible explanation of the Russian enthusiasm; it is conceivable, as will be argued in the next chapter, that folly for Christ's sake arrived in Russia from the West.

The first Russian fool for Christ's sake was St Isaac Zatvornik (d. 1090), a hermit of the famous Monastery of the Caves at Kiev.[24] The considerable influence and prestige of this monastery in Kievan Russia is due to its creative synthesis of the desert spirit with that of Mount Athos and the Studite Rule of Constantinople. Like the monasteries of the Cistercians, being founded at the same time in France, the Monastery of the Caves developed a high spirituality of monastic poverty, which was seen both as union with Christ in his poverty and as solidarity with the destitute. St Theodosius (d. 1074), who established the Studite Rule, conceived of a monastic *imitatio Christi*:

> Our Lord Jesus Christ became poor and humbled Himself, offering Himself as an example, so that we should humble ourselves in His name. He suffered insults, was spat upon, and beaten, for our salvation; how just it is, then, that we should suffer in order to gain Christ.[25]

It will be apparent when we come to consider the Cistercians that Russian monks and holy fools, with ideals such as these, would have been completely at home under Abbot Aelred in Rievaulx, that city of the poor.

St Procopius of Ustyug (d. 1302) is described as being 'of the western countries, of the Latin tongue, of the German land', in other words, a foreigner and Roman Catholic. His life was spent in wandering from town to town, across the plains and through the forests, looking for a mysterious country—the lost homeland. He sought the company only of the poor and scorned the rich. He walked naked and slept in the porches of churches. During the day his life was one of complete imbecility; the night he spent entirely in prayer.[26]

The greatest era of the *yurodivye*—fools for Christ—in Russia is the sixteenth century. Nearly all travellers to Muscovy at this time mention them, including the Englishman, Giles Fletcher, who wrote as follows:

> They have certain hermits, whom they call holy men, that are like gymno-

sophists for their life and behaviour, though far unlike for their knowledge and learning.

They use to go stark naked save a clout about their middle, with their hair hanging long and wildly about their shoulders, and many of them with an iron collar or chain about their necks or midst, even in the very extremity of winter.

These they take as prophets and men of great holiness, giving them a liberty to speak what they list without any controlment, though it be of the very highest himself. So that if he reprove any openly, in what sort soever, they answer nothing, but that it is *po graecum*, that is, for their sins.

And if any of them take some piece of saleware from any man's shop as he passeth by, to give where he list, he thinketh himself much beloved of God and much beholden to the holy man for taking it in that sort. Of this kind there are not many, because it is a very hard and cold profession to go naked in Russia, especially in winter. Among other at this time they have one at Moscow that walketh naked about the streets and inveyeth commonly against the state and government, especially against the Godunovs, that are thought at this time to be great oppressors of that commonwealth.[27]

The most greatly venerated fool is St Basil the Blessed (d. 1552), who led the life of a vagabond and walked naked through the streets of Moscow. Like St Simeon and, indeed, Jesus himself, he scandalized the righteous by his compassion for the morally reprobate; he threw stones at the houses of respectable people and bathed with tears those of sinners. Basil unmasked the devil wherever he tried to hide himself, even when it meant challenging the authority of princes. Nearly twenty years after his death he is supposed to have appeared to Ivan the Terrible at Novgorod which the Tsar was then razing to the ground. Basil offered the Emperor a meal of fresh blood and meat. When he refused, Basil showed him in the sky the souls of those whom Ivan had butchered and who now went before him into heaven.[28]

The last Russian fool for Christ's sake was canonized in the seventeenth century. After this period the fool became suspect not only during his lifetime but also after his death; not even the cultus of the *yurodivye* was sufficient for the Church to admit another subversive to the ranks of the blessed.[29] However, the literary motif, and the living reality, of the fool for Christ's sake was not eradicated from Russian tradition. Fools make their appearance in Pushkin's *Boris Godunov* in the figure of 'Nicky, Nicky, Iron nightcap', Tolstoy's *Childhood, Boyhood, and Youth*, and above all in the writings of Dostoievsky, where in the figure of *The Idiot*, Prince

• Myshkin, with his outspokenness and 'fellowship with publicans and sinners', we have the compassionate folly of a *yurodivy*.[30]

Contemporary with Dostoievsky is Alexis Bukharev (1822-1871),[31] whose life resembles not only the holy fools of Byzantium and Russia but the western apostles of self-abasement, especially Surin and Boudon, whom we shall consider later. Until the age of 40 Bukharev was Archimandrite Theodore, a monk and scholar at the Moscow Theological Academy, a favourite of Metropolitan Philaret. In and through his monastic discipline Bukharev developed a great knowledge of the intellectual and literary currents of his day, being an admirer of Gogol, Turgenev, and Dostoievsky. In 1862 he decided on the unprecedented and scandalous step of laicization, and a little later the scandal was intensified when he decided to marry. Students of his life say that this was not an act of infidelity to the monastic life but an expression of Bukharev's ascetical desire for self-abasement and communion with the Lord Jesus in his self-emptying. Bukharev's was a courageous witness to Christ in the midst of poverty, both material and spiritual, for laicization meant the deprival of civic rights, academic degrees, all money connected with previous occupations, and, most painfully, the loss of all public esteem. It was a deliberate act of folly for Christ's sake. In his book *On Modern Spiritual Needs* the former Archimandrite wrote as follows:

The true fools in Christ follow the words of 1 Cor. 4: 9–10: they become a spectacle to angels and to men. . . . The passage, 'death worketh in us, life in you', refers to the same also. As fellow workers of the loving Christ's spirit, the holy men of God bear, by the grace of Christ, human sinful weaknesses and humiliations, as if they themselves were liable to spiritual foolishness. According to such heroes of faith and love, the grace of God does not abandon men who (*freely*) give themselves to these dishonouring weaknesses and silliness; but meekly and patiently he brings them on the path of truth and clear understanding. (Ordinary) men pass gradually from their childish mind into the *life* of sane intelligence because those others, in their gracious love, offer themselves to the hard *death* of frank madness in the eyes of men. Such is the mystery or significance of foolishness for Christ's sake.

Mme Gorodetsky, from whom this quotation is taken, then comments: 'May not this passage be an explanation of his own strange destiny?'[32]

The Elements of Holy Folly

This brief sketch of the history of holy folly in the Christian East enables us to distinguish a number of elements which, as we shall see in the next chapter, are common both to the East and to the less conspicuous but equally developed tradition in the West.

The first and most important of these elements is the *Christocen-tricity* of the fools: the inspiration of all their actions is identity with Christ crucified, participation in the Lord's poverty, mockery, humiliation, nakedness, and self-emptying. The fools follow St Paul in 'completing what is lacking in Christ's afflictions' (Col. 1: 24), in sharing in the Lord's death that they may 'know him and the power of his resurrection' (Phil. 3: 10). Their folly is the folly of God himself (v. 25), who became man and poor and was crucified in his great love for us.

> [The fool] is a poor, inadequate being, deserving of jest and even brutality . . . But the memory of the Cross and the Crucified, the memory that *he* was slapped, spat upon and scourged, lives in his heart and compels him for Christ's sake to endure at every moment disgrace and persecution.[33]

Secondly, folly for Christ's sake is a *charisma*, a vocation and gift from God; it is therefore to be distinguished sharply from simple eccentricity or pathological madness. Ernst Benz writes: 'Folly itself is understood as *charisma*, as a special gift of the Spirit and of grace, as an arming with special spiritual power.'[34]

Thirdly, holy folly is *simulated*; the holy fools *play* at being mad. The fool for Christ is a sacred jester, clown, or mimic. He leads a double life: 'on stage' (in the streets, by day) he is imbecile; 'in private' (in church, at night) he is a man of prayer.

> This theatrical, mimic character of the fools' existence practically expresses itself in the fact that the saint who plays the madman leads a complete double life. By day he wanders around the streets and market-places, in the inns and taverns, and plays his tricks. But at night he withdraws to a hidden place, to some corner, or, if he has one, to his hut, and there he takes off the mask of his folly and sinks down into unbroken prayer, which continues till the next morning.[35]

Moreover, there is hardly anyone, perhaps only his spiritual guide, who knows the truth about him. After his death the secret is known to all, and the faithful begin to venerate him.

The simulated, or theatrical, nature of holy folly is problematic.

It clearly connects the hagiographical phenomenon in some way to the profane; it is surely significant that the profane fool disappears from the courts and streets of Europe at precisely the time when the holy fool becomes rarer in the Christian community. The main difficulty is one of definition, the question of what we mean by 'madness'. The Byzantine literature implies that 'sane' men simulated 'madness'; later on, we shall encounter fools who 'really' were mad, but who transcended their madness, or made of it a humble self-oblation, for the sake of Christ. The difficulty of asserting overconfidently that the folly of the *saloi* is feigned or simulated is that it assumes as absolute some already available definition of what madness and sanity are. It overlooks the fact that the fools' special vocation, like that of the apostles, is to reveal to men befuddled by the world's delusive wisdom where true sanity and wisdom are to be

• found; they show us that we cannot absolutize the criteria of wholeness offered by this present world, 'for it does not yet appear what we shall be, but we know that when he appears we shall be like him' (1 John 3: 2). Our humanity is a mystery that cannot be reduced to prosaic definition by the world: we are made in the image, and restored in Christ to the likeness, of a mysterious and incomprehensible God; man must therefore be, as St Gregory of Nyssa

• teaches, nearly as much of a mystery as God;[36] in St Augustine's words, God and man are two unfathomable abysses of mystery.[37] To the world, with its ungodly idea of sanity, the fools 'really' were mad; to God, they 'really' were wise. The Christian tradition of holy folly does not condone every form of madness on the specious grounds that the world's judgements are always wrong; it is not a licence for irrationality and abnormal behaviour. While there are examples not only of saints who simulated madness but also of others who endured psychological illness, we shall not try to mimimize the real horror of psychiatric illness. Some madness may be 'breakthrough' rather than 'breakdown', but it is undeniable that there is a madness which destroys, enslaves, and causes untold suffering; there is also, moreover, a madness caused by demonic possession, a 'folly for the sake of Satan'. It is imperative to follow

• the holy fools themselves in exercising discernment of spirits and, by the criteria here presented, to distinguish the life-giving folly of the cross from both the madness of the world (called wisdom) and the madness of those possessed by evil spirits. We shall also try and distinguish these three kinds of spiritual folly (for Christ, for the world, for Satan) from mental illness as such.

Then, fourthly, folly for Christ's sake is always *eschatological*. The holy fool proclaims the conflict between this present world and the world to come. As we have already noted in the last chapter, according to St Paul's account of *mōria* in 1 Cor. 1: 18ff, it is in the eyes of the world and of its ruling powers that the word of the cross appears as 'folly'. *The folly of the cross is the wisdom of the world to come.* As a modern Greek theologian has said: 'The fool is the charismatic man who has direct experience of the new reality of the Kingdom of God and undertakes to demonstrate in a prophetic way the antithesis of this present world to the world of the Kingdom.'[38]

Fifthly, one of the most frequently encountered eschatological motifs in the lives of the holy fools is *pilgrimage*, the quest for a lost country, the Promised Land. The fool is a nomad, who never settles anywhere in this present world but wanders, like the pilgrim people of God in the wilderness. The fool for Christ is nearly always a stranger or foreigner. St Simeon wanders from Edessa to Jerusalem and Emesa; St Andrew is a Scythian in Constantinople; St Procopius is a German. According to a study by Peter Brown,[39] this 'beduinisation of the ascetic life' had its origin in Syria where, because the desert is conducive to human habitation, identification with it was more realistic. In the howling, dead awfulness of the Egyptian desert, the monk had simply to survive; in Syria a deeper communion was possible. The desert became a republic of monastic freedom, where the monk might wander, detached from all ties, eating the food nature gave him, making friends only with animals and birds. On Brown's view, then, the Syrian desert is the birthplace of the wild wanderers, 'grazers', and pilgrim-fools of later hagiography.

Brown also claims that this 'strangeness' endowed the holy man with great power in society; the outsider turns out to be close to the centre; the stylite is in every sense the 'man at the top'. Here we meet the sixth element of folly for Christ's sake: the *political*. Brown argues thus:

For the society around him, the holy man is the one man who can stand outside the ties of family, and of economic interest; whose attitudes to food itself rejected all the ties of solidarity to kin and village that, in the peasant societies of the Near East, had always been expressed by the gesture of eating. He was thought of as a man who owed nothing to society. He fled women and bishops, not because he would have found the society of either particularly agreeable, but because both threatened to rivet him to a distinct place in society.[40]

If it is true that the holy fool's political power is dependent upon his being an unstable and strange element in an otherwise harmonious and closely knit society, it follows that when the stability and peace of Church and State are disrupted, the fool's distinctive witness is out of place. And this would appear to be so. The fool appears most commonly at a time of political tranquillity, when the Church adapts herself to the political *status quo*. Peter Hauptmann, writing on the Russian fools, says:

We encounter them only in the context of a Church protected by a Christian government. With the incursions of the Arabs and later the Turks they disappear in the devastated parts of the Byzantine empire. Their expansion in Russia, too, shows clearly enough dependence on the decline of Mongol supremacy. Apart from the one case of Isaac in the Monastery of the Caves at Kiev, they are found in the thirteenth and fourteenth centuries only in the free north and do not appear in the area of Moscow until the fifteenth century.[41]

When the Church is persecuted, her opposition to the present age is starkly revealed, and martyrdom, prophecy and holy folly are the vocation of all. But when the peace comes and the Church conforms, the prophets and holy fools emerge to proclaim to their fellow Christians the destiny and vocation of all: 'if only all the Lord's people were prophets' (Num. 11: 29). The fool is regarded as such *by his fellow Christians*: the apostle is mad, but the Corinthians are 'such sensible Christians'. Yannaras comments:

[The fools] appear outside the Christian establishment, which has compromised with the agreed criteria and sensibility of the world and measures the regeneration of man and new life with the yardstick of . . . public decency.[42]

But the fool is a faithful son of the Church, not a schismatic. He belongs to, and is ultimately recognized by, the Church. Like the secular jester, he judges the social group of which he is a loyal, albeit restless, member.

The seventh element of holy folly is one we have already noted in the case of St Basil of Moscow: the *discernment of spirits*. Here is the secret of his apparent moral outrages: 'The saint who has renounced all appearances of reason and morality is capable, by virtue of a special clairvoyance, of discovering and denouncing all forms of pious hypocrisy, all false virtues which conceal a profound vice.'[43] The fool for Christ's sake penetrates the façade of conventional respectability, which those conformed to the world use to hide their disloyalty to the gospel. By his words and actions, the fool reminds the Church of the terrible goodness of God, which judges not only ostensible sin but the evil that hides behind self-righteousness and pharisaical superiority. The fool confronts man with his true nature beneath the layers of self-deception: 'In his very acts of madness, in his jokes (like the fools of medieval kings), he manages to teach people the bitter truth of their inner selves, and through these strange lessons confirmed by miracles and, particularly, by fulfilled prophecies, some people are converted.'[44]

Eighth: the holy fools are *ascetics*. But their asceticism is of a particular kind—that of an extreme *apatheia*. In them the growth of *apatheia*, which must accompany all spiritual endeavour, helps them to resist the lure of worldly respect and honour. They aspire to become the little ones of Christ, the last of all, the least, the forgotten, the despised, so that they may conquer pride, renounce self, and live only to the Lord; folly for them is the last stage or highest grade of humility—the loss of all reputation and esteem. The fool has 'gone out of his mind', the mind obsessed with self, the mind 'set on the flesh' (Rom. 8: 7); he has unlearnt the egotistical prudence of the world; he has exorcized Satan from his inner self, has taken conversion deep into his heart, and in his inmost being he is remade. His holiness is known only to God, and he is deprived of any cause for proud boasting; like Paul, he can boast only of what shows up his weakness. Folly, whether 'real' or 'simulated', is gladly embraced, so that the saint may find wholeness and wisdom only in Christ; 'it is no longer I who live, but Christ who lives in me; and the life I now live in the flesh I live by faith in the Son of God, who loved me and gave himself for me' (Gal. 2: 20).

The holiness of the fool shows itself in his solidarity with the outcasts of society; he is not content with 'social work' but identifies himself completely with the wretched of the earth. The beggar, the leper, the prisoner are not simply 'cases' to be helped but brethren in whom Christ is present and waits to be served. The fool lives with them, feels close affinities with them; he is on their side and shares their fate. He feels especially drawn to the moral and mental out-casts, those whose behaviour makes them intolerable in normal society. He does not condone their behaviour; on the contrary, like St Andrew Salos, he is fervent in his denunciation of sin while unfailing in love of the sinner and in determination to suffer with him the superior disdain of the self-righteous. He makes friends of prostitutes, not to approve their behaviour or become their client, but to bring them to salvation without the cold hand of pride to pervert his mission. In all such 'dangerous' encounters the fool is guarded by his spiritual discipline and *apatheia*, which do not destroy warm and loving relationships but rather protect him against the tyranny of the instincts, enabling such relationships to exist without exploitation.

Finally, the fool for Christ's sake is protected above all by his *childlikeness*, his purity and simplicity of heart. Spiritual infancy cannot be simply equated with holy folly but is its constant companion. As we saw in the first chapter, Our Lord himself teaches us that his mysteries are revealed only to babes and hidden from the worldly wise (Matt. 11: 25). As our story progresses, we shall continually discover that beneath the wild and apparently ferocious exterior of the fool is the gentle, trusting heart of a child. 'If you want to know the truth, ask a child or a fool.'

3

Folly from East to Far West

In Christ there is no East or West. The Church's catholicity is not
the modern 'pluralism', which it is hard sometimes to distinguish
from anarchy but the rich unity-in-diversity of a community made
one through the blood of Christ, given personal identity and
character by the work of the Spirit. In its 'Decree on Ecumenism'
the Second Vatican Council urges Latin Catholics to 'realize that it
is of supreme importance to understand, venerate, preserve, and
foster the rich liturgical and spiritual heritage of the Eastern
Churches in order faithfully to preserve the fulness of Christian
tradition, and to bring about reconciliation between Eastern and
Western Christians'.[1]

For the Catholic Christian, for whom the 'communion of holy
things' is a law of the mystical Body, there can only be the surprise
of delight when he discovers that something so apparently Eastern,
so Byzantine, as folly for Christ's sake, is also one of the features of
a Christian tradition in the very Far West, at 'the end of the
world'—in Ireland. Such a discovery can open the eyes of his mind
to the fact that what is 'different' in another tradition is already
found in his own: that the *salos* and *yurodivy* had their equivalent in
the early Irish 'wild man' or *geilt*, that monastic 'marginality' was no
less the ideal of ascetics at the edge of the known world, where the
desert was a rocky cave by a wild sea, a cabin in a forest, or a shelter
in the glen.

Ireland and the East

We have seen that the term 'folly' came to be associated with those
who had withdrawn from 'normal' society to live a life of prayer in
the desert. Folly was properly ascribed to anchorites or solitaries as
such but developed as a vocation peculiar to certain individuals
within the *coenobium* or society at large. Early Christian Ireland
had the most thororoughgoing monastic Church in Christendom.
We will not be surprised, then, to learn that folly became a feature
of its spirituality and fools the regular companions of monks.

Perhaps nothing shows more clearly Ireland's affinities with the primitive monasticism of the East. As a distinguished student of the Celtic Church has said, 'already in the traditions of the sixth century, Ireland comes before us as an Island of Saints (*sancti*), thickly studded with anchoritic and monastic settlements, and . . . *as the outermost ripple of the great monastic movement of the Greek and Coptic Churches of the East*'.[2]

Ireland was never cut off from the rest of Europe, neither was contact with Christian faith and culture lacking before St Patrick (*c*.390–*c*.460) went there as a missionary, as we know from the long tradition of saints anterior to or independent of him who are still venerated. It is significant that they are associated with Munster and the coastal region of southern Ireland, which had ancient trading links with Gaul and Spain.[3] Despite these contacts, Ireland never formed part of the Roman Empire, and this most certainly affected the structure and ethos of the Irish Church. Since there were no cities, the basic social unit remained the small, familial, rural community. Diocesan episcopacy on the continental model, with its hierarchy of urban and provincial bishops, proved incapable of adaptation to the tribal system, and so there developed in Ireland an almost wholly monastic church polity. By the sixth century 'almost all jurisdiction . . . was exercised from the monasteries'.[4] However, if in this respect its social organization was idiosyncratic, Irish monasticism, in its spirituality, offered abundant proof of continuity with Eastern asceticism. For monks in both the Far West and the East, monastic life was spiritual warfare, *militia Christi*. The hard words of the British abbot, Faustus of Riez (*c*.408–*c*.490), to his monks on the Mediterranean island of Lérins, where St Patrick is thought to have been a novice, would have been fully endorsed by cenobites from Tabennisi to Tallaght: 'It is not for quiet and security that we have formed a community in this monastery, but for a struggle and a conflict.'[5] Moreover, as we shall see, in Ireland, as in Egypt, such struggle and conflict included the vocation to be a fool for the sake of Jesus Christ and to accept humbly and without resentment the ridicule and contempt of men.

Before taking a closer look at the connection between Irish and Eastern folly, we should consider the more general problem of how Eastern monastic ideals were transmitted to the Far West. Many scholars have suggested Visigothic Spain as the intermediary. Edmund Bishop drew attention a long time ago to the similarities between Mozarabic and Celtic liturgical customs, and Charles Beeson demonstrated the Irish contribution to the transmission of the works of St Isidore of Seville.[6] More recently, J. N. Hillgarth has taken the analysis a stage further.[7] Spain was a natural meeting-place for Far West and East. The south of Ireland had ancient commercial links with the north-west of Spain, which in turn, on its other seaboard, had dealings with the eastern Mediterranean. It was not unheard of for a vessel to make the whole voyage from the East out to the British Isles.[8] The crucial area is Galicia, from which Egeria travelled to the East in the fourth century and which was thought to be of Greek origin.[9] Galicia is also the province closest to Ireland and linked to it by the ancient trade route already mentioned. Furthermore, it included the Celtic see of Britonia, probably founded from Brittany and attested from the late sixth century. We know that the monastery of Santa Maria de Bretoña near Mondoñedo in the northern part of Galicia retained Celtic customs and privileges until a comparatively late date.[10] Slightly further south, in Braga, there is evidence of a continuing influence of Byzantine thought and letters, even after the expulsion of the last Byzantine troops from the Iberian peninsula in 624.[11] In St Martin of Braga (fl. 550), we have, as it were, a 'Janus-faced' Iberian Father, with connections to both North-west and East: a monk-bishop on the Celtic model but born in Pannonia and formed in the monastic tradition of the East, he was also the compiler and translator of selections from the *Sententiae Patrum Aegyptiorum*.[12] The hypothesis that Spain was an intermediary between Ireland and the East is further strengthened by the fact that, while the centre of Europe was dark and dead, submerged beneath barbarism, religious life and culture were flourishing at the periphery in Spain and Ireland. Moreover, the Arian Suevi and Visigoths did not persecute the Church. North-west was the only direction in which letters and spirituality from the East might travel.[13]

The evidence supports the plausibility of this hypothesis, but it does no more than that. We have no solid grounds for supposing that books containing stories of the holy fools were actually transported from, as it were, Byzantium to Braga and thence to Bangor, County Down. All that the 'Spanish connection' does for us is to render more tantalizing the parallels we shall now describe between the *salos* of the East and the *geilt* of Ireland.

The Wild Men of Early Christian Ireland

Madmen are constantly encountered in early Irish hagiography. As Robin Flower has written:

> We are told of practically every Irish saint that he lived in an intimate converse with lepers and people of troubled wits . . . These madmen, the legend related, roamed the woods, living in tree-tops and sharing their couches with the creatures of the wild. They could go under the water and take the fishes in their hands. Their utterance was a medley of obscure folly and inspired wisdom. If one part of their mind was dim from the quenched reason, another part was illuminated by the divine light. The tales of them are wild and strange, and much of the most beautiful poetry of the time is associated with them.[14]

Mrs Chadwick has described these wild men as 'the most extreme form of Irish asceticism' and compares them with the Syrian 'tree-dwellers' and 'grazers'.[15] I believe that a closer parallel is to be found in the Eastern 'fools for Christ's sake', but there is no need to press any particular theory of literary dependence. Not only is 'The Wild Man of the Woods' a widespread tale, to be found in many cultural settings (the biblical Nebuchadnezzar is one variant), it is obvious that the most important Christian sources, such as the Pauline writing about folly, were as accessible to the Irish monks as they were to those of the East. No elaborate theory of literary filiation is required to account for what, to the Christian, is the inspiration of the Paraclete.

The word *geilt*, usually translated 'wild' or 'mad', may be derived from the root **gel-*, 'to graze'; if so, its etymology resembles that of the Greek *boskos* or 'grazer'.[16] It would seem that the seventh century was the great age of the *gelta*, but in the early eighth century they are still active, though less numerous; soon after they would seem to disappear from Irish history, although they haunted the imagination of the medieval monks responsible for the texts recounting their exploits. The most notable saga is *Buile Shuibhne*, which tells of the madness of the king Suibne in the seventh century.[17] In its present form it was compiled and edited in a monastic *scriptorium* in the twelfth century, probably in the territory of Airgialla.[18] The traditions with which it deals, however, are much older: as early as the ninth century we have indirect evidence of the cultivation of the Suibne story at the southern monastery of Tech-Moling. The famous manuscript of that period and place, the Carinthian Codex Sancti Pauli, contains, side by side, poems of Suibne and of the seventh-century St Moling.[19]

Suibne, king of Dál nAraide by Lough Neagh, went mad in consequence of a curse from St Rónán, whose psalter he had flung into a lake. While taking part in the battle of Magh Rath in 637, Suibne looked up into the sky and felt such horror that he fled the battlefield and, abandoning all human society, sought solitude and quiet. The twelfth-century text paints a vivid picture of the violent descent of madness upon Suibne:

Now, when Suibne heard these great cries together with their sounds and reverberations in the clouds of Heaven and in the vault of the firmament, he looked up, whereupon turbulence, and darkness, and fury, and giddiness, and frenzy, and flight, unsteadiness, restlessness, and unquiet filled him, likewise disgust with every place in which he used to be and desire for every place which he had not reached. His fingers were palsied, his heart beat quick, his senses were overcome, his sight was distorted, his weapons fell naked from his hands, so that through Rónán's curse he went, like any bird of the air, in madness and imbecility.[20]

It is God, working through the saint, who has made him mad. He laments:

> Frequent is my groan,
> far from my churchyard is my gaping house;
> I am no champion but a needy madman,
> God has thrust me in rags, without sense.[21]

Suibne lives a wandering, restless life but is a voluntary exile, driven on by some mysterious longing. Like Nebuchadnezzar, the mad king of the Book of Daniel, he 'returns to nature': he grows feathers and then flies from place to place, haunts the tops of trees, and subsists on a diet of herbs, roots, and cresses. It is his communion with wild nature that provides the inspiration for the poems ascribed to him, some of the most beautiful in Early Irish. In one poem he compares his tree-top home to a hermit's oratory:

> My little oratory in Tuaim Inbir:
> a full mansion could not be more delightful—
> with its stars in due order,
> with its sun and its moon.[22]

He describes the beauty of *Glenn mBolcáin*.

> If I were to wander alone

> over the mountains of the great world,
> I should prefer the site of a single hut
> in *Glen mBolcáin buirr*.

> Good is its pure blue water;
> good its clean fierce wind;
> good its cress-green water-cress;
> better its tall water-parsnip.[23]

Much of the poetry, however, contains Suibne's complaints.

> I am in great grief tonight;
> the pure wind has pierced my body;
> my feet are wounded; my cheek is pale;
> great God, I have good cause to be so . . .

> Restless my wandering from region to region;
> it has befallen me to be without reason or wits;
> from Moylinny I wander over Mag Lí,
> from Mag Lí over the rough Liffey valley . . .

> Gloomy is the life of one who has no house;
> it is a wretched life, good Christ;
> everlasting green-topped cress for food;
> cold water from a clear stream for drink.[24]

Suibne is befriended by St Moling, the Leinster saint (d. 697), whom he often visits. Finally, he meets his death, having been mortally wounded by one of Moling's servants. Moling gives him the last rites and then, finally, praises the holy fool.

> The tomb of Suibne here;
> remembrance of him has wrung my heart;
> dear to me, out of love for him,
> each place in which the holy madman used to be.[25]

The folly of Suibne seems fairly complete, and the saga has certain obvious resemblances to those of the *saloi*. But to what extent is Suibne a *holy* fool, a fool for Christ's sake? O'Keeffe, the editor of *Buile Shuibhne*, claims that 'the distinctly Christian passages could be omitted without any serious distortion of the tale'.[26] P.Ó Riain has, however, argued against this.[27] The story is, of course, coloured by many elements from the pre-Christian religious tradition of Ireland; it may be that Suibne is half-way between an old pre-Christian *fili* and a Christian ascetic, but a distinctly Christian orientation remains. The key to understanding the specifically religious nature of Suibne's madness is to be found in the Moling episode where he is associated with an historical saint and is indeed described as 'the king, the saint, the saintly madman'.[28] We cannot, in fact, probe further the Suibne enigma without examining in detail the history of the attractive saint of the Barrow.

St Moling is the 'familiar pet saint' of the *céili dé*, the 'servants of God', that great movement of renewal in Irish monasticism in the eighth century.[29] St Moling, the outstanding saint of the seventh century, became almost the patron saint of the Culdees of the next.

Moling was born the son of a landholder named Fáelán in 'capacious Luachair' (near Castleisland, Co. Kerry). His mother was his father's sister-in-law, Emnat, who in her shame and despair at her sinful union with Fáelán tried to kill Moling at birth. He was saved, however, by a dove, which flew into his mother's face so she could not hurt him. Then came Brénainn, son of Findlug ('with his clerical students'), who baptized him and brought him up.[30] Moling was endowed with prodigious athletic ability, being able to leap great heights and distances, hence his name *Mo ling* ('my leap'). He studied at Ferns but then withdrew to the bank of the River Barrow where he founded the monastic settlement of St Mullins; he himself lived some distance away from the main community in a small hermitage. He is famed for his love of animals and had a fox and a fly as companions. He loved the unlovable; on one occasion, he wiped a leper's nose by sucking it, and in a well-known story, he puts the devil right on the social doctrine of those who believe in the Incarnation.

Once upon a time Moling was at prayers in his church, and he saw a lad coming towards him, a goodly lad arrayed in purple raiment.

'Hail, cleric!' says he.

'The same to thee,' says Moling.

'Why greetest thou not me with a blessing?' says the lad.

'Who art thou?'

'I am Christ, Son of God.'

'I know not that,' says Moling. 'When Christ would come to have speech with the Culdees, 'twas not in purple raiment or in kingly guise that he would come, but after the fashion of hapless men, as a leper or a man diseased.'

'Is it doubt of me thou hast?' says the lad. 'Who thinkest thou, then, that I am?'

'Methinks,' says Moling, 'thou art the devil come to do me injury.'

'Ill for thee that unfaith,' says the lad.

'Well,' says Moling, 'here is thy witness after thee, Christ's gospels.' And he lifted up the gospel.

'Lift it not, cleric,' says he. 'Perchance I am he thou thinkest. I am, indeed, the man of tribulation.'[31]

An important element in the Moling traditions is the theme of folly: it would seem that if his companion, Suibne, is a fool with a tendency towards asceticism, then he himself is an ascetic with a tendency towards folly. According to the Irish 'Birth and Life of St Moling', in his wanderings the saint encounters some evil spirits.

> The cleric said to the spectres: 'Grant me a boon'. 'What boon dost thou ask?' say they. 'Easy (to say): to let me have my three steps of pilgrimage towards the king of heaven and earth, and my three steps of folly also, so that death may be the farther from me.' 'It is granted to thee', says the hag, 'for thou wilt never get away from us; since we ourselves are as swift as wild deer, and our hound is as swift as the wind'.[32]

James Carney has maintained that this element of 'wildness' in Moling has contributed to the fusion of the two traditions of Moling and Suibne. The original Suibne story, in some form, passed into Ireland from the British kingdom of Strathclyde; Suibne is identical with his British counterparts described as 'wild men', viz. Myrddin, Lailoken, and the Arthurian Merlin. On Carney's view, the most archaic form of the story is of a king and a hermit-saint, who acts as the king's adviser. There are many poems in early Irish which, in subtle counterpoint, demonstrate the contrasts between the 'life-styles' of the two. Carney mentions that this external contrast between two separate figures (the king in his palace, the hermit in the wild woods) was later interiorized as a contrast between the two halves of the life of a single individual (the king who goes wild and mad).[33]

Another important early text is the Life of St Cuimine Fota contained in a medieval manuscript in the Royal Irish Academy, which relates the adventures of St Cuimine (592–662) and Mac-dá-Cherda, the fool of the Déisi.[34] According to this story, Cuimine was a bastard, born of the incestuous union of the king of Iarmuma and his daughter, Mumain. Like Moses, the unfortunate child was consigned to the river in a box and was found by a virgin, who brought him up at her hermitage. At first the boy was slow and

stupid but then determined to become an educated man, and 'all
wisdom and learning was bestowed upon him'.[35] His natural mother
then married Mael-Ochtair and went to live with him at Lios
Rudrach in the land of the Déisi. She bore him a son, Comgan,
Mac-dá-Cherda.

The two half-brothers went their different ways. Cuimine was
ordained priest and celebrated his first Mass in the presence of the
parents of Mac-dá-Cherda; eventually he was made bishop of the
two provinces of Munster. Mac-dá-Cherda, on the other hand,
came to excel at athletics and military arts. However, he attracted
the attention of Mael-Dub, the second wife of Mael-Ochtair, his
father, but he rebuffed her. In her anger the lascivious lady
persuaded a druid to curse Mac-dá-Cherda at a fair where he usually
carried off the prize. He was knocked off his horse, and sickness
came upon him.

And he was brought home and spent a year in the weakness of disease
with the physicians of the country and the world in attendance on him, but
they could not cure him. His hair fell out and he lost his mind and reason and
sense, so that he became a mad foolish senseless fool, who preferred any
other fool to all the people of the world. When his household saw that, they
deserted him and went to another master. From that time forward he used
to get a fit of foolishness and a fit of wisdom, and for that reason he was
called Mac-dá-Cherda, for he practised both the art of foolishness and the
art of wisdom.[36]

Like Suibne, Mac-dá-Cherda recites poetry of great beauty, but he
is far more self-conscious in his folly than the fool of Moling, and
sees it as a gift bestowed upon him by God.

My madness,
I thank the King of Heaven for it;
though I am mad, by the people's will
I am well able to turn a good verse.

Three people
who are the most foolish in the world:
infatuated young woman—by strength of deed,
a small child, and a fool.

I am the third of these,
I give thanks to the King.
God took away my reason without asking my permission
and condemned me to foolishness.

It is unjust to call me a fool,
God endowed me with the best of sense.
When I am foolish, I strike heaven;
when I am wise, I am repentant.

Periods of my reason come to me,
so that I am the wisest under the sun,
so that I pass judgements with effect
for all the men of the world.

Other periods come to me of foolishness
and of madness; when they (the men of the world)
come to me after that,
I do not follow the true path.

If there is truth in the happy end
which Jesus has ordained for the fool,
if foolishness is what God loved,
is wisdom any better than foolishness?[37]

This poem is strongly reminiscent of the folly of the eastern fools. Mac-dá-Cherda's madness, like theirs, conceals, or is accompanied by, a profound spiritual discernment and wisdom, 'the best of sense'. Mac-dá-Cherda is prophet and judge.

In a story from the life of St Brigit in *The Book of Lismore*, a madman is called upon to prophesy and deliver the word of God.

Once Brigit went over Sliab Fuait. There was a madman biding on the mountain who used to harry the congregations. When the nuns beheld him, fear and great dread seized them. Said Brigit to the madman: 'Since I have come to thee here, preach God's word unto us'. 'I cannot', saith he, 'avoid ministering unto thee, for thou art merciful unto the Lord's household, both the miserable and the poor.' Then said the madman: 'Love the Lord, O Nun! and everyone will love thee. Revere the Lord and everyone will revere thee. Pray unto the Lord, and everyone will pray unto thee.'[38]

Here, then, are three examples of holy madmen or wild men in early Christian Ireland. In order to facilitate our comparison with the Eastern evidence, it will be useful to reproduce Professor Ó Riain's list of the structural components of madness in the sagas of the *gelta*.

(A) THE OCCASIONS OF MADNESS: (i) the curse of a *sacerdos*; (ii) a battlefield experience; (iii) consumption of contaminated food or drink; (iv) the loss of a lover.

(B) THE STATE OF MADNESS: The madman (i) takes to the wilderness; (ii) perches on trees; (iii) collects firewood; (iv) is naked, hairy, covered with feathers or clothed with rags; (v) leaps and/or levitates; (vi) is very swift; (vii) is restless and travels great distances; (viii) experiences hallucinations; (ix) has a special diet.

(C) THE OCCASIONS OF RESTORATION TO SANITY: (i) intervention by a *sacerdos*; (ii) consumption of blessed food or drink; (iii) the act of coition.[39]

There are obvious parallels with the Eastern material. In section (A), while madness in the East does not follow a curse, it usually follows self-accusation or conviction of sin; folly for Christ's sake has a strongly penitential aspect. Likewise, considering A (ii), many of the fools are 'drop-out' soldiers. This was indeed a constant motif in early monastic literature—perhaps the most famous example being St Martin of Tours, whose life by Sulpicius Severus was known at an early date in Ireland.[40] The well-known story of Martin's conversion involves voluntary departure from military life as well as compassion for the poor; moreover, bystanders laugh at Martin when they see him clad in only half a cloak, the other half having been given to a poor man.[41] In Ireland there is a tradition that St Columba (Columcille) went on pilgrimage to Britain as a penance, out of 'fear of hell', following his instigation of the battle of Cul Dremne fought somewhere in northern Connacht in 561; the hymn *Altus Prosator* is presented as a prayer for forgiveness.[42] However, Adomnán, in his life of Columcille, written a hundred years after the saint's death, seems to deny this tradition as he mentions several return trips made to Ireland by the saint.[43]

It is in his 'life-style' that the Irish fool most closely resembles the Eastern *salos*. For Ó Riain the pivotal element in the saga is the *wilderness*. The wild life of the madman is a thoroughly natural one; it extends his communion with nature and animals and also his solidarity with others, for, while he flees human society, his influence (for example, his inspired judgements) is ultimately beneficial to the community. In this respect the Irish wild man closely resembles the holy men of Syria analysed, as we have seen, by Peter Brown; the strangeness of the wild man, his 'separation from wonted status' (for Ó Riain, a more fundamental category than his madness), endows him with considerable social and spiritual power. The relation with the created order is also noteworthy. The Irish *dísert* was more like the Syrian *erēmos*: it could support life; it was not an enemy. Suibne may complain of his lot, but the beauty of his poetry reflects his positive appreciation of God's creation. Similar themes appear in the Eastern monastic literature. The desert may be the place of spiritual battle with the devil, but the monks *love* it: as Fr Chitty has pointed out,[44] while they were aware of the negative aspect, the monastic saints 'had at the same time a positive love for the stark beauty of their wildernesses'—even, *pace* Brown, the Egyptian wildernesses. When a philosopher asked St Antony how he could endure without books in his long solitude, he would point to the mountainous wilderness around him: 'My book, O philosopher, is the nature of created things, and it is present, when I will, for me to read the words of God.'[45]

Ó Riain relies on anthropological interpretation and claims that the key concept in the *gelta* sagas is separation from wonted status: the king in the desert, the royal one gone wild. He sees the madness as a 'rite of passage' and regards the wilderness as the point of departure for reintegration into society. While such an inter-pretation cannot be accepted uncritically, it is a warning that we may be dealing with a more generalized phenomenon than folly for Christ's sake. While the Irish stories have several points of contact with the Eastern, it must be admitted that explicit references to the Pauline texts are rare, and folly is never seen as an active apostolate. Nevertheless, as we have seen, the *gelta* were of interest to monks; their lives were written in monastic *scriptoria*, probably in southern monasteries whose spirit may well have been influenced by Spanish and thus ultimately Eastern monastic literature. St Moling, the almost-foolish friend of Suibne the madman, is the patron saint of the *céili dé*; the saga of the Battle of Allen, in which *gelta* appear, is written 'from the standpoint of one who is earnestly concerned to uphold the prestige of the Culdees and St Columba'.[46] Moreover, the constant association in Ireland of monks with fools, lepers, and outcasts preserved a sense of monastic marginality, a fervent resistance to conformity to the wisdom of the world. This, after all, is what we isolated as one of the key elements in Eastern folly, and it may be this generalized sense, rather than a completely developed hagiographical category of 'holy fool', which is most characteristic of early Irish Christianity.

The Wandering Saints

In the last chapter it was said that the Eastern fools were wanderers and strangers, restlessly seeking some lost homeland. Being a constant traveller meant always being 'the odd man out', a constant fool because a perpetual stranger. Wandering, or *peregrinatio*, is also found in early Christian Ireland; indeed, it has been described as 'the chief legacy' of Irish monasticism.[47] During the sixth and seventh centuries we find Irish monks travelling everywhere: St Columba to Scotland; St Columbanus (*c.*543–615) to Gaul, Switzerland, and Italy; St Gall (d. 645) to Swabia; St Kilian (d. 689) to Franconia. St Brendan (b. 484), according to the ninth-century Latin *Navigatio S. Brendani*, set out on an amazing voyage to the *terra repromissionis sanctorum*.[48] The motives of such peregrination were ascetical, rather than missionary or exploratory. The monk left his home and kindred, not to settle down somewhere else, but to detach himself completely from human ties of any kind and come closer to God in solitude. In human terms the wandering of the Irish monk, like that of the holy fools of Russia, is aimless. The *Anglo-Saxon Chronicle* for the year 891 tells us of three Irishmen who had this sacred wanderlust:

> And three Scots came to King Alfred from Ireland in a boat without oars. They had left home bent on serving God in a state of pilgrimage, they cared not where. Their boat was made of two and a half hides and contained enough provisions to last them seven days, and within a week they landed in Cornwall and shortly afterwards came to King Alfred. They were called Dubslane, Macbeth, and Maelinmun.[49]

These Irish monks are 'wanderers for Christ's sake'. Adomnán tells us that Columba left Ireland for Scotland 'wishing to be a pilgrim for Christ'.[50] Walafrid Strabo,the biographer of St Gall, tells us that he was engaged in 'peregrination for the love of God'.[51] If there is a land that the Irish monks seek, it is their heavenly homeland, the Jerusalem on high. There is a poignant quality in all Irish writing on the theme of exile—exile at once from Erin and Heaven. But this, says St Columbanus in a homily, is the way it must be:

> Then, lest we be concerned with human things, let us concern ourselves with things divine, and as pilgrims ever sigh for and desire our homeland; for the end of the road is ever the object of hopes and desires, and thus since we are travellers and pilgrims in the world, let us ever ponder on the end of the road, that is of our life, for the end of our roaming is our home. . . . Let

us not love the roadway rather than the home-land lest we lose our eternal home; for we have such a home that we ought to love it. Therefore let this principle abide with us, that on the road we so live as travellers, as pilgrims, as guests of the world, entangled in no lusts, longing with no earthly desires, but let us fill our minds with heavenly and spiritual impressions, singing with grace and power. When shall I come and appear before the face of my God?[52]

In the Irish Life of St Brenainn an angel describes heaven as home in these lyrical terms:

A place wherein ye shall find health without sickness, delight without quarrelling, union without wrangling, princedom without dissolution, rest without idleness, freedom without labour, luminous unity of angels, delights of Paradise, service of Angels, feasting without intoxication, avoidance of pain, faces of the righteous, partaking of the Great Easter. A life blessed, just, protected, great, loveable, noble, restful, radiant, without gloom, without darkness, without sin, without weakness, in shining, incorruptible bodies, in stations of angels, on plains of the Land of Promise.[53]

But the spirit of Irish peregrination is best captured in the Old Irish *Life of St Columcille*, where Abraham is taken as the type of the perfect pilgrim.

God counselled Abraham to leave his own country and go in pilgrimage into the land which God had shown him, to wit, the 'Land of Promise'. . . . Now the good counsel which God enjoined here on the father of the faithful is incumbent on all the faithful; that is, to leave their country and their land, their wealth and their worldly delight, for the sake of the Lord of the Elements, and go in perfect pilgrimage in imitation of Him.[54]

Irish pilgrimage integrates the eremitical life of the first monks with a restless wandering and attempts to realize a *stabilitas in peregrinatione*. Like folly for Christ's sake, peregrination is a way of practising self-abasement, for unlike the pilgrim to the Holy Places, who has a definite earthly destination, the exile or *peregrinus* has a dangerously vagabond air and so is despised; he is a voluntary outlaw. Peregrination is a way of imitating, and growing in union with, the humiliated Christ. As Dom Jean Leclercq has said: 'Peregrination is always a form of solitude, a quest for exile and destitution, a way of imitating Christ in his poverty, an authentic evangelical life: did not the Lord praise, in the gospel, the one who becomes a stranger for him?'[55]

The dependence of Ireland on the East has been challenged in recent years by Dr Joseph Raftery, who has pointed out that a mass of theory has been built on minute scraps of evidence.[56] Perhaps, he suggests, the influence went the other way. In an earlier chapter we spoke of folly for Christ's sake in Russian Christianity; was this Russian enthusiasm generated simply by contact with Byzantium, or could it be that this component of Celtic spirituality was integrated in Russian monasticism at an early period? A. Parczewski has shown the considerable influence of Irish monks in the early days of Polish Christianity in the tenth, eleventh, and twelfth centuries.[57] Poland, of course, is not Kiev, but we do know that the Irish monks who came to Poland were from Ratisbon, and that monastic 'Scots' came from that city to Kiev in the twelfth century to minister to the German community there.[58] Indeed, towards the middle of the twelfth century a Latin rite church dedicated to the Blessed Virgin was erected there, together with a Benedictine monastery with monks drawn from the Scots community at Vienna; we know the monastery survived until the Mongol invasion in 1241.[59] There is always the possibility that wandering monks from Ireland might have reached Kiev earlier than this, and that 'wandering Germans', like St Procopius the holy fool, had been formed in, or at least had had some contact with, the Irish houses in central Europe.

Apart from peregrination, there was much else in Irish spirituality with that quality of foolish excess we associate with the most ancient monasticism and the ascesis of the fools for Christ's sake. One common practice was to spend long periods of prayer standing in cold water to quench the flames of lust and grow in *apatheia*. In the preface to his *Martyrology* we are told of Oengus that he 'was an humble, lowly servant to God, and 'tis he that used to chant his psalms thus, while he was at Dísert Oegusso, to wit, fifty in the river with a withe round his neck and tied to the tree, fifty under the tree, and fifty in his cell'.[60] Indeed, this folly of the monks of the Far West and Far East led God's athletes to organize a kind of ascetical Olympics, of which the following story is an example:

There was a pious monk who came across from the East to compete in devotion with Comgall of Bangor, and whatever act of devotion Comgall would perform, the foreign monk would do the same, until Comgall went into the river to chant his psalms, and the monk that had come from the East went into the same river. When he was on the side below Comgall, the monk could not endure it, because of the greatness of the heat of the water. When he was on the side above Comgall, the monk could not endure it, because of the greatness of the cold. So that hence he was not able to compete in devotion with Comgall.[61]

But not all Irish asceticism was of this athletic kind. The early monastic literature constantly reminds us that the goal of all ascesis is imitation of, and union with, Our Lord. To be rejected and reviled as a fool is not a Christianized Stoicism but fidelity to the gospel text where the Lord reminds his followers that serious discipleship involves persecution. In a letter St Columbanus writes: 'As it is written, he who says that he believes in Christ ought also himself to walk even as Christ walked—that is, be both poor and humble and ever preaching truth under the persecution of mankind'.[62]

The Irish ascetics were famed for their sympathy and identification with the poor, with lepers, and madmen. This, once again, was a truly evangelical ideal. It was grounded in the doctrines of the Body of Christ and the Communion of Saints, an expression of obedience to the apostolic precept about bearing one another's burdens and making up the afflictions of Christ. In the Body of Christ there is a rhythm of exchange of sorrow and joy, pain and happiness; when one member is hurt, the rest of the Body feels it too (1 Cor. 12: 26). It is significant that one of the earliest Irish texts we possess, the 'Cambrai homily', just before speaking of the three kinds of martyrdom (red—by blood; white—by abandonment of everything for the love of God; green—by fasting, toil and penance), asserts:

> Thus it is fitting for us ourselves, that every suffering and every ailment that is on his neighbours should inflame every part, for we are all members unto God, as saith the apostle: *Quis scandalizatur et ego non uror? quis infirmatur et ego non infirmor?* . . . the holy apostle has said this from the abundance of his charity; everyone's sickness was sickness to him, offence to anyone was offence to him, everyone's infirmity was infirmity to him. Even so it is meet for everyone of us that he suffer with everyone in his hardship and in his poverty and in his infirmity. We see in these wise words of the sage that fellow-suffering is counted as a kind of cross.[63]

The Irish fools radiate paschal joy and peace; there is a lightness, gaiety, good humour, about the greatest of the Irish ascetics. Adomnán says that Columcille was 'merry' in the midst of his pious exercises, his fasts and vigils: 'In all this he loved everybody, there was mirth on his face, and he was happy in his inmost heart in the joy of the Holy Spirit.'[64]

Like the great hesychast saints of the East, he was transfigured in the Uncreated Light. One night, we are told, a young man, Virgno, went into the church on Iona and prayed in an *exedra* that adjoined the oratory wall.

After some space of time, as it were of one hour, the venerable man Columba entered the same sacred building; and along with him there entered a golden light, descending from highest heaven and wholly filling the inside of the church. Also the enclosed space of the *exedra*, in which Virgno tried to conceal himself as well as he could, was filled with the brightness of that heavenly light, which streamed through the partly open inner door of that room, not without some effect of terror. And just as none can look with direct and undazzled eyes upon the summer midday sun, so also Virgno, who saw that heavenly brightness, could not at all endure it, because the brilliant and incomparable radiance greatly dazzled his sight. When he saw this flashing and terrifying effulgence, that brother was so greatly overcome by fear that no strength remained in him.[65]

Here, in the Far West, is a classic portrait of a saint transfigured in Christ by the power of the Holy Spirit. In the wild men and fools of early Ireland we learn to recognize a no less radiant beauty.

4

Joy, Mirth, and Folly in the Hermits of the Eleventh Century

Hermits have nearly always been written off as fools; their austerities have been regarded as destructive of health, their rigour as fanatical, their desire for uninterrupted silence and solitude as subversive and anti-social. Cut off from all earthly ties of kinship and friendship, exposed to dangers from wild animals and to the unpredictable movements of the weather, forced into a kind of savagery, the hermit looks like the enthusiast, the extremist, *par excellence*. If there is a fool in the Church, it is the hermit. He has left all prudence and wisdom behind.

The late Thomas Merton, who himself spent the last years of his life as a hermit in Kentucky, epitomizes, in his description of the modern world's contempt of the hermit, a response that has been all too common, not only outside but also inside the Church.

In the eyes of our conformist society, the hermit is nothing but a failure. He has to be a failure—we have absolutely no use for him, no place for him. He is outside all our projects, plans, assemblies, movements. We can countenance him as long as he remains only a fiction, or a dream. As soon as he becomes real, we are revolted by his insignificance, his poverty, his shabbiness, his total lack of status. Even those who consider themselves contemplatives, often cherish a secret contempt for the solitary. For in the contemplative life of the hermit there is none of that noble security, that intelligent depth, that artistic finesse which the more academic contemplative seeks in his sedate respectability.[1]

In eleventh-century western Europe there was a reawakening of interest in the solitary life. Not surprisingly, perhaps, its main protagonists have much to say about the wisdom of a life which looks like sheer lunacy. However, we would be wrong in thinking that the folly of the hermits is a species of fanaticism: on the contrary, there is a gay, joyful, almost humorous quality in their writings and the accounts of their lives. They exude paschal joy and an immovable faith that the Lord Jesus conquers and reigns, that 'all shall be well'. The style is detached, remarkably free of neurotic tension or repressed emotion. There is mirth (*hilaritas*) and good humour (*iocunditas*) in the hermitages.

In the middle of the twelfth century, William of St Thierry
(*c.* 1085–1148), friend and biographer of St Bernard and mystical
theologian, wrote his 'Golden Epistle' to the Carthusian monks of
Mont Dieu, whose life combined both eremitical and cenobitic
elements. William boldly describes their vocation as 'folly for
Christ's sake'.

> Look, my brethren, look upon your vocation. Where is there one wise
> among you? where a scribe? where a disputer of this world? For though
> there be some wise among you, yet through the simple hath He added to
> Him the wise, who once by men that were fishers subdued unto Himself the
> kings and philosophers of the world. Leave therefore, leave the wise of this
> world, that swell with the spirit of this world, and whose conceit is of high
> things and whose tongues lick the dust, wisely to go down into hell. But as
> for you, while the pit is being digged for the sinner, as ye have begun so
> continue, being made fools for Christ's sake, in the foolishness of God
> which is wiser than all men, and by Christ's guiding learn the meek discipline
> of ascending into heaven.[2]

Thus William exhorts his friends in the Charterhouse. But his words
of folly have been prefaced by a lyrical opening address, in which
evangelical good humour is well to the fore.

> To the brethren of the Mount of God, by whom the eastern light and
> ancient Egyptian fervour of religion are brought into this western darkness
> and cold of France, namely the pattern of solitary life and form of heavenly
> conversation—to them go forth, O my soul, yea and join with them in the
> joy of the Holy Spirit, in merriment of heart, in fervour of piety, and in all
> service of devout will.[3]

In what follows we shall see something of such 'merriment of
heart' and folly for Christ's sake in the eremitical spirituality of the
West in the eleventh century and especially in St Romuald, St Peter
Damian, and the founders of the Carthusian Order.

St Romuald (c.950–1027)

St Romuald began his monastic life at the abbey of Sant' Apollinare
in Classe, but a year after being appointed abbot he resigned in
order to practise a more rigorous eremitism. The later years of his
life were spent in a wandering apostolate, making disciples and
calling men to perfection. Two monastic institutes survived him
as a memorial: Fonte Avella, a congregation of hermits in the

Apennines, and Camaldoli, near Arezzo, where monks to this day
live an eremitical life in a single group of buildings, coming together
on certain days for liturgical prayer and common meals.[4]

St Romuald neither founded a religious order nor wrote a rule.
Such developments belong to the more centralized form of Church
government established by the reforms of Pope St Gregory VII in
the second half of the eleventh century. St Romuald was essentially
a spiritual father, an 'elder', in the Eastern sense, one whose distinctive spiritual teaching was never written down by himself and then
later codified, but rather communicated through personal teaching
and example to his disciples, who were thus encouraged to share his
vision and practice of the life of prayer.

We know St Romuald only through the writings of others,
notably St Peter Damian, who entered the monastery at Fonte
Avella in 1035 and wrote the *Vita Sancti Romualdi* some fifteen
years after the saint's death. Damian did not know Romuald, but
they were both from Ravenna and Damian knew many of the
monks who had taken part in the events he recounts. It is obvious
from the tone of his writing that he attempted, as best he could, to
introduce the authentic Romuald to his readers.

The Romuald thus presented is an attractive, warm and good-
humoured spiritual father. Like all hermits, he is at war, engaged in
spiritual combat, but he fights with irony and a sense of fun. When
evil spirits descend upon him, Romuald simply laughs them away.

> Christ's great champion insulted them with these words, 'Look, I'm
> ready, come on; let's see your power, if that's what it is! Or are you really
> powerless? Are you already defeated, don't you have some secret weapon
> to bring out against God's little servant?' In the end with these and similar
> words, he confounded the spirits and sent them on their way, like so many
> arrows from a bow.[5]

Jean Leclercq has described Romuald's treatment of the devils in
this and other incidents as 'contemptuous drollery'; Romuald exor-
cizes by satire and jest.[6] Most endearing of Romuald's qualities is
his compassion for sinners; for example, his kindness to thieves,
which is free from any trace of condescension and combines
resolute spiritual direction with a playful sense of fun. One day a
thief breaks into Brother Gregory's cell.

> In his mirth (*hilariter*) the holy man said 'Brethren, I just do not know
> what to do with such a wicked man. Shall we tear out his eyes? But then he

won't be able to see. Shall we cut off his hand? But then he won't work any
more and will probably die of hunger. Shall we chop off his foot? Then he
couldn't walk. No, take him inside, and give him some food, so that
meanwhile we can work out what to do with him.' And so the holy man,
exulting in the Lord, fed the thief and then humbly chided him and
admonished him with sweet words, letting him return home in peace.[7]

Damian gives many instances of this gentle, good-humoured spirituality: we are told of Romuald's *alacritas*, a suggestive word, which
might best be translated as 'spiritual bounce'. It is said that the holy
man loved giving presents, not as a kind of compensation for what
the saint called his preference for the austerity of the eremitical life,
but as a fruit of it. Above all, we are told of Romuald's gift of tears
and his unceasing invocation of the name of Jesus.

Frequently he was ravished by so much contemplation of the Godhead,
that, almost dissolved in tears and burning with the ardour of divine love, he
would cry out: Dear Jesus, my sweet honey, ineffable longing, sweetness of
the saints, delight of the angels. . . .[8]

A fervent devotion to Our Lord in solitude and contemplation
makes Romuald a true fool for Christ's sake not so much in the style
of the wild ascetics of Byzantium or Ireland but with a new and
perhaps distinctively Italian quality of good humour, charm, and
joy. Romuald is, perhaps, more of a clown for Christ's sake.

'The Impossible Man'

St Romuald's biographer, St Peter Damian (1007–1072), was, by
any reckoning, a giant of the eleventh century, outstanding as
Church reformer, social prophet, theologian, poet, and writer on
spiritual and monastic subjects. He has the reputation of being a
man of ferocious intransigence and verbal violence, 'an impossible
man', anticipating St Bernard as much in his vehemence as in his
spiritual influence. And yet the vehemence of St Peter Damian is
rather like that of his namesake, the Prince of the Apostles, whose
fiery personality was harnessed to the service of the gospel, trans-
gressing sometimes the limits of propriety and good taste, but
always full of enthusiasm and passion for the truth. There is good
humour in Damian, as there was in Romuald, and there is an
explicit revelling in folly for Christ's sake, but the overall
impression is of a holy extravagance, a calculated extremism for

the sake of the gospel. Damian is very much the prophet. But it is as a contemplative that St Peter Damian makes his appearance in Dante's *Paradiso*, and that is surely how he would have wished it.

> Between the two shores of Italy and not far distant from thy native place rise crags so high that the thunder sounds far below them; and they make a ridge that is called Catria, beneath which is consecrated a hermitage which once was wholly given to worship. . . . There I became so constant in God's service that with food seasoned only with olive-juice I passed easily through heats and frosts, content in contemplative thoughts.[9]

For him, the hermit's life of contemplation was the hardest but surest way to perfection; by contrast, the Rule of St Benedict was the easier route, a mere propaedeutic. Damian was unashamedly partisan in his support of the eremitical movement, and his language often verges on what one might call the 'eremolatrous'!

> What more shall I say of you, O solitary life, blessed life, pleasure-garden of souls, holy life, angelic life, hall of heavenly jewels, court of the senators of heaven? Your fragrance excels the fragrance of all spices, your taste is sweeter to the tongue of the enlightened heart than the dripping honey-comb or any honey. . . . Those who know you love you; those who have rested in the delight of your loving embrace know the merits of your praise.[10]

The richness of this language should not beguile us into imagining that Damian saw the desert as a beautiful escape from the awfulness of humankind in the tradition of the Cynics and recluses of the ancient world. There is no trace of 'preciousness' in Damian's celebration of the desert. Jean Leclercq has put it well:

> Solitude is opposed to insularity, which is a form of bombast, a real cancer. The humble hermit has a gay, smiling, relaxed face. He is pleased at the arrival of a brother, even if the visit prevents him fulfilling his daily programme of prayer and austerity. He is forbearing, peaceful, always full of good cheer. He does not irritate, he does not know what malice is; he radiates peace, concord. . . . The solitary is not an isolated man: animals live isolated lives; but the Christian life is a communion with all the members of the meek and humble Christ; one is filled with Jesus Christ only by means of those two virtues. Those who go to the hermit to find Christ will find him there if the hermit possesses the virtues, and if Christ truly abides and presides in his soul.[11]

The eremitical way is a form of *imitatio Christi*; on entering the desert, the hermit is in the line not only of Moses and the children of

Israel, of Elijah and Elisha, of the monks in Egypt and Syria, but also of Our Lord himself, whose ministry was constantly sustained by silent prayer in the desert.

One strand in the fabric of early monasticism also to be found in the writing of St Peter Damian is that of holy idiocy, which he expounds in terms of holy simplicity. To some, Damian appears to be opposed to rational inquiry or learning of any kind, and there are, indeed, some scathing passages about letters.

I spurn Plato, the searcher into the hidden things of nature, who set a measure to the movements of the planets, and calculated the courses of the stars; Pythagoras, who divided the round world into its regions with his mathematician's rod, means nothing to me; I renounce the much-thumbed books of Nichomachus, and Euclid too, round-shouldered from pouring over his complex geometrical problems; the rhetoricians with their syllogisms and the cavillings of the sophists are useless in this matter. Let the gymnasts shiver in their nakedness for love of wisdom, and the peripatetics seek truth at the bottom of a well. . . . Let the simplicity of Christ instruct me, and the true humility of the wise loose me from the chains of doubt. For, as St Paul says: 'When God showed us his wisdom, the world, with all its wisdom, could not find its way to God; and now God would use a foolish thing, our preaching, to save those who will believe in it.'[12]

Damian, however, is no obscurantist. His own works are elegantly written and cogently argued; he was formed in the schools of Lombardy, and his renunciation of the philosophers and poets reveals a considerable knowledge of them; he does not reject them without first succinctly summarizing their contribution to learning. The import of Damian's polemic against Plato, and of his advocacy of simplicity, is that it demonstrates his militant independence, as a theologian, from cultural trends, ideologies, and movements of thought.

There are theologians and historians writing in our own time who hold that 'the whole tradition from Abraham to Schleiermacher' has a craven and submissive attitude to its various cultural settings: the Fathers, we are told, 'constructed' Catholic Orthodoxy because of their 'Platonism'; St Thomas Aquinas wrote his *Summa* because of his 'Aristotelianism'. Such over-simplification disregards the truth that the Church's theologians and spiritual writers have always been fully conscious of the problems of cultural determination and have striven to overcome them, some more successfully than others. They have attempted to strike a balance between the two extremes, on the one hand, of rejecting all secular wisdom, and, on the other, of being submerged beneath it.

The ideas of the *saeculum* are assessed according to the criteria of the Church's teaching office; where they are good and true, such ideas may contribute to the rearticulation of Catholic truth; where false, they are rejected or corrected. Origen compares this Catholic approach to culture with the Israelites 'spoiling the Egyptians' (Exod. 3: 22), who, by appropriating the 'gold and silver' of their former masters, demonstrate their liberation in the very act of theft; while the heretics, 'who, from their Greek studies, produce heretical notions, and set them up', are like those who erected the golden calf at Bethel.[13] Damian uses the same image and commends the one who 'seizes the treasures of the Egyptians to construct a dwelling for God, the one who reads the poets and the philosophers in order to be more vigorous in penetrating the mystery of the heavenly word'.[14] These words are intended to remind those who have been bewitched by learning and scholarship that education is secondary to, and should be ordered towards, the worship of God. He endeavours to achieve the right relationship between faith and knowledge, to prevent learning developing cancerously to the detriment of godliness.

The concept Damian uses to confront the complexity of worldly wisdom is *simplicitas*, which already had a venerable history. For Tertullian, it was equivalent to the truth of Scripture and tradition in contrast to the *curiositas* of the world.[15] It was further developed by the Latin Fathers of the fourth century: for St Ambrose, simplicity is greater than all argument.[16] Damian recapitulates this long Latin tradition of *sancta simplicitas* in many of his writings, notably in a short work concerning the need to value holy simplicity above the knowledge that puffs up.[17] He calls us to admire the mystery of God's grace, which transformed the apostles, who were not wise and learned men but ignorant fishermen, *idiotae* and rustics. Preaching on the feast of St Andrew, the first-called of the apostles, he says:

> Yet he did not choose for his service those distinguished by triumphant titles, nor energetic warriors, nor riders of roaring steeds, nor, lastly, philosophers and men of eloquence, but the masters of nets and oarsmen of a wretched little boat, so that victory might be ascribed, not to human prowess but to divine power alone.[18]

And on another occasion:

The captain of a ship was appointed the key-bearer of heaven; the disciples of fishermen became the masters of orators; and the wisdom of the world has been defeated by the simplicity of Christ, as the apostle says: 'Seeing that in the wisdom of God, the world,' by wisdom, knew not God, it pleased God, by the foolishness of our preaching, to save them that believe'. By this simplicity Paul, who judged himself not to know anything among the Corinthians except Christ Jesus and him crucified, triumphed over Dionysius the Areopagite at Athens.[19]

The monk, says Damian, must be 'simple, pure and ignorant of the depravity of the world' and see himself as called 'to the wise folly of Christ'.[20] Above all, the monk must have a vivid sense of his unworthiness and littleness: Damian's favourite description of himself, to be found at the head of most of his letters, is 'sinner monk',[21] 'lowest servant of the cross of Christ'.[22]

Damian was an 'impossible man', not a boor or a churl, but a prophet, a shocking but redemptive sign to Church and world of the radical demands of the gospel. His great attacks on corruption and simony in the Church, his proclamation of the need to flee ecclesiastical dignity, and his dissertation on the inevitable 'shortness of the Roman pontiffs' life' (because all life is short and all temporal glory must be despised),[23] are but an expression of the fervour of the Holy Spirit, who kindled an unquenchable flame in the heart of this great lover of God. What makes Peter Damian an extremist, a prophet, is his relentless pursuit of the one thing needful, the art of arts, the worship and adoration of God. It is the primacy of contemplation which stirs Damian to fight humbug and hypocrisy and the worship of false gods. His epitaph, which is also the rationale of a peculiarly vehement sanctity, is the phrase of Dante: *diposto a sola latria*. St Peter Damian is wholly given over to worship.

The Carthusians

'Never reformed because never deformed' is the famous claim made for the Carthusian order, founded by St Bruno (*c.* 1032–1101). With its sensitive combination of cenobitic and eremitical ideals, it has preserved the 'ancient Egyptian fervour of religion' and 'merriment of heart'. Carthusian solitude could not be further removed in spirit from the lugubrious religiosity implied by the secular English usage of the word 'recluse': above all, it is a spirituality of joy.

Joy is the keynote of the first pontifical document addressed to the Carthusians by Pope Urban II (*c.*1042–1099):

> Urban, bishop, servant of the servants of God, to his dear sons, Bruno, Landuin, and the other brothers: greeting and apostolic blessing. It is written: 'Joy and happiness are his companions; they dwell with him in his tent: thanksgiving and songs of praise are found at his side.' Dear sons, called by the Lord to inhabit the place he has prepared for you on the mountain of Chartreuse in the diocese of Grenoble—live there full of 'joy and happiness' through the contemplation of heavenly things, so that you may unceasingly raise up your hearts to God and rejoice in the Lord.[24]

It would seem that this papal command was faithfully obeyed by the saintly founder of the Charterhouse. In his panegyric for St Bruno, Landuin says that 'he always had a mirthful expression on his face'. In one of his letters Bruno speaks of monks as spiritual market-gardeners, who go out into the wild places of the desert to cultivate joy, the fruit of the Spirit.

> There strong men may be recollected as much as they like, abiding within themselves, assiduously cultivating the seeds of the virtues, and feeding on the goodness of the fruits of paradise. There they strive to acquire that eye whose clear look wounds the divine Bridegroom with love and whose purity leads them to see God. There one is devoted to a truly fulfilled leisure, and is at rest in a tranquil action. There God gives his athletes, for the toil of combat, their desired reward: a peace that the world does not know and joy in the Holy Spirit.[25]

At the end, as he approached his death, Bruno wrote a charge for his brethren in the Dauphiné, a letter in which we find the distillation of his teaching in the litany-like repetition: *gaudete . . . gaudete . . . gaudete.*[26]

In conclusion, then, we can see that monastic solitude, misinterpreted by some as soulless and anti-human, was regained by the eleventh-century Western doctors of the eremitical life as the cultivation of exuberant joy in the Lord, the proclamation of the gospel of good humour, a revelling in holy folly. In an almost Chestertonian way they saw Catholic Christianity in its divine foolishness both as a weapon of attack against the citadels of worldly wisdom and also as a repository of paschal mirth and joy, that 'gigantic secret of the Christian'.[27] Firm and fearless in the witness to divine truth, on fire with heavenly joy: what better description of the vocation, not only of the religious, but of every Christian? For the man who flees the world, said Bernard the

Carthusian, 'joys are not lost but transformed. . . . They are not without humour (*iocunditas*) who say: "I am happy in the way of thy testimonies, as if in all riches".'[28]

.

5

God's Jesters: The Cistercians

In one of his longest letters St Bernard of Clairvaux (1090–1153) describes himself as a jester.

It is very dangerous for anyone to hear himself spoken of above what he knows he deserves. Who will grant me to be deservedly humbled before men for the truth, just as much as I have been undeservedly exalted for what is not true? I could rightly apply to myself these words of the prophet: 'being exalted, I have been humbled and troubled' (Vulgate Ps. 87: 16); and again: 'I will play and make myself meaner than I have done' (2 Sam. 6: 22). Yes, I shall play, that I may be mocked. A good game, this, by which Michal is enraged and God is pleased. A good game, I say, which is ridiculous to men, but a very beautiful spectacle to the angels (cf. 1 Cor. 4: 9). I say it is a good game by which we become 'a reproach to the rich and a contempt to the proud' (cf. Ps. 122: 4).

For what else do worldlings think we are doing but playing about, when what they desire most on earth, we flee, and what they flee, we desire? We are like jesters and tumblers, who, with heads down and feet up, exhibit extraordinary behaviour by standing or walking on their hands, and thus draw all eyes to themselves. But ours is not the play of children or of the theatre, which excites lust and represents sordid acts in the effeminate and shameful contortions of the actors. No, ours is a joyous game, decent, grave, and admirable, delighting the gaze of the heavenly onlookers. This chaste and religious game he plays who says: 'We are made a spectacle to angels and to men' (1 Cor. 4: 9). And let us too play this game now, so that we may be made game of, discomfited, humbled, until he comes who casts down the mighty and exalts the humble, who will gladden us, glorify us, and exalt us for ever.[1]

This eulogy of holy 'play' is the peroration of a strongly worded and clearly written letter, the objects of which are not to afford amusement or light relief. It is addressed to Ogier, a Canon Regular of Mont-Saint-Éloi near Arras, with whom St Bernard was in regular correspondence. It would seem that the Abbot of Clairvaux held his friend in great respect. He had submitted his Apology to him for his approval, even before William of St Thierry had seen it. In 1125 the Bishop of Noyon had chosen Ogier to introduce the Canons Regular into the parish of St Médard in Tournai. He remained as superior for fourteen years but then resigned in order to lead a more contemplative life at his original monastery. When asked for his opinion, Bernard had advised him to remain as abbot, but Ogier ignored the advice. Then he wrote to Bernard asking him to draw up a rule of life for him. It is quite clear that Ogier regarded Bernard as an unimpeachable authority on monastic questions, a source of spiritual wisdom and discernment. In the letter that was to prompt Bernard's reply he urged the Abbot of Clairvaux to show his full talent and God-given greatness.

Bernard responds with characteristic emotion and astonishing self-irony. He begins by showing that he will not tolerate flattery. Throughout your letter, says Bernard, you go too far with your praise: 'You praise me a great deal and exalt me above myself. I am unconscious of deserving all this, and so I put it down to your benevolence and forgive you for your ignorance.' He will not accept Ogier's apologies for disregarding his advice; he always feels relieved when people reject his admonitions: 'Whenever my advice is followed, I confess that I always feel oppressed with a great burden of responsibility, and I can never be confident and always await the outcome with anxiety.'[2]

Bernard dismisses Ogier's image of him as the wise, all-knowing master of the spiritual life. No, says Bernard in the phrase beloved of St Peter Damian, I am a 'sinner monk' (*monachus peccator*), one who knows himself only to be a fool. Bernard seeks to expose the subtle and pernicious pride lurking behind Ogier's apparently admirable decision to renounce the dignities of abbatial office and retire to a simpler monastic life.

I congratulate you on having disburdened yourself, but I very much fear that in so doing you have dishonoured God (*quod sis exoneratus . . . exhonoratus sit Deus*). Without doubt you have, so far as you could, opposed his designs by casting yourself down from the post to which he had promoted you. If, by way of excuse, you allege the necessity of poverty, I reply that necessity wins a crown (*Reg.* 7); if you allege the difficulty or impossibility of your position, I reply that all things are possible to one who believes. Better tell the truth, and admit that your own quiet pleases you more than labouring for the benefit of others.[3]

But Bernard will not simply warn of the dangers of pride disguised by humility; the Abbot of Clairvaux must demonstrate that 'humiliation is the way to humility'. And so, having rejected flattery, Bernard goes further in self-renunciation and vehemently asserts his own stupidity and foolishness. The great Abbot of Clairvaux calls himself a jester or jongleur (*ioculator*) and speaks of himself being 'made game of' (*illudamur*), a word that recalls the ridiculing of Jesus in the Praetorium and at the cross (*illudebant ei*; Vulgate Matt. 27: 29, 31, 41). In the letter to Ogier there is no explicit allusion to the mocking of Christ but rather to the dance of David before the ark: the humble jest of the servant of God is contrasted with the postures of the proud. It is not to endear himself to his correspondent that Bernard calls himself a jester; *ioculator* had no sympathetic connotations. As we shall see later, to call someone a jester in the monastic milieu of the mid-twelfth century was to insult him. Not only had a long series of conciliar decrees condemned the jongleurs and forbidden the profession to the clergy, but also at the time of writing this letter Bernard was using the language of jest in a pejorative sense to insult Abelard. Indeed, in that controversy, there were mutual accusations of childishness and clowning, although we should note that it was St Bernard who took the initiative in using the vocabulary of jest to insult his adversaries.[4]

It is thus not only surprising, but also moving, to find Bernard using this language against himself, for, in a deliberate and well-argued way, he calls himself *ioculator, saltator*, the player of a game. Bernard turns the tables against himself, teaching Ogier the lesson of humility by applying satire to himself.

Humiliatio est via ad humilitatem; humiliation, being laughed at and written off as a clown, is the way to true humility. St Bernard's message in this letter might seem at first sight to qualify him for recognition as a fool for Christ's sake, for unselfconsciously he transforms the secular motif of the jongleur into an image of the true disciple of Jesus Christ. However, to understand more fully its implications, we must consider this letter within the general context of Cistercian spirituality.

The Foolish Extremism of the Cistercians

The Cistercian tradition is characterized, from the beginning, by its extremism. Like the movements of monastic renewal and reform we studied in the last chapter, like the first monasticism in Egypt, the Cistercians sought to wrench religious life away not simply from corruption or moral decadence but even from worthy, respectable moderation. The Cistercian, like the Old Testament prophet, is 'marginal man', on the very edge of Church life, because of his fidelity to its heart and centre.[5] The Cistercians became 'outsiders' in order to recall the Church and monasticism to its true interiority, its roots and sources. This meant, first of all, a return to an uncluttered and straightforward observance of the Rule of St Benedict; the first Cistercians intended to maintain 'the purity and simplicity of the holy rule purely and simply'.[6] But this return to sources did not end there. Fidelity to the Rule was but part of a more general desire for the pristine spirit of the desert, of St Antony and St Pachomius and St Basil, who in turn would point beyond themselves to the life of the apostles and of the Lord himself. In a word, it is the passionate yearning for an uncompromised following and imitation of Christ which makes the first Cistercians 'extremists'.

It is this Christocentric extremism which underlies St Bernard's conception of the sacred jest. For authentic conformity to the Word Incarnate means imitation of that divine excess and folly which took God to the crib and the cross. As William of St Thierry (*c*. 1085–1148) said:

> From him a new wisdom has come into the world, a wisdom that transcends all worldly wisdom and makes it mad, the new wisdom of those who understand and appreciate that what is foolish or weak with God is wiser and stronger than men, the wisdom of those who taste, in the sweet savour of the Spirit, the humility of the Son of God, who was obedient unto death, even death on a cross, that Passion which he bore for our sakes, the derision, the slaps on the face, the spittings, the scourging, the thorns, and the nails.[7]

According to William, the love manifested in the Incarnation and Passion is 'amazing and divine', a foolish love, which enkindles a like love and folly in men. The redemptive works of Christ are 'amazing mysteries of eternity', which stir the believer to imitate the Lord's sufferings.[8] In his treatise *De natura et dignitate amoris* William shows how the stupendous wonders of God's love of man account for the 'holy madness' of our love of God (*sancta . . . amoris insania*).

> If those who have the souls of beasts or sheep, 'whose flesh', according to the prophet, 'is like the flesh of asses', if those are driven to madness by the seduction of transitory things, how much more fitting is it that they should

go mad in the fervour of spiritual youth who are possessed of true love and are led by its spiritual prompting. Is it not a sad thing indeed, if those who corrupt nature are more successful in doing evil than the lovers of truth are in doing good? Listen to holy madness (*Audi sanctam insaniam*): 'If we are out of our mind', says the apostle, 'it is for God; if we are sane, it is for you' (2 Cor. 5: 13) . . . Listen to the same apostle: 'For I could wish to be anathema for Christ, for the sake of my brethren' (Rom. 9: 3). However holy his motives may be, does not the apostle seem to be mad? For he is firmly resolved to desire that which is impossible—to be anathema from Christ for Christ's sake. Such was the drunkenness of the apostles when the Holy Spirit came upon them; such was the madness of Paul, when Festus said to him: 'Paul, you are mad'. Is it surprising if he was called mad who even at the point of death strove to convert to Christ those men by whom he was being judged for Christ's sake? It was not great learning that created this madness in him, as the king claimed who knew the true reason but pretended that he did not. No, as we have said, it was because he was drunk with the Holy Spirit that he longed to make those who judged him like himself in great things and in small. What madness could there be greater or more surprising than that of a man who has left the world behind because of his yearning for Christ, yet cleaves to the world for Christ's sake, that is, under the compulsion of obedience and brotherly love? He strives after heaven and yet sinks himself in the mire. He is young Benjamin, completely carried away. . . . Such was the madness which made the martyrs laugh in the midst of their torments. I can even use the fervent and daring words of the poet: 'it is good to be mad'.[9]

'Holy madness' for the Cistercian Fathers, the rationale of their extremist renewal, is grounded in the dogmas of the Incarnation and Redemption. We are saved by God's weakness, poverty, humiliation and foolishness. Thus union with God, growth in grace, and sanctification must involve an increase in these hard virtues, must mean participation in the excess and foolishness of God.

With the Cistercian Fathers we shall now explore the mystery of holy folly in the models or archetypes of Christian perfection which they saw in the child, the idiot, the pauper, the humiliated man, and the fool.

The Child

As we saw in Chapter 1, the tradition of folly for Christ's sake is inseparable from that of spiritual childhood, the little way. In the Cistercians, the notion of folly for Christ's sake, with its robust sense of a 'counter-culture' in conflict with the wisdom of the world, is epitomized, not in delinquency or violent mania, but in childlike simplicity and weakness. St Bernard, in particular, in his sermons on the Nativity of Our Lord, makes us contemplate the infancy of God; he will not let us forget that the Word assumed the flesh of a child: 'The Word was made flesh, weak flesh, infantile flesh, young flesh, helpless flesh.'[10] But why, he asks, should the God of majesty have done such a thing? Why should God be a child? The answer is to be found in the teaching of Christ: the example of his infancy foreshadows the doctrine of his maturity—the necessity of conversion to spiritual childhood: 'Why was it necessary that he should so empty himself, so humble himself, make himself so small (*sic abbreviaret se*), but that you should do likewise?'[11] And again, in his 'Sermon to the Clergy on Conversion', he speaks thus:

> Our true life is found only through conversion; nor is there any other entrance into life, as the Lord says again: 'Unless you be converted and become as little children, you shall not enter into the Kingdom of heaven' (Matt. 18: 3). Fitting indeed is it that only little children enter in, for it is a little Child who leads them (Isa. 11: 6), he who to this very end was born and given to us. [12]

The truly converted man is thus one of the 'little ones' (*parvuli*), to whom God reveals what he hides from the wise and understanding. As in the tradition of Theophilus of Antioch and Irenaeus, Bernard sees the infancy, youth, and manhood of Christ as successively recapitulating and sanctifying the ages of human life. Infancy occupies a special place in this process simply because it is the beginning, the first age; growth to maturity must be preceded by regeneration and rejuvenation: 'For this reason also a child was born and came to manhood through the successive ages of human life, so that he should be absent from none.'[13]

Guerric of Igny (d. 1157), a contemporary of Bernard and another whose desire for solitude had been overruled by the Abbot of Clairvaux, meditates at great length on the infancy of God and its causal role in man's rejuvenation and redemption. Moreover, he explicitly connects spiritual childlikeness with folly for Christ's sake. For Guerric, spiritual infancy requires us to unlearn the delusions of our godless maturity; becoming a little child means going out of our adult mind. The infancy of God 'granted us the mystery of a second birth'.[14] The infancy of God is thus efficient, instrumental, for our salvation.

Unto us therefore a little Child is born, and emptying himself, the God of majesty has conformed himself not only to the earthly body of mortal men but even to the age of childhood in its weakness and littleness. O blessed childhood, whose weakness and foolishness is stronger and wiser than men; for it is, in truth, the strength and wisdom of God that works in us, does the work of God in man. It is the very weakness of this Child that triumphs over the prince of this world, binds the strong man armed, takes the cruel tyrant captive, looses our captivity and sets us free. This Child's simplicity, which seems mute and speechless, makes the tongues of children eloquent, makes them speak with the tongues of men and angels, dividing the tongues of fire. It is he, who seems to know nothing, who teaches knowledge to men and angels, for he is the very God of all knowledge, the Wisdom of God, the Word. O sweet and sacred Childhood, which brought back man's true innocence, by which every age may return to blessed childhood and be conformed to you, not in physical weakness but in humility of heart and holiness of life.[15]

In this sermon the themes of childlikeness and folly are linked with simplicity, humility, and 'learned ignorance'. It is important that we distinguish these several strands and do not conflate them. In one sense, they are all expressions of the self-emptying of the Son, but in their application to men they have quite distinct characteristics. Holy folly, childlikeness, ignorance are specific graces, each with its own ascesis; Guerric is not commending any of these conditions for their own sake; he will not let us confuse holy folly with pathological madness, or childlikeness with childishness, or ignorance with irrationality. Holy folly and spiritual infancy are the marks of a life thoroughly converted to Christ and unconformed to this world. Fallen, worldly man seeks grown-up autonomy from God by virtue of his own prowess and achievements. The man of God, by contrast, strives to be like a child, trusting only in God, rejecting the arrogant, falsely adult mind of the worldling. Guerric delivers a broadside against man in his fallen maturity.

Sons of Adam, you are so grand in your own eyes, your pride has made you grow to the enormous size of giants, but most surely, if you are not converted and become like this little child, you will not enter the Kingdom of heaven. 'I am the door of the Kingdom', says this little child. If men in their great height do not bend down, this humble door will not let them in. That is why, without doubt, it 'will crush the heads (of many) in the land' (Ps. 109: 6); and those who arrive at the door with head held high will be pushed away and fall backwards, with their heads smashed.[16]

Guerric's account of spiritual infancy is militant, with no trace of a sentimental or nostalgic cult of childhood. The Holy Child invades the fantasy world of Adam's adolescence and confronts him with the truth that seems like madness. There can be no substitute for fidelity to the wild paradoxes of the gospel—littleness as the only way to greatness, death as the road to life, for this is the way taken by God himself, who 'emptied himself, to the point of almost seeming to be nothing, without whom nothing would have been'.[17] The Christian way of wisdom is the little way of the childlike fools. Guerric concludes his first sermon for Christmas with a doxology:

> So be it! Like new-born babes, we shall worthily praise the new-born infant Lord, and with the conduct of our lives and our voices in consort, from the mouth of babes and sucklings shall proceed the perfect praise of the babe and suckling, the Lord Jesus Christ, to whom be ascribed, with the Father and the Holy Spirit, praise and jubilation for ever and ever. Amen.[18]

The Idiot

Closely connected with the idea of the spiritual child is that of the *idiota*, the unlettered 'rustic', whose spiritual knowledge surpasses the booklearning of scholars. As we have already seen, the emphasis in early monastic literature, both Greek and Latin, is on the idiot's simplicity and lack of sophistication, rather than on any psychological inadequacy.

It is in highly literate societies that we observe a certain fascination with the idiot, and in some of the literature there is a slight suspicion of *de haut en bas*. Such a patronizing approach is, however, quite absent from our Cistercian sources. In the *Exordium magnum* the idiots are lovingly described as *friends*, unlettered *conversi* with a firm place in the monastic family, men of no education who, by God's grace, become masters of the spiritual life. The stories radiate Easter joy and convey a strong sense of faith in Our Lord's promise that his power is made perfect in weakness, that he chooses for his purposes 'mere nobodies' to shame the wise. The following is the account of the death of an illiterate lay brother, who had suffered greatly from cancer. On his death-bed he was given something to drink.

> He tasted this, and then, as if drunk on heavenly wine, he straightway broke out into a jubilant outpouring of heavenly praise. With a serene face this 'idiot', who had never learnt to sing or read, began to sing certain new

and utterly delightful hymns and canticles from the Songs of Sion, with a most beautiful melody. Hearing this, a great crowd of the brethren assembled to see, with great wonder, a man oppressed with so much misery and misfortune and yet greeting the approach of death with song and dance, insulting death and, as it might be, saying: 'O death where is thy victory? Here am I, a great sinner and poor little beggar man. Since I have borne patiently the marks of the Lord Jesus in my body for his name's sake, I do not fear you, ghostly shade, mother of sorrow, exterminator of joy and waster of life. No, I despise you, because I know you have been swallowed up and utterly destroyed in the victory of the cross of my Lord Jesus Christ'. So this precentor of ours, chanting Alleluia, that song of the streets of the heavenly Jerusalem, as it were anticipating it, revealed in wonderful prophecy what would happen to him after the death of the flesh, while still lodged in the corruptible flesh. Thus rejoicing and praising with a voice of exultation and testimony he gave up his blessed spirit. Blessed Bernard, in great fervour, preached a most religious sermon to the brethren in chapter concerning this happy consummation, commending in him a worthy fruit of penance and proposing for the imitation of all his amazing patience.[19]

Another story tells of the *conversus* upon whom God conferred the knowledge of holy scripture, even though he was a 'rustic, who never learnt letters'. Such miracles demonstrate that '. . . in the eternal blessedness of his Kingdom, according to the word of the apostle, there will be neither Jew nor Greek, Barbarian or Scythian, slave or free, literate or illiterate, but according to the prophet all shall be taught of the Lord (John 6: 45), and all from the greatest to the least of them will know me, says the Lord'.[20]

Concern with 'holy ignorance' is not confined to Cistercian hagiography but is frequently discussed in the writings of the Cistercian Fathers. The most important concept is that of the 'school of Christ', which infinitely transcends the schools of worldly learning.[21] St Bernard returns to the theme time after time: 'We are in the school of Christ, and there we learn a twofold doctrine: one which the only true Master teaches us himself, and the other through his ministers. Through his ministers, fear; from himself, dilection'.[22] Jesus Christ, our 'Master and Lord', whose 'school is here on earth, whose seat is in heaven',[23] teaches us not the wisdom of ancient Greece and Rome but the ineffable doctrine of true love and fear of him. In the 'school of the Holy Spirit', says Bernard, we may come to say with the psalmist 'I have understood more than all my teachers': 'why [are you making such a boast]? . . . Is it because you have understood or have endeavoured to understand the reasonings of Plato and the subtleties of Aristotle? "God forbid", I say, "it is because I have sought your commandments, O Lord" (Ps. 118: 100).'[24]

Again, St Aelred says: 'In his school our Master Christ did not teach us grammar, rhetoric, or dialectic but humility, gentleness, and justice.'[25] Moreover, the apostles chosen by Christ for preaching the gospel and leading the Church were themselves idiots, as William of St Thierry says, 'ignorant of the liberal arts and of everything appertaining to worldly learning, rough men, unfamiliar with grammar, not trained in dialectic'.[26] And St Bernard asks:

> What did the apostles teach us and what do they teach us still?. . . Not to read Plato, nor to turn and return to the subtleties of Aristotle, or how always to be learning and never arriving at the knowledge of the truth; they have taught me to live. Do you believe it is a little thing to know how to live? It is a great thing and indeed the greatest.[27]

Bernard's understanding of the higher *sapientia, philosophia* and *schola* is in the tradition of Peter Damian and the other doctors of *sancta simplicitas*. It reflected itself in the communal life of the monastery in the great reverence shown to the holy idiot. This was part of the glory of Rievaulx under Aelred: 'At table, in procession, at Communion, and in other liturgical observances, all of them, small and great, young and old, wise and ignorant (*prudens et ydiota*), are subject to one law.'[28] And we are told of a secular clerk who left Rievaulx because he had not mastered the science of true ignorance: he went 'ignorantly ignorant, unwisely unwise'.[29]

To appreciate the full significance of this cultus, in life and letters, of the idiot, we should recall that in the twelfth century there was a new spirit of intellectual adventure. It was the age of the Schools—of Paris, Rheims, Laon, Chartres. It was the age of the *moderni*, of Roscellin (d. *c.*1125) and Abelard (1079–1142), of daring, and often heterodox, experiments in speculative thought. There was a growing enthusiasm for logic and for systematic inquiry into theological questions. John of Salisbury (*c.* 1115–1180) tells us of a certain William of Soissons, whose self-confident logical system served as 'an engine for storming the citadel of the old logic, building up unexpected links of argument, and demolishing the opinions of the ancients'.[30] It is no exaggeration to speak, as many

have done, of a twelfth-century Renaissance. In such a historical
context, the Cistercian ideal of the holy idiot can be seen to have a
truly prophetic quality: it warned against the dangers of a purely
self-generating intellectualism and narrow scholasticism. Of course
monastic spirituality in the twelfth century was never obscurantist;
St Bernard was insistent that the spouse of Christ must not be a
simpleton and that there was a proper place for the pursuit of
knowledge.[31] But he was equally insistent that the pursuit must be
subordinated to the love and service of God, that the mysteries of
God, the folly of God, wiser than men, could never be confined
within the syllogisms of Aristotle.

The Pauper

Folly for Christ's sake is a kind of dispossession, the surrender of
worldly wisdom for Christ's sake, and thus is intimately connected
with poverty. The converse is equally true. Poverty, especially
voluntary poverty, can seem like madness. The poor man, whether
voluntarily or involuntarily poor, is a challenge to the established
wisdom of a society based on the desire for profit and acquisition;
but the one who deliberately chooses to be a fool in the eyes of
the world becomes a sign to that world of the real madness of
worshipping Mammon.

According to William of St Thierry, in his life of St Bernard,
poverty of spirit was, from the very beginning, the distinctive
Cistercian ideal: 'They began to serve God simply, in poverty of
spirit, in hunger and thirst, in cold and nakedness, and in long
vigil.'[32] For the monks of Cîteaux, the *spiritual* poverty of the New
Testament was fundamental, but physical poverty, the renunciation of wealth, was an essential outward and visible sign of the
spiritual reality. Roger of Byland, an early English Cistercian,
wrote to a prospective postulant: 'Poor we follow the poor Christ,
so that we may learn to serve him with minds that are free. We
work, we fast, we keep vigil, we pray; Christ does not ask for gold
and silver from us—only that we love him with a pure heart and
body.'[33]

The original aim of the founders of Cîteaux was to enable the
monk to become like one of the *anawim* of the Old Testament,
one of God's poor, voluntarily stripped of everything; they felt
themselves called not only to be poor, but 'to feel it, to experience

it'.[34] They wanted to know the poverty and nakedness of Christ crucified in their inmost being, in the depths of their hearts, and to trust in God alone. Cistercian spirituality sees the monk's physical poverty as a sign of that total dispossession, that death of the acquisitive ego, which Jesus tells us is the only way to eternal life. It is death for which poverty, both physical and spiritual, prepares us. Not only is the pursuit of wealth inimical to life, it is also inimical to a holy death. For Jesus teaches us in all four Gospels that 'he who finds his life will lose it, and he who loses his life for my sake will find it' (Matt. 10: 39; cf. Mark 8: 35; Luke 9: 24, 14: 26; John 12: 25). Jesus expands an Old Testament theme in his parable of the rich man who hoards and saves and accumulates as much wealth as possible, only to die and lose it all (Luke 12: 16ff; cf. Ps. 39: 6, 52: 5ff). Wealth makes us cling to what we have and what we are, it buttresses our egos with economic power and privilege, makes us self-protecting, cautious and calculating in the way we live. This is the reverse of Jesus's way, which throws caution to the winds and proceeds by self-abandonment and obedience to do the Father's will, a way which leads to life through death. The material dispossession of the poor man is the efficacious sign of that total dispossession which is faith: dying with Christ, sharing his sufferings in order to know the power of his resurrection. Life comes through letting go; death is the inevitable result of holding on.

St Bernard makes the same point when he compares men of the world, men conformed to the present age, to people who have suffered shipwreck and battle for their lives in the water: they cling. The worldlings cling to the unstable goods of nature and fortune, instead of letting go of them and holding fast to God alone. All of the world's securities must be renounced, if there is to be true faith and hope; God alone is our hope. Commenting on Psalm 90, St Bernard says:

Others may put their trust in different things—some in the science of letters, others in worldly cleverness or in all manner of vanity; but I, for your sake, have suffered the loss of all things and count them as refuse: 'For you, O Lord, are my hope'. Let others trust in the uncertainty of riches; I look not even for the bare necessities of life except from you, trusting most surely in your word, for which I have abandoned all things: 'Seek first the Kingdom of God and his justice and all these things shall be added unto you' (Matt. 6: 33).[35]

In the *Exordium magnum* the 'form of perfect penitence' given by

Our Lord is his command to those who would follow him to renounce all they possess. The so-called 'communism' of the apostles (Acts 2: 44f) is commended as 'this school of the primitive Church'; the abandonment of the desire to possess property is a sign of true learning. The *Exordium magnum* also gives us several hagiographical examples of the meaning of Cisterian poverty. In the story of the ascetic in Germany visited by Acardus we may detect some of the elements already noted in the stories of the *gelta* of Ireland and the *saloi* of the East: a return to nature and a total detachment from material comfort of every kind.

> When the servant of God was staying for a time in Germany in order to establish a monastery . . . in the region of Trier, heaven granted him to see and speak with a holy man, a truly rich man, a certain great solitary, who, for some time in those parts, had run about naked in the name of Christ, through the mountains and woods, without shelter or clothing, sustaining the life of his mortal flesh with wild herbs and their roots, enduring the heat of summer and the most bitter frosts of winter with incredible patience. . . . Dom Acardus held up the virtues and superhuman endurance of this blessed man for the admiration of his novices, thus magnificently strengthening the beginnings of their formation and not a little enkindling their love of virtue.[36]

To a world that 'clings', such dispossession seems foolish; by the standards of worldly *astutia*, such recklessness is insanity. No matter, for the poor man has already turned his back on that world and its wisdom. The monk has let go of every security, even the security of being of one mind with the world. The Christian must be poor in spirit, simple-hearted, and divinely foolish. William of St Thierry conjoins poverty and folly thus:

> The wealth of the poor in spirit who seek God is simplicity of heart. They perform with constancy what is commanded, await with strong faith what is promised, anticipate in the certainty of hope what is awaited and therefore think of God in goodness. They set not their minds on high things but condescend to the lowly; they neither refuse the Lord's yoke nor kick against the goad of his discipline. All this is far from the spirit of the world and its peddling wisdom, Assyrian conceit, and ornamental eloquence.[37]

The Infirm

'The weakness of God', says St Paul, 'is stronger than men' (1 Cor. 1: 25). The powers of hell have been conquered by the impotence of

God incarnate on the cross, who would not save himself but silently accepted calumny and insult from the mighty. Likewise, the Lord tells his apostle Paul: 'My grace is sufficient for you; and my power is made perfect in weakness' (2 Cor. 12: 9). It is a general law, then, for those who live in Christ that 'when I am weak, I am strong' (ibid., v. 10); that our infirmities are our only cause for pride (v. 5). My weakness is my greatest treasure.

This law was taught by the Cistercians and applied practically in their communal life. Each Cistercian house became a haven for a wide variety of the 'weak'—the physically sick, the morally vulnerable, the mentally subnormal or abnormal, outcasts and social misfits of every kind. Teaching and practical application of the Pauline principle of strength through weakness were conjoined at Rievaulx under the abbacy of St Aelred, who must surely qualify for the title of 'apostle of the weak'. His biographer describes his transformation of Rievaulx as follows:

He turned the house of Rievaulx into a stronghold for the sustaining of the weak, the nourishment of the strong and whole; it was the home of piety and peace, the abode of perfect love of God and neighbour. Who was there, however despised and rejected, who did not find in it a place of rest?. . . And so those wanderers in the world to whom no house of religion gave entrance, came to Rievaulx, the mother of mercy, and found the gates open, and entered by them freely, giving thanks unto their Lord. If one of them in later days had taken it upon himself to reprove in angry commotion some silly behaviour, Aelred would say, 'Do not, brother, do not kill the soul for which Christ died, do not drive away our glory from this house. Remember that "we are sojourners as were all our fathers" (1 Chron 29: 15), and that it is the singular and supreme glory of the house of Rievaulx that above all else it teaches tolerance of the infirm and compassion with others in their necessities. . . . All . . . whether weak or strong, should find in Rievaulx a haunt of peace, and there, like the fish in the broad seas, possess the welcome, happy, spacious peace of charity, that it may be said of her, "Whither the tribes go up, the tribes of the Lord, unto the testimony of Israel, to give thanks unto the name of the Lord". There are tribes of the strong and tribes of the weak. The house which withholds toleration from the weak is not to be regarded as a house of religion.'[38]

It would seem from this that among the *infirmi* were many who might now be described as 'subnormal' or 'mentally handicapped'. Aelred regards toleration of their behaviour in all its 'silliness' as a test of authentic spirituality. It is the monastery's capacity to welcome and integrate both the weak and the strong which constitutes its claim to be a house of religion. It is not to be forgotten that the vast majority of the members of the Rievaulx family were 'idiots', the unlettered rustics who made up the numbers of the *conversi*. A modern historian writes as follows:

> Clearly for Aelred the Cistercian way of life was no garden enclosed, in which only rare and pure souls would find green pasture, but rather something in its way as catholic as the Church, a home for souls of every kind who should find each the help most suited to him. And it must not be forgotten that three out of every four who came were simple, unlettered, stolid labourers, come to swell the ranks of an army of *conversi*. [39]

Aelred was acclaimed by one of his biographers for his 'sympathy for the infirmities, both physical and moral, of others'.[40] In a homily on the Solemnity of SS Peter and Paul, his description of the apostle of the Gentiles is an unintended self-portrait.

> It seems as if, having extended the arms of charity, having opened the bowels of piety, having opened the bosom of compassion to embrace the whole world, and like the hen in the gospel who gathers her chicks under her wings, having expanded the toga of his love to bring together Greeks and barbarians, wise and foolish, he brooded over them, he fed those still young with the smoothest cup of milk, strengthening those who are adult with solid food. Sorrowing with some, making merry with others, he appeared to others like a doctor of heavenly wisdom descended to earth. He fulfilled the office of mother, nurse, and teacher. You might see him, above all in holiness, below all in humility, with all in equality, in all in love. Someone was sorrowful, nothing but tears was seen in Paul; someone rejoiced, he shared their joy; someone was ill, Paul helped like the most compassionate doctor. He worked with all, shared sorrow with all, shared joy with all. 'If anyone is weak', he says, 'do I not share their weakness? If anyone is made to stumble, does my heart not blaze with indignation?'[41]

The special place accorded to the weak in the monastic community reflects not so much moral as Christological truth. We have been redeemed by the strong weakness of God; in the power of the Spirit the incarnate Word waits to be served in the hungry and thirsty, the naked, the sick and the prisoner. Moreover, weak and strong are bound together in the community of salvation, the Church, to bear one another's burdens, so that the comfort or affliction of one helps to promote the salvation of the other (2 Cor. 1: 4ff). The sympathy of an Aelred or Paul is an expression of the 'way of exchange' established by the paschal mystery.[42] By the operation of the Paraclete, the limbs of the Body mediate grace and salvation to one another, not in competition with Christ the one mediator but precisely in and through him. Such is this solidarity of the Communion of Saints that the monk may truly be said to become one of the weak; there is a 'family resemblance' between the 'weak' and 'foolish' who come to the monastery to be helped and the 'weak' and 'foolish' brethren who welcome them as icons of Christ.

The Cistercians and Worldly Wisdom

The child, the idiot, the pauper, the weak man—these were for the Cistercians the models, the paradigms which, as we have seen, depend for their truth on dogma and spirituality rather than on ethics and psychology. Each highlights an aspect of that holy folly outlined with such wit in Bernard's letter to Ogier. We will now consider the Cistercian understanding of the relation between that folly and the death-dealing wisdom of the present age.

Cistercian folly is not, as has already been stressed, a sacralization of enthusiasm or a flight from reason. On the contrary, the Cistercians, like St Paul, offer precisely *rational* criteria for distinguishing true folly from false, true wisdom from false. The fundamental concept is not folly but the wisdom of God; it is only when that wisdom is judged by worldly wisdom that it appears foolish. Likewise, when worldly wisdom is judged by the standards and criteria of the gospel, its intrinsic insanity appears. To the worldly wise, the Christian is a fool; to the godly wise, the worldling is mad.

What, then, is worldly wisdom, and in what way is it foolish? Is it so mad that it regards the wisdom of God as foolish? Who is playing the fool? Worldly wisdom is not to be confused with intellectual inquiry or the pursuit of knowledge; these may be idolatrously perverted and so become part of the 'diabolical wisdom of the world', but in themselves they are good, say the Cistercians, and an important part of sacred theology. Worldly wisdom, so our authors would seem to suggest, is not logic but ideology, the prevailing prejudices of a culture, the unwritten law by which men live in a world organized in opposition to God. Worldly wisdom is not to be equated simply with intellectual activity or speculative thought; intellect and speculation become worldly wisdom only when they

are constrained to serve the interests of the age rather than of God.
John of Ford (d.*c*.1214), the English Cistercian, speaks thus of the
false wisdom claimed by 'the world's propagandists' (*conquisitores
saeculi huius*).

Its pretensions are fourfold. It either probes the hidden nature of things,
or the subtleties of language, or the foundations of morality, or the secrets
of divine power. Now we do not condemn the pursuit of learning so long as it
draws its inspiration from the fount of wisdom and flows smoothly along the
river-bed of humility, returning to its source by practising virtue and
thanksgiving. But when it is a question of 'ascents' of this kind (cf. Vulgate
Ps. 83: 6), great and wonderful beyond the reach of man, which they
'arrange' in their heart, from the power of their own heart, without the help
of God, then they are not being guided by the true wisdom of God. From
false wisdom they rush headlong into real madness, from pride into
ingratitude, from ingratitude to impiety, and from this last to that
horrendous abyss of vice attacked by the Apostle.[43]

A particularly devastating critique of 'worldly wisdom' is,
significantly, to be found in the most scholastic of the Cistercians—
Blessed Isaac of Stella (b. *c*.1110). In his All Saints' sermons on the
Beatitudes, he 'preaches good news to the poor' and exposes the
wisdom of the world as the insane logic of the expropriating rich.

The false wisdom of this age, which is really folly, pronounces judgement
without understanding what it says or what it affirms; it declares blessed the
'strange children' whose 'right hand is full of iniquity' and whose 'mouth
speaks iniquity' (Vulgate Ps.143: 7f); but only because of their 'storehouses
full, flowing out of this into that', because of 'their sheep fruitful in young',
'their oxen fat', their uncertain riches, their peace which is not peace, their
stupid joy. Against all this, the wisdom of God, the only-begotten Son, the
right hand of the Father, the mouth which speaks the truth, proclaims that
the poor are blessed, destined to be kings, kings of the eternal kingdom.[44]

Worldly wisdom, according to Isaac, is contentious and divisive. Its
intellectualism is nothing but a disordered curiosity, a faithless and
ruthless pursuit of earthly prestige and influence.

The evil of curiosity results in the vice of pride. This is the wisdom that is
not from on high, but which is 'earthly, animal, diabolical' (cf. Jas. 3: 15),
full of jealousy and contention, which 'buys a farm' (cf. Luke 14: 18) in
order to have dominion over others and be involved constantly in chicanery,
finding its beatitude in domination. This, then, brethren, is that truly
diabolical wisdom, the eldest daughter of the devil himself, who is ambitious

of placing her throne above the stars (Isa. 14: 13), that troubled and troublesome wisdom, which the disciples forsook when they left the 'tribe'.[45]

Not surprisingly the gospel of Christ crucified looks crazy to this self-absorbed 'wisdom' of exploitation and domination. Christ, divine wisdom, has commanded his disciples to carry neither purse nor scrip, to give more to those who steal from them and not to ask for anything back. Such generosity seems absurd to calculating self-interest. Isaac cries out to Our Lord:

O Lord Jesus, who *today* will believe our report, and to whom then, in the course of his life, has this way of yours been revealed? O way so narrow that few can follow it! This is your 'way' in that immense ocean, and 'your footsteps shall not be known' (Ps.76: 20). This way, called by your apostle wisdom, is regarded *today* as extreme foolishness, sloth, and inertia.[46]

The repeated 'today' in the above has considerable force. Isaac is here addressing himself to a specific historical situation, the place and time in which he lived, to that feudal society whose values, whose 'prudence' and 'wisdom', were beginning to affect adversely the primitive Cistercian ethos; the sons of Robert and Alberic were now becoming powerful landowers in their own right, a monastic class of *nouveaux riches*, and would soon be the economic success-story of the Middle Ages. It was perhaps his fellow Cistercians, as much as secular landlords, who were the target for Isaac's invective. In contrast to any such capitulation to Mammon he holds up the noble example of the strict poverty of the Carthusians and the monks of Grandmont. The latter inspire him to quote the poet Juvenal: ' "In the presence of the thief of this world", the heavenly traveller, the monk of Grandmont, denuded of all, will be singing in joy, and yet they will save many of those they meet on the way' (Luke 10: 4).[47] Isaac, then, states firmly that the worldly wise can only be saved by abandoning their unwise wisdom and embracing divine folly, a folly seen in the paradoxes of the Sermon on the Mount: 'In a word he says: sorrow is the way to joy, by desolation we come to consolation, it is by losing one's life that one finds it, by rejecting it that one possesses it, by hating it that one loves it, by despising it that one keeps it.'[48]

In another sermon Isaac compares Our Lord's changing water into wine at Cana to God's transformation of folly and weakness into wisdom and strength.

For it has pleased him to save those who believe by the folly of preaching, and by the weakness of suffering, and thus to, as it were, inebriate those who drink at the wedding. For this folly and weakness are perhaps the water, the water nonetheless changed to wine, that is, to wisdom and power; for what is folly for God is wiser than men and what is weakness for God is stronger than men. The world, it has been said, could not know God by wisdom, for it did not have any wine; therefore it pleased God to use folly, that is to give the guests water to drink, only first changing it into wine, transformed that is into wisdom.[49]

Worldly wisdom is the wine that is served first. Its inadequacies are shown up by God's grace.

Mention is made of the best wine, and truly. It is in comparison with that, and in its praise, that one criticizes the wine served first, that is, the wisdom of this age, made folly by the wisdom of God, the wisdom of the philosophers, a wisdom found wanting. For 'truths are decayed from among the children of men' (Vulg. Ps. 11. 2) and that is why they have spoken vain things, each to his neighbour, the master to his disciple. The pagan philosophers have been dashed on the stone, which is Christ.[50]

The contrast here is one made often in the Middle Ages between the philosophy that is only a theoretical knowledge and the philosophy that is a way of life. The former is characterized by 'curiosity', which reduces, 'decays', the truths of the gospel. The latter, *philosophia coelestis, spiritualis, divina*, is fulness of life in Christ, the wisdom of God.[51]

According to Isaac, the wisdom and philosophy of the world (the old wine) must be emptied, and new wine (which looks like folly) brought in: ' "If there is one among you who seems wise"—that is, seems to have wine—let him empty it thoroughly so as to be filled with the best wine, that is, "let him become a fool, that he may be wise".'[52] Isaac reveals the true nature of what the world counts folly (water) to be renunciation of self. 'Let him be a fool to become wise. Let him accept water so that he may drink wine, let him renounce himself, that is his own sense and his own will, so that he may progress in wisdom and love through the virtue of obedience.'[53]

The Cistercians teach us that the only real madness is to mock Christ for surrendering himself to the Father and to refuse the way of self-renunciation. It is St Bernard who makes this point most clearly in a passage which reads like a prose poem.

Brethren, the tears of Christ overwhelm me with shame and fear and sorrow. I was playing out of doors in the street, while sentence of death was being passed upon me in the privacy of the royal council-chamber. But the King's only-begotten Son heard of it. And what did he do? He went forth from the palace, put off his diadem, covered himself with sackcloth, strewed ashes on his head, bared his feet, and wept and lamented because his poor slave was condemned to death. I meet him unexpectedly in this sad condition. I am astonished at the woeful change in him and inquire the cause. He tells me the whole story. What am I to do now? Shall I continue to play and make a mockery of his tears? Surely I am insane and devoid of reason if I do not follow him and unite my tears with his.[54]

Monks on the Margin

In this chapter we have described how the early Cistercians found models for spirituality in a series of unlikely figures—the jester-fool, the child, the idiot, the pauper, and the weak. We saw that this identification depended on the dogma of the Incarnation, in which God saved us through *his* foolishness, childhood, ignorance, poverty, and weakness. In union with the poor Christ the Cistercian monk begins to discover a profound solidarity with the poor, weak, childlike, ignorant, and foolish. The monk does more than idealize the outcasts; he discovers a special relationship with them, with all those on the margin, all excluded from the centre of life, activity, and power. The monk voluntarily goes to the margin in order to realize a closer relationship with other 'marginals', and also, indeed, with those at the centre; he withdraws from all men to be more closely united to all men. He is called to share the burden of all outsiders despised and rejected of men, all whom the world writes off as mad, foolish, weak, idiotic, or just plain bad. To illustrate this I would like to refer here to an event in the life of the great French novelist, Georges Bernanos. In his own experience he knew the reality of Christian, and especially of monastic, solidarity with the suffering, through substitution and exchange in the Body of Christ. In 1936 Bernanos wrote a letter to the defence lawyer of Eugène Weidmann, a convicted murderer, later publicly guillotined at Versailles. Bernanos had been haunted by this young man after seeing his photograph in a newspaper. While in no way condoning his terrible crime, Bernanos felt great compassion for one so oppressed by sin, guilt, and fear, so completely separated from his fellow men, not only by prison walls but also by the more

impenetrable barriers of hatred and condemnation. The more
Bernanos considered the enormity of the crime, the more tragically
absolute Weidmann's alienation from the rest of mankind seemed
to become. It seems that the novelist spoke of Weidmann to some
monks, and in his letter to the lawyer he mentions this conversation:
'I would like him to be able to understand that there are monks,
lonely like him, who do better than just pity him, but who will from
now on take over, as brothers should, part of his appalling
burden.'[55]

From solitude the monk establishes a deeper union—not by
occult power or psychological technique, but through communion
with Jesus Christ, the head and heart of the Body, the Saviour of the
lost and the last, the divine marginal killed outside the camp.

How, then, in conclusion, are we to relate Cistercian folly to the
classical paradigm of the Eastern tradition? There is an obvious
correspondence between the components of Eastern hagiography
and the characteristic themes of Cistercian literature; the same
Christocentricity, nonconformity to this world, poverty, simplicity,
and so on. However, there is this difference: like the desert monks,
especially the anchorites, the Cistercians had too vivid a sense of the
absolute nature of every monk's vocation to admit the possibility of
a more extreme way of life within their own monastic family. As we
have seen, the nearest parallel we may find to the *salos* or *geilt* is the
kind of solitary held up for the admiration of the brethren by
Blessed Acardus. Moreover, just as the hermit or holy fool comes to
have a social influence precisely because of his marginality, so,
likewise, this cenobitic order, 'the world forgetting, by the world
forgot', within a short time began to play an active role in public life.
Ironically, as Dom David Knowles has pointed out, this was the
doing, albeit unconscious, of the great Abbot of Clairvaux, the saint
so embarrassed by respect as to play the fool for God's sake.

The extraordinary personal ascendancy and activity of Bernard, which
gathered force year by year in the second and third decades of the century,
not only set a precedent for lesser men but attracted to Clairvaux and its
daughters many of unusual administrative abilities, and thus made of the
Cistercian order at once a nursery from which rulers of churches might be
taken and a centralized organization standing for purity of administration
and ready to serve any reforming prelate or pope who might wish to use it.[56]

This influence should not be thought of cynically as a betrayal of the

primitive Cistercian ideal to the standards of the present age. For
Bernard at least, the rigorous idealism of Cîteaux could not be
subordinated to the pragmatism of Church or state politics. There
is, of course, a real tension in Bernard between being, for example,
both God's jester and the preacher of the Second Crusade, but the
tension does not invalidate the heroism of his sanctity; his was a
painful journey towards holiness through the vehemence of his own
personality.[57] Like the Prince of the Apostles and St Peter Damian
before him, he was an 'impossible man', a man of contradictions,
but one whose witness reveals, more dramatically than do more
tranquil temperaments, God's ability to do the impossible, to
transform our weak and foolish human nature. It is, then, perhaps
in the more problematic features of St Bernard's life and teaching,
in that which, from our twentieth-century viewpoint, seems
most contradictory, that we should look for the analogue of Eastern
folly for Christ's sake. As Louis Bouyer has said, the violence of St
Bernard's denunciation of 'moderate monastic humanism' is
attributable not to the choleric disposition of a mere bigot but to the
passionate vision of one who 'saw and denounced with biting clarity
the perpetual risk of sinking from that "humanism" into a bourgeois
unawareness of the foolishness of the cross'.[58] It may be that St
Bernard and the other Cistercian Fathers sometimes misinterpreted
their monastic call to marginality; it may be that it was sometimes
tissued with the less desirable traits of their personalities; but never
for one moment did they lose their sense of the radical demand the
Lord Jesus makes· on his disciples, his urgent call to let go of
everything, possessions, wisdom, even life itself, and follow him.

6

The Golden Age

The thirteenth century is the beginning of the golden age of the fools, both sacred and secular. Henceforth the fool is well established; he has arrived. In the alehouse or the palace, fools, buffoons, and jongleurs are a familiar sight. Whether their sage-folly be greeted with anger or delight, it now has a recognized place within medieval society. Moreover, this is as true of the fools for Christ as it is of the court fools. In the later Middle Ages there is an unselfconscious revelling in the mirth, joy, and good humour of life in Christ. The star of the fools will be in the ascendant for the next three centuries. Their vogue steadily increases in the fourteenth and reaches its zenith in the fifteenth and early sixteenth centuries: then there is a crisis; the fool, whether sacred or secular, is under attack, and soon 'Poor Dick, alas! is dead and gone'.[1]

The fortunes of the sacred and secular fools are inextricably bound up together, and the forces that destroyed the one had no sympathy with the other. It has been argued that the medieval court jester is the result of a fusion between the ancient Roman fool and the Celtic *geilt* or *gwyllt*, who was shown above to be closely analogous to the Eastern holy fool.[2] The court fool was often deemed to be in possession of spiritual powers, of clairvoyance, prophecy, or healing. Many jesters were tonsured clerks, and in the annual Feast of Fools at the New Year buffoonery and religion were well and truly intertwined.[3] It was not the case, however, that no distinction at all was made between kinds of folly, or that the intermingling of religion and mirth was officially and unambiguously endorsed. It would seem that the Elizabethan distinction between the 'natural' and 'artificial' fool goes back at least to the twelfth century,[4] and it is important with regard to what we isolated in an earlier chapter as one of the elements of holy folly: its simulated nature. It might seem reasonable to assert that the fool for Christ's sake is the hagiographical equivalent of the 'artificial' fool or mimic: he 'plays the part of the fool' on the stage of life as the servant of his heavenly Lord, just as the professional entertainers fooled about in the courts and castles of princes and barons. But this comparison has its limitations and the relation between the sacred and secular fools is more complex. The simulating fool for Christ occasionally crosses swords with his opposite number at court and then upstages him and shows that his foolish tricks are only serving the world's wisdom and fall far short of the reckless, redemptive, foolishness of God.

Folly and Scholasticism

In this chapter, then, we shall journey with the fools from the world in which they had a fixed and honourable place to the harsh age which regarded them as fit only for Bedlam. We must first confront what appears to be a major paradox: why was it that the golden age of the fool coincided with the age of scholasticism? At a time when the sober wisdom of the schoolmen was of such influence, surely, it might be argued, the holy fool could be little more than a freak phenomenon on the edge of the Church, untypical and thus unreliable as a guide to medieval spirituality. In the last chapter we saw that such a dichotomy between holy folly and the pursuit of learning is at least not characteristic of the Cistercian tradition and that, in the sermons of Blessed Isaac, monastic folly and scholastic wisdom are reconciled. In the thirteenth century we have an even more striking reconciliation of the two in the Angelic Doctor, St Thomas Aquinas (c. 1225–1274).

St Thomas gives us precise rules for distinguishing folly for Christ's sake from that other folly which he says quite unequivocally is a sin. He speaks of a 'good folly' opposed to an 'evil wisdom', the worldly wisdom, the wisdom denounced in the Letter of St James as 'earthly, unspiritual, devilish' (3: 15). This evil wisdom, St Thomas says, 'takes some worldly good to be the highest cause and ultimate end'. And he continues: 'So too there is a kind of good folly that stands against this evil wisdom, and sets little store by worldly goods. It is of this that the Apostle speaks.'[5] Evil wisdom, then, is a kind of idolatry, substituting Baal, or the belly, or Mammon, for God. Commenting on St James, St Thomas says:

If he fixes his end in the external earthly goods, it is called 'earthly wisdom'; if in goods of the body, it is called 'animal wisdom'; if, however, in some creaturely grandness, it is called 'devilish wisdom', because, as Job says, it imitates the pride of the devil, 'and of all the sons of pride, he is the king'.[6]

In the article on irony St Thomas speaks even more emphatically of the need to distinguish between the two kinds of wisdom and the two kinds of folly: 'One who is strengthened by God professes himself to be an utter fool by human standards, because he despises what the wisdom of men strives for.'[7]

These texts illustrate St Thomas's profoundly faith-full approach to reasoned inquiry and the way he explored, from the position of that faith, the possibilities offered by Aristotle for clarifying and rearticulating the central doctrines of God, human nature, and salvation. In this process, as Chesterton put it, St Thomas did not reconcile Christ to Aristotle; he reconciled Aristotle to Christ.[8] At the very outset of the *Summa theologiae*, St Thomas demonstrates how little the slave of secular wisdom he is and how much the 'plunderer of the Egyptians'. He contrasts the self-evident premises of other sciences with the truth of theology that comes from revelation.

On this account establishing the premises of other sciences is none of its business, though it may well be critical of them. For whatsoever is encountered in the other sciences which is incompatible with its truth should be completely condemned as false: accordingly the second epistle to the Corinthians alludes to the pulling down of ramparts, destroying counsels and every height that rears itself against the knowledge of God.[9]

It is an entailment of the Catholic doctrine of creation that the wisdom of the sciences has real value as truth; that not only the physical and biological sciences, but also philosophies such as that of Aristotle or Plato, may offer materials serviceable to theology. But the Holy Spirit, working through the Magisterium, 'bringing to remembrance' the truths of scripture and tradition, is the determinative influence, the ultimate guide to all truth.

At the end of his life St Thomas had a mystical experience, which in some ways resembles the 'astonishment' of the holy fools, an experience that transformed his understanding of his theological project. According to the evidence of Bartholomew of Capua, the following incident took place on the morning of the feast of St Nicholas:

While the said Friar Thomas was celebrating Mass in the said chapel of St Nicholas at Naples, he was suddenly moved by a wonderful change, and after this Mass he never wrote or dictated anything, but rather 'hung up the instruments of writing' in the *tertia pars* of the *Summa* in the treatise on

Penance. And when the same Friar Reginald saw that Friar Thomas had ceased writing, he said to him, 'Father, why have you put aside such a great work that you began to the praise of God and for the enlightenment of the world?' To which Thomas replied, 'Reginald, I cannot'. Friar Reginald, fearing lest so much study had unbalanced his mind, insisted that Friar Thomas should continue his writing. But Thomas replied, 'Reginald, I cannot, because all that I have written seems like straw to me'.[10]

A few weeks after this conversation, Thomas went to visit his sister, the Countess Theodora of San Severino. However, when his sister went to greet him on his arrival, he could scarcely say a word. In this dazed and mute state Thomas remained at his sister's home for three days. 'Then, greatly upset, the Countess said to Friar Reginald, "What is the matter with Friar Thomas? He is completely out of his senses (*totus stupefactus est*)". Reginald replied, "He has been in this state since about the feast of St Nicholas".'

Various historians have speculated on the nature of Thomas's 'stupefaction' and have suggested that he might have had a mild stroke, without obvious paralysis, after such a long period of intense mental strain and concentration.[11] Others, meditating on the muteness of the 'dumb ox' who had spent so many years in careful articulation and communication, have seen a deeper significance in his silence. Josef Pieper, writing on *The Silence of St Thomas*, has pointed to the apophatic element in St Thomas, his reverence for mystery and the divine darkness. And he sums up the work of St Thomas in these words: 'The man who does not use his reason will never get to that boundary beyond which reason really fails.' In St Thomas, a Dominican vowed to communicate to others the fruits of his contemplation, we see language consummated in adoring silence, the best of intellectual wisdom fulfilled in holy stupefaction and folly.

The last word of St Thomas is not communication but silence. And it is not death which takes the pen out of his hand. His tongue is stilled by the superabundance of life in the mystery of God. He is silent, not because he has nothing further to say; he is silent because he has been allowed a glimpse into the inexpressible depths of that mystery which is not reached by any human thought or speech.[12]

The various accounts of Thomas's last days are truly moving to read. The big, heavy man, as silent and still as a babe asleep; the scholar at last without his pen. We can see Thomas and Reginald

together, the friend anxious but finally accepting, the saint lost in
contemplation of the divine beauty. By the 'faithful testimony' of
Reginald we are told that the last confession of Thomas was like that
of a 'five year old boy',[13] suggesting not only the purity of infancy
but also that childlike trustfulness commended by the Lord, who
reveals his mysteries not to the clever but to babies.

Franciscan Folly

St Francis of Assisi (1181/2–1226) is one of the most popular and
attractive saints of the Middle Ages, and indeed of all times. The
reasons for this are not hard to find. Not only are the details of his
life full of excitement and delightful detail, but his joy in the Lord
and radiant spirituality powerfully communicate themselves in all
that we know of him.

Much that is distinctive in the life of St Francis corresponds to the
spirituality of the fools for Christ's sake.[14] In him we find all the
elements of holy folly. Like the *gelta* of Ireland, he was converted as
the result of a battle—during a long illness following his imprison-
ment after a military engagement between Perugia and Assisi. Like
the *saloi* and *yurodivye*, he stripped himself naked, disowning his
own father in the presence of the Bishop of Assisi. He identified
himself with beggars, lepers and the lowest of human kind. He was a
wanderer and pilgrim, travelling at different times to Rome,
France, Spain, Eastern Europe and Egypt. He joyfully endured
humiliation and contempt. Again, like so many fools of East and
West, his wildness gave him a profound rapport with all living
things: he preached to the birds, converted a wolf, and sang the
praises of the wonders of creation. If St Bernard of Clairvaux is
God's jester, then St Francis is his minstrel and troubadour. In the
Mirror of Perfection we are told how he sang French songs in praise
of Jesus Christ.

Intoxicated by the love and compassion of Christ, blessed Francis
sometimes used to act as follows. The sweetest of spiritual melodies would
often well up within him and found expression in French airs, and the
murmur of God's voice, heard by him alone, would joyfully pour forth in
the French tongue. Sometimes he would pick up a stick from the ground,
and laying it on his left arm, he would draw another stick across it with his
right hand like a bow, as though he were playing a viol or some other
instrument; and he would imitate the movements of the musician and sing in

French of Our Lord Jesus Christ. But all this jollity would end in tears, and his joy would melt away in compassion for the sufferings of Christ. And at such times he would break into constant sighs, and in his grief would forget whatever he was holding in his hands, and be caught up in spirit into heaven. [15]

The most conspicuous parallels between Franciscan and Eastern folly are Christological, for both are concerned to obey the Lord's commands without compromise or conformity to this world and to share as deeply as possible in the sufferings of Christ crucified. In a moving passage of the *Fioretti* Francis explains to Brother Leo that participation in the Passion of Christ, above all enduring the contempt and hostility of the world, is the source of perfect joy.

And therefore mark down the conclusion, Brother Leo: the highest gift and grace of the Holy Spirit that Christ grants to his friends is to conquer oneself and, out of love of Christ, to endure willingly sufferings, injuries, insults, and discomfort. We cannot glory in all the other gifts of God because they are not ours but they are of God, because of which the Apostle says, 'What do you have that does not come from God? If you have had it from God, why do you glory in it as if it were your own?' But we can glory in the cross of tribulation and affliction, for this is ours, and the Apostle therefore says, 'I will glory only in the cross of our Lord Jesus Christ'. [16]

For St Francis himself this taking up of the cross, this total identification with the crucified, was consummated when he received the stigmata, the marks of the precious wounds in his own body. [17]

There are many occasions when Francis behaved in an apparently foolish or eccentric way to illustrate some truth of the gospel. Like the fools of Russia, Francis and Brother Ruffino on one occasion preached naked and were mocked by the people who thought they 'had gone mad out of an excess of penance'. However, when Francis spoke to them from the pulpit of the nakedness and humiliation of Jesus Christ, they wept and repented. [18] That Francis regarded such folly as explicitly folly for Christ's sake is illustrated in the account of the Pentecost chapter of 1222. Five thousand friars attended, including the most learned members of the order. The most urgent item on the agenda was whether Francis could be entrusted with the writing of the Rule. Some argued that it would be preferable to adopt the rule of one of the existing orders, as the Dominicans had done. And so pressure was put on Cardinal Ugolino by a group of

learned brothers to persuade Francis to follow the same course. The
saint replied as follows:

> My brothers, my brothers, God has called me by the way of simplicity and
> humility, and he has shown this way in truth for me and for those who want
> to believe in me and imitate me. And I do not want you to mention to me
> any other rule, neither that of St Benedict, nor of St Augustine, nor of St
> Bernard, nor any other major form of living except the one which has been
> mercifully shown and given to me by the Lord. The Lord told me that he
> wanted me to be a new fool; and he did not want to lead us by any other way
> than by that learning. But by your learning and wisdom God will confound
> you.[19]

M. Sabatier, in a note, comments perceptively that the chapter in
which this passage occurs 'seems inspired and sustained by the
memory of the beginning of the first letter of St Paul to the
Corinthians' and then lists from the Vulgate the verses about folly
that lie not far from the surface of the text.[20] The issue of choosing
folly for Christ's sake in preference to the wisdom of the world was
to be central to the dispute in the Franciscan order between the
'spirituals' and 'conventuals' of which the Pentecost chapter conflict
was a kind of harbinger.[21] Be that as it may, from what we have
learnt already of holy folly, idiocy, and simplicity, Francis is in a
classical tradition. When criticizing the wisdom and 'prudence' of
this world, he uses language that could come straight from St Peter
Damian. In a letter he says that 'we must not be wise "according to
the flesh" and prudent, but we must rather be simple, humble, and
pure'.[22]

St Francis is a fool for Christ, not only in this sense, but also as an
exponent of what was called above 'the gospel of good humour'. In
the early Franciscan literature there is constant use of the terminology of joy: Francis both exhibits and commends *laetitia, hilaritas,
iocunditas.*

> It was always the supreme and particular desire of blessed Francis to
> possess continual joy of spirit outside times of prayer and the Divine Office.
> This was what he especially loved to see in his brethren, and he often
> reproached them when they showed signs of gloom and despondency . . .
> 'For it is the lot of the Devil and his supporters to be sorrowful, but ours
> always to be happy and rejoice in the Lord'.[23]

The joy of St Francis was a rich, full-blooded, enthusiastic *mirth*
in the Lord Jesus. Francis wanted his disciples to be the Lord's

merry men, his *joculatores*, as he called them. After he had sung his canticle *Altissimu, onnipotente bon Signore*, we are told:

His spirit was then filled with such consolation and sweetness that he wanted to send for Brother Pacifico, who in the world was called 'the king of verses' and was truly a curial doctor of the cantors; and he wanted to give him some good and spiritual brethren to go with him through the world preaching and singing the praises of the Lord. He said that he wanted the best preacher among them to give a sermon and after that for them all to sing the Lord's praises together, like jongleurs of the Lord (*joculatores Domini*). When the praises were over, he directed the preacher to say to the people: 'We are the jongleurs of the Lord, and we want to be paid for it by you, that is, we want you to be true penitents'. And he said: 'Who else but his jongleurs are the Lord's servants who lift up the hearts of men and move them to spiritual joy?'[24]

This passage is decisive for the development of our argument. In the last chapter we saw how St Bernard called himsef a *ioculator* at a time when he was using the same term to vilify his opponents in the Abelard controversy, and we noted the remarkable humility implied in that self-ascription. Now we must consider who these *ioculatores* were and why they were so despised.[25]

The word *iocus* in classical Latin means a joke or jest; an object of derision or laughing stock; or a trifle, a child's plaything, of no importance. *Ioculator* is very rare in classical usage, one of the few examples being a letter of Cicero to Atticus where an old man, Scaevola, is described as a 'joker'.[26] In the Middle Ages, however, it is much more common and is frequently found in the vernacular as *jogleor* (Old French) and *jogelour* (Middle English), from which the modern English 'juggler' is derived. The jongleur was essentially an itinerant entertainer with many skills and accomplishments. He could be a jester, clown, tumbler, dancer, actor, mimic, minstrel, singer, or poet. Frequently, sleight of hand or prestidigitation formed part of his act, so *jogelour* often means 'conjurer' or 'illusionist'.[27] With talents such as these, it is not surprising that the jongleurs soon earned a reputation for being charlatans and con-men, and in Middle English the word is often used to mean 'parasite, deceiver, or rascal'. Moreover, being 'footloose and fancy-free', detached from normal society and employment, the jongleur was regarded with something like the suspicion aroused by the beatniks and hippies of the 1960s.

Ioculator first appears in Christian literature at the beginning of the sixth century in the canons of the Council of Agde (506), where it was decreed that 'the jeering, joking foul-mouthed cleric is to be removed from office'.[28] This is the first occasion on which our term *ioculator* was applied to a class of churchmen condemned by councils and individual bishops: the so-called *vagi*, the wandering clerks.[29] They were not condemned for being wanderers as such; as we have seen, the *peregrini* were a venerable ascetical institution. No, the *vagi* were reprehended precisely for being *ioculatores*, for their outrageous behaviour, their vagabond way of life, above all, for dancing and singing—for being, in other words, clerics in 'show-business'.

Not all *ioculatores* were in orders, but it would seem that the majority were, if only because as professional entertainers they had to be able to sing, which was still very much a clerical skill. Moreover, the tonsure gave them a certain protection and guaranteed status.[30] The reaction of the Church authorities was, nevertheless, violent in the extreme. The vagabond clerics were denounced with all the ferocity which in the sixteenth and seventeenth centuries the Puritans directed against the stage. And yet there was considerable ambivalence in the official attitude, for, while the profession was officially frowned upon, the possibility of its making a legitimate contribution to human happiness was also acknowledged. For example, Pope Innocent IV said that a clerk could, without sin, 'make gesticulations' for some good cause, like comforting a sick person. St Thomas, following Aristotle, defends play and insists that 'playful' or 'humorous' pleasure (*delectatio . . . ludicra vel jocosa*) is necessary for relaxation (*ad quamdam animae quietem*). The acting profession is not in itself unlawful, he says, although like everything else it can be perverted from its true dignity.[31]

Whether the official attitude was hostile or simply ambivalent, it was daring of Bernard and Francis to call themselves *ioculatores* for Christ. Like the evil wisdom criticized by St Thomas, what went wrong with the entertainment provided by the jongleurs was that it was not all for the glory of God and was directed towards some lesser and unworthy end. Francis consecrated merry-making to God's service, so that the devil might not have all the good tunes. The *laudi* which he directed his jongleurs to sing for the Lord are the songs of the troubadours transposed into a theological key but in form and melodic delight the same. The Franciscan lay brother Iacopone da Todi (*c.*1230–1306) wrote beautiful *laudi* of this kind, some in Latin and some in the Umbrian dialect. One of them celebrates the divine jest, folly for Christ's sake. It is entitled *Como è somma sapienzia essere reputato pazo per l'amor de Christo* ('That it is the highest wisdom to be thought mad for the love of Christ'):

> Sense and nobleness it seems to me to go mad for the beautiful Messiah.
> It seems to me great wisdom in a man if he wishes to go mad for God;
> in Paris there has never been seen such great philosophy as this.
> Whoever goes mad for Christ seems afflicted and in tribulation;
> but he is an exalted master of nature and theology.
> Whoever goes mad for Christ certainly seems crazy to people;
> it seems he is off the road to anyone without experience of the state.
> Whoever wishes to enter this school will discover new learning,
> he who has not experienced madness does not yet know what it is.
> Whoever wishes to enter this dance will find unbounded love;
> a hundred days' indulgence to whoever reviles him.
> But whoever goes seeking honour is not worthy of his love,
> for Jesus remained on the cross between two thieves.
> But whoever seeks in humility will, I am sure, arrive quickly;
> let him not go to Bologna to learn another doctrine.[32]

Ramón Lull

The history of the Franciscans is a mystery and a wonder: a band of holy beggars, idiots, and jongleurs transformed almost overnight into a world-wide order numbering among its members some of the intellectual giants of the age—St Bonaventure, Duns Scotus, and William of Occam. It would be wrong to exaggerate the contrast. As we have noted several times, the vocation of folly for Christ's sake has never meant the exaltation of unreason. In the Franciscan Tertiary, Ramón Lull (*c.*1233–*c.*1315), the 'Apostle of Africa', we have one who is jongleur, poet, missionary, and philosophical theologian. In recent years interest has been steadily growing in this man who combined so many vocations in a full and exciting life and who wrote prolifically in Catalan, Latin, and Arabic. Lull's importance for us lies in his use of the motif of folly for Christ's sake in his writings and in the way that motif is intertwined, though not equated, with that of the jongleur.

The salient facts of his life[33] are that he was born in Majorca shortly after its liberation from Islamic rule; that he was of noble blood, entered the service of King James I and later James II of

Majorca; married and had two children. He became something of a
philanderer and on one occasion was stunned when the beautiful
and devout lady whose attentions he sought showed that her breast
was being slowly eaten away by a hideous cancer. Shortly afterwards, a vision of Christ crucified made him decide to devote his life
to preaching the faith throughout the world. He conceived a host of
ambitious projects, including the writing of books whose incontest-
able logic would confute and convert heretics, Jews and Moslems.
Following his conversion, he spent nine years in study, at the end of
which he wrote his *Ars magna*. In 1276 he persuaded James I to
establish at Miramar a missionary college in which thirteen friars
would devote themselves to the study of Arabic. From about 1287
onwards he was constantly on the move, importuning kings and
popes for support of his plans for the conversion of Islam, and often
being dismissed as a fanatic or idle dreamer. He travelled inces-
santly in Italy and France, lecturing at the universities on the *Ars
magna*, disputing in public with the Averroists. He travelled to the
islands of Malta and Cyprus and even as far as Armenia. On three
occasions he went on missions to North Africa, landing first at Tunis
in 1292, where he convinced and converted many of the people and
so brought upon himself the wrath of the Caliph; but a sentence of
death was commuted to banishment at the intercession of a local
man of influence. Finally, according to a late tradition, he went to
Bugia in North Africa, where he defiantly preached the gospel in
public and was stoned to death.

Lull's life was full of hectic enthusiasm, a foolish impetuosity for
the sake of the gospel. What is truly amazing about him is that in the
midst of all his journeyings he was able to write so prolifically. It is
in his great romance, *Blanquerna*, that the motif of folly most
frequently occurs.[34] This semi-allegorical novel tells the story of
how a gallant and wealthy youth named Evast marries a pious and
beautiful girl Aloma. They live happily and devoutly but, to their
great sorrow, have no children. Aloma prays to God and is
rewarded with the birth of a son, Blanquerna. The child is brought
up religiously and grows up to be a young man of wisdom and
perception. Evast decides to withdraw from the world, but Aloma
disapproves and says that they can practise ascetical discipline in
their own home, with Blanquerna in charge of the household. But
the son tells his parents that he wants to be a hermit. His mother
then panics and attempts to marry him off to a beautiful girl called

Natana, whom Blanquerna then persuades to become a nun. Blanquerna himself is ordained priest and becomes abbot of his monastery. In the third book he becomes a bishop, and in the fourth, Pope. As Pope, Blanquerna has Lull's own vision of the conversion of the heathen and yearns that 'all infidels and schismatics may be brought into the union of the Holy Catholic Church'. At length there comes to the papal court 'a man with shaven head and clothed in the garb of a fool', with a sparrowhawk and leading a dog. This is Ramón the Fool. He addresses the court concerning his vocation to holy folly.

'I was aforetime', he says, 'in the Court of the Emperor and I learned to be a fool, to the end that I might gather together money; and the Emperor has spoken to me so often of the Passion of Jesus Christ and of the nobility of God, that I desire to be a fool that I may give honour and glory to Him, and I will have no art nor device in my words by reason of the greatness of my love.'[35]

Ramón is God's jongleur (*juglar*) and, like the holy fools of the East, believes he has a vocation to simulate folly for the sake of prophecy and preaching and to the greater glory of God: 'In praise of God and to reprove the vices of the Court of Rome Ramón the Sage has taken the office of fool.'[36] In these words we may detect the feelings of frustration and disappointment that Lull felt when time after time he was rebuffed by popes and high ecclesiastics, who lacked his vision and burning sense of urgency. Somehow he had to make them *see*, even if it meant appearing before them in the motley of the fool.

Blanquerna is a masterpiece of European literature. It is a century older than Froissart and Chaucer and yet has many of the qualities of the *Chronicles* and *Canterbury Tales*. It is more, however, than a piece of satire or propaganda, although it is both of those. It also contains mystical teaching. At the end of his life Pope Blanquerna renounces his high office and becomes a hermit, devoting his last days to contemplation. The fruits of this are presented in *The Book of the Lover and the Beloved*, which describes the mystical longing of the soul (the Lover) for God (the Beloved) and offers simple and homely guidance in the way of loving contemplation.

The heart of such prayer is love, and love is the uniting of our wills with God, the giving up of self-will, an ecstatic 'going out' of self and

finding fulfilment in communion with the Beloved. This is the
'excess' which overflows in the *juglar's* folly and joy.

> As one that was a fool went the Lover through a city, singing of his
> Beloved; and men asked him if he had lost his wits. 'My Beloved,' he
> answered, 'has taken my will, and I myself have yielded up to Him my
> understanding; so that there is left in me naught but memory, wherewith I
> remember my Beloved.'[37]

Here is that 'memory of God' of which the Desert Fathers speak,
the murmuring recollection of God's presence. But the fool of love
is a fool not only because he loves God with a foolish excess but also
because he is despised by the world and, folly of follies, has no care
for human respect.

> 'Foolish Lover! Why dost thou weary thy body, cast away thy wealth,
> leave the joys of this world, and go about as an outcast among the people?'
> 'To do honour to the honours of my Beloved,' he replied, 'for He is
> neglected and dishonoured by more men than honour and love Him'.[38]

Ramón Lull has been judged an immortal for many reasons: the
discovery of nitric acid, of a great elixir, even of America, are
among the exaggerated claims made for him. 'He has been represented as a troubadour, a disillusioned Don Juan, a naturalist, a
jurisconsult, a musician, a mathematician, a chemist, a navigator, a
theologian . . . as everything except what he was', writes Allison
Peers, going on to say that he was, in fact, a patriarch of Catalan
literature, an outstanding active-contemplative, a typical Franciscan. But above all, the life and character of this great lover of
God is summed up in the title of Peers's later study of him: *Fool of
Love*.[39]

'Blind Men for Jesters'

We have observed several times that the holy fools, while they may
be said to have 'played' at their folly, nevertheless shared the
common lot of the madmen of their time and were dedicated to
serving Christ in the persons of the poor and despised, the lepers
and other 'untouchables' of their day. We have seen this at every
stage of our story—in Greece and Russia, in the fools of Ireland, in
the Cistercians, in St Francis of Assisi. The same is true in a
spectacular way of Blessed Giovanni Colombini (*c*.1300–1367), the
founder of the Gesuati. Born into a noble Sienese family, he

married and lived in a grand and luxurious manner until he was converted by reading the life of St Mary of Egypt, whereupon he committed himself to a life of prayer, penance, and poverty. His desire was to be a mendicant and to 'follow the poor Christ'. Despite his wife's reluctance, he abandoned all his worldly respectability and privilege, gave away his money, despised himself in the sight of others, and cared for the sick and poor. When his wife complained of the prodigality of his almsgiving, he told her that the world was mad: 'Giovanni affirmed that everyone was in a dream and raving, and that human life was like smoke, and a wind that passes away; and that he who has gathered most riches has the worst bargain.'[40] On one occasion he carried a disgusting leper home on his shoulders, and when his wife protested, he replied:

> I pray thee to have patience. This is one of God's creatures, redeemed as we are by His precious blood . . . Know that the poor and the sick represent the person of Christ, because he says in the Holy Gospel, 'Whenever you remember and do good to one of these my least ones, you do it unto me'.[41]

He even drank some of the water with which he had washed the leper. His wife visited the leper's room and it smelt sweetly fragrant; on her return it was empty, and she knew that the leper cared for by her husband had been Jesus Christ.

From then on, Giovanni and his companion, Francesco, set about reversing their way of life. Instead of strutting in finery through the palaces of the city, they dressed in rags and worked as menials. And they played the fool, so that they would be despised and lose all worldly honour and respect. To atone for his former privileged life, Giovanni rode an ass round the market-place inviting the derision of the city merchants. '"You laugh at me," he says, "and I at you", as if he would say, "You despise me because I follow Christ, and I despise you, because you follow the world".'[42] He and his companions possessed the gift of tears and the power of spectacular jumping, like St Moling and the seventeenth-century St Joseph of Copertino. One of them, Bartoluccio di Santi, was converted while listening to a sermon: 'Such fervour was kindled in him that he could no longer contain the ardour of his spirit: he ran out of the church, and leapt into the square, without touching any of the church steps. Many times against his will he made the bystanders laugh with astonishment.'[43]

In one interesting respect Colombini is distinct from other fools, at least, from the *gelta* of Ireland: he was critical of wildness for its own sake. Francesco became rather like Suibne, grew his hair long, let his nails grow like talons, and never shaved. Giovanni believed this to be a useless penance and appeared to Francesco in a dream to tell him to stop. His companion obeyed and was assured that his obedience was a worthier ascesis.

While it is true that the destinies of the sacred and secular fools are strangely intertwined, and their positions in Church and society were similarly transformed in the Reformation era, we must insist that the two cannot be simply equated; on the contrary, they are to be distinguished. Whereas the secular fool very often did little more than meet the requirements of powerful men for entertainment, Francis and his friends are *God's* jongleurs, and Bernard insists that his game is *serious*. If many of the secular fool's songs and jokes were satirical, he nevertheless remained happily conformed to the *status quo*. Like the bizarre behaviour of the prophets of Baal in the Old Testament (1 Kings 18: 19ff), the frothing, cavorting and excesses of these 'wild men' could conceal a deeper conservatism, an attachment to a privileged and protected life at court. They could, more often than not, be the wisest of the worldly wise, and if, consequently, the secular fools sometimes became 'men at the centre', the fools for Christ were always 'outsiders', identified with the outcasts of society, with the natural fools and half-wits, the beggars and lepers and rural poor, in whom they believed Christ was truly present to be served and loved.

In fourteenth-century England, at a time of political chaos and economic distress, in the century of the Black Death and the Peasants' Revolt, William Langland (?b. 1332) inveighed against the 'japers and jonglers' whom he believed to be social parasites and 'children of Judas'. He was convinced that 'Jesus Christ of heaven, in a poor man's apparel pursueth us ever' and so, if the rich wanted 'fools' at their table, let them give hospitality to the real outcasts.

Knights and scholars welcome the king's minstrels, and out of love for the king, their lord, they listen to them at their feasts. How much more, then, should the rich entertain beggars, who are the minstrels of God. For Christ says, in the Gospel of St John, 'He that despiseth you despiseth me.' So you rich men, I counsel you, at your banquets, to refresh your souls with minstrels like these: to have a poor man sitting at your high table, in place of a foolish 'wit', and a priest to sing you ballads of the suffering of Christ, and so to save your souls from your enemy Satan; and let him, without flattering your vanity, fiddle for you the story of Good Friday. And for your jester, you should have a blind man or a bed-ridden woman, who would cry to our Lord for alms for you, and sing your praises to God. Such minstrels as these might make you truly merry, and if you would listen to them and appreciate their music, they might bring you great comfort at the hour of death. For your soul would be full of hope, knowing that you acted so towards God's holy ones.[44]

At the end of the Middle Ages folly for Christ's sake is as evangelical, moral and spiritual as ever. It does not beatify every kind of madness, eccentricity or jest; it does not take a patronizing or morbid interest in the mentally ill. The tradition continues to affirm that God works through weakness, failure and suffering and that the way to true life and joy is the way of the cross. Above all, the holy fools proclaim that Christ, in Langland's word, has won his 'joust' against the devil, and now all shall be well. Holy folly is a celebration of holy *mirth*—a word used frequently in English spiritual writing of the fourteenth century. It has an important place in the vocabulary of Walter Hilton (d. 1396), whose *Scale of Perfection* anticipates much of the doctrine of the great sixteenth-century Carmelite mystics. At the end of his translation of the *Stimulus Amoris*, a popular work of medieval piety, he adds some of his distinctive convictions and a resounding peroration to the golden age of the gospel of good humour:

> Then (in the heavenly Jerusalem) shall we joy and have mirth, each man of other's joy as of his own, and sovereignly we shall have joy of the unmeasurable mickleness of God's nature and of his wisdom and of his goodness . . . Let us say with the prophet thus: 'Joying I shall joy in our Lord, and mine heart shall be merry in our God' (Isaiah 61.10). Make we aye merry in our Lord, and yield we to him thankings for his benefits.[45]

The Fools' Finest Hour

If the High Middle Ages are the golden age of the fools, both sacred and secular, the sixteenth century is their finest hour, the dramatic climax before they are submerged beneath the cold, relentless sanity of the new age. At the moment when the world to which the fool belonged was collapsing, the men in motley stepped forward for a final flourish, a triumphant display of their sage-folly. Henceforth, they would not be treated so kindly. No longer would the fool be the guardian of truth; foolishness is now a disease or a crime, not to be celebrated, but removed from normal society by cure or punishment.

The sixteenth century was an age of transition and conflict in the history of the fool. Folly, whether sacred or secular, real or feigned, had now to contend with a new, strident and essentially hostile worldly wisdom. It is against this background that we shall briefly consider folly in two saints, Thomas More (1478–1535) and Philip Neri (1515–1595), who exemplify what has been our concern throughout this book, namely, a holy folly practised firmly and loyally within Catholic orthodoxy.

More was famed in his lifetime for his sense of humour and love of jokes. His friend, Erasmus, dedicated his *Praise of Folly* to him for this reason; indeed, its very title is a pun on his name (*Encomium Moriae*). At the end of the preface, Erasmus solemnly adjures his friend: 'Farewell, learned More; be a stout champion of your name-sake Folly.'[46] More was most certainly that. As the poet, Francis Thompson, wrote:

> Ah happy Fool of Christ, unawed
> By familiar sanctities,
> You served your Lord at holy ease!
> Dear Jester in the Courts of God . . .
> To the keen accolade and holy
> Thou didst bend low a sprightly knee,
> And jest Death out of gravity
> As a too sad-visaged friend;
> So, jocund, passing to the end
> Of thy laughing martyrdom;
> And now from travel art gone home
> Where, since gain of thee was given,
> Surely there is more mirth in heaven.[47]

Stapleton, in his *Life*, records that 'even by his most intimate friends he was thought to be speaking in earnest when he was simply joking'.[48] Edward Hall, writing his *Chronicle* in the reign of Edward VI, confessed his difficulty in making a proper judgement of More and said that he was not sure whether he was a foolish sage or a wise fool.[49]

The supreme act of More's folly was his death. To many, even to those closest to him, it was an act of irresponsible prodigality, the unnecessary waste of a life so full of distinction and glory. There is, of course, always an element of absurdity in martyrdom. Judged by the canons of caution and self-regarding prudence, the man who gives away his life is a wastrel. The world protects the ego behind the fortifications of pride and encourages the soul to forget death. To the world the martyr is a bitter joke. It is significant that in this respect More's own household fool, Henry Patenson, reacted like one of the worldly wise. He urged his master to acknowledge the royal supremacy: 'Why, what aileth him that he will not swear? Wherefore should he stick to swear? I have sworn the oath myself.'[50] More went to his death as a 'laughing martyr', a fool of love, made merry by the love of Christ, mocking the death-dealers because of his sure faith in Christ's victory, the faith that believes that 'all shall be well'.

St Thomas More has the *iocunditas* and *hilaritas* of medieval spirituality, a mirth founded on the power of God's grace to transform human weakness, even in the face of death: 'If God draw me to (death) himself, then trust I in his great mercy that he shall not fail to give me his grace and strength.'[51] For More, mirth is the joy which fills the hearts of the saints and overflows from heaven to earth. He believed Christians were knit together by Christ into one communion and fellowship of holy merriment, encouraging and cheering one another through works of charity and by prayer. More was shocked by the Protestant rejection of prayer for the dead, for to him it was the rejection of the bonds of love that unite the members of the Body of Christ, both in heaven and on earth. As his death approached, More constantly returned to these two ideas—of heaven as a place of mirth, and of the necessity of bearing one another's burdens, before and after death, as a consequence of our incorporation into Christ. Thus, in his last and most touching letter to his daughter, Meg: 'Farewell, my dear child, and pray for me, and I shall for you and all your friends, that we may merrily meet in heaven',[52] and to his young friend, Thomas Pope, who brought him the news that he was to die: 'Quiet yourself, Master Pope, and be not discomforted; for I trust that we shall, once in heaven, see each other full merrily, where we shall be sure to live and love together, in joyful bliss eternally.'[53]

St Philip Neri (1515–1595), the founder of the Oratory and 'apostle of Rome', was famed, like More, for his infectious sense of humour, which grew greater, rather than less, in direct proportion to his holiness.[54] He was for ever playing tricks and telling jokes, sometimes to prick the bubble of other people's pomposity, more

commonly to bring mockery upon himself, to conceal his sanctity
and thus overcome pride. The stories of his delightful folly are
legion. He performed ridiculous dances in the presence of cardinals; he wore his clothes inside out and dressed in a cassock and
large white boots. He had his hair cut once during High Mass and
shouted at the astonished onlookers, 'See if my hair is not being well
dressed'. He often took hold of people by the chin, hair, or beard,
and on one occasion, when surrounded by a group of women, he
gravely took off his spectacles and placed them on the nose first of
one and then of another.

St Philip had what the Italians called *festività*, a word his
twentieth-century biographers define as signifying an 'expansive
good humour and, above all, cordiality and natural bearing
. . . an attitude which extends to everything, both things and
people, and especially to the vicissitudes of life. In the daily affairs
of life *festività* denotes the absence of anxiety . . . accompanied by
the power of treating as a joke what one cannot really enjoy'.[55]

In the face of adversity or suffering, Philip rejoiced in the Lord.
His austere asceticism was famed, yet those who met him saw only a
radiant paschal faith. His prayers, we are told, bubbled out of him in
fervent acts of affective repetition, *Jesus sis mihi Jesus, Jesus sis
mihi Jesus*. He was convinced of the harm done to the soul by
melancholia: gloomy and pensive people, he said, 'wronged the
Spirit and hampered his action'. Throughout his life he took special
delight in the joke-book of Piovano Arlotto, the remarkable
fifteenth-century priest-buffoon. On one occasion, when visited by
a party of Poles, he declaimed extracts from this joke-book in mock
solemnity. Such good humour had extraordinary evangelistic
effects: 'there was no limit to his goodness and cheerfulness . . . it
was rarely that anyone escaped him', we are are told in the Process
of Canonization. Moreover, Philip's jests did not dull his sensitivity
to human suffering or deaden his social conscience. At a time when
Pius V was persecuting the Jews, Philip showed them kindness and
gentleness. He also organized a petition to prevent gypsies being
rounded up and used as galley slaves for the fleet the Pope was
mustering to sail against the Turks.

St Philip Neri is a classical fool for Christ's sake: a saint of Easter
mirth, a practitioner of jests to ward off the world's esteem, a
champion of the oppressed. As one of his most devoted sons has
written:

Come sinners! ye need not forego
　Your portion of light-hearted mirth;
He came unthought-of roads to show,
　And plant a paradise on earth.
All praise and thanks to Jesus be
For sweet Saint Philip's charity![56]

The New Intolerance

During the Middle Ages, the fool, whether sacred or secular, whether feigning or real, *belonged*. Of course, as Langland reminded us, the court fool belonged just a little too comfortably and could become a social parasite. The 'natural' fool, however, belonged in a deeper and more important sense: he had a home. At Rievaulx, and at other religious houses, the physically and mentally infirm were given a refuge and true family life. At the close of the Middle Ages it is unlikely that this high ideal was universally maintained. The fools to be found in monasteries in the early sixteenth century may have been members of Aelred's 'tribes of the weak', but they may equally well have been the domestic fools of religious superiors whose manner of life was more baronial than monastic. However, whether or not the presence of fools is a sign of decadence, what we must grasp is that the fool's place in medieval society was natural and normal; he was neither an outcast nor a monster.

With the dissolution of the monasteries, the situation in England changes radically. Once the monastic refuges have been destroyed, where does the poor, weak fool find fellowship? His home has gone; he does not belong. The professional fool may still find employment in the houses of great men, but the 'lunatik lollers' are no more than filthy vagrants, a social nuisance, and from now on can expect incarceration rather than incorporation. One of the most far-reaching effects of the dissolution was the institution of the asylum. In 1247 Bethlehem Hospital had been founded in London as a priory hospice for brethren of the Order of the Star of Bethlehem visiting England. Given the fatiguing nature of travel at that time, it is not surprising that what began as a lodging-house developed into a hospital. Later it became concerned with the care of the mentally ill, but in the Middle Ages this was only one of its functions, for it remained primarily a confraternity, hospice, and refuge. In 1547,

however, it was handed over to the City of London for no other
purpose than the confinement of the insane. The poor of England
were not slow to perceive the implications of the end of monastic
hospitality. A contemporary ballad includes this lament:

> Alacke Alacke
> For the church sake
> Pore comons wake
> And no marvell.
> For clere it is
> The decay of this
> How the pore shall mys
> No tong can tell.
>
> For ther they hade
> Boith ale and breyde
> At tyme of nede
> And succer grete
> In alle distresse
> And hevyness
> And wel intrete
>
> In troubil and care
> Where that we were
> In maner all bere
> Of our substance
> We founde good bate
> At churche men gate
> Without checkmate
> Or varyaunce.[57]

The new intolerance was also applied to the fool-entertainer, less
often in the early period under Henry VIII, who had his own court
fool, but very commonly at the end of the century when Calvinist
influence was extending itself. Of course, the Middle Ages had not
been without its critics of folly. In early chapters mention was made
of the definitely pejorative associations of the vocabulary of jest
in the twelfth century. Nevertheless, there was some continuum
between sacred and secular folly. The mirth of heaven, of which
Walter Hilton and Thomas More spoke, far exceeded that of earth
but did not condemn it; laughter on high fulfilled the merriment
below. The more extreme Calvinists rejected any idea of a
continuum and resolutely opposed any intermingling of faith and
fun: the mystery plays were suppressed, and the morris dancers

were driven out of sanctuary and churchyard. While medieval
hagiographers delighted in the *hilaritas* of the saints, the English
Puritans at the end of the sixteenth century regarded mirth as the
product of human weakness and sin, a consequence of the Fall.
Bernard, Francis, Iacopone, Ramón could rejoice in being God's
jongleurs; the Calvinists saw only sin and degradation in the jester's
art. Above all, they condemned what we have noted as one of the
universal features of holy folly—the feigning of madness to conceal
sanctity. The English Puritan, Christopher Fetherston (fl. 1580s), in
a diatribe against dancing, sport, May games, and jesting, wrote:
'What mere madness is this, that a man whome God hath endued
with witt and reason, woulde put on a noddies coate, and feigne
himselfe to bee a foole, and to be destitute of both these most
precious giftes.'[58] Fetherston would have been unmoved by the
suggestion that, in condemning secular mirth and feigned folly, he
was writing off a whole *tradition* of spirituality. In the same tract he
maintains that man is now wiser than he was before, and the
precedent of our forefathers' beliefs is irrelevant: 'Wee may boldely
say wee are wiser than our fathers, if it haue pleased God to bestow
upon us greater store of knowledge and wisedome than hee gaue
unto them.' The Puritan is sternly independent of the semi-pagan
mummery of England's past, whether in religious or secular dress.
Man's natural play, delight, gladness of heart, feigned folly, have
no equivalent or antitype in the kingdom of grace and stand
condemned by God.

It would be wrong to give the impression that the new intolerance
was manifested only by Puritans; as we shall see a later chapter,
it was to be found in Catholic France as well. While the Calvinists'
belief in the total depravity of human nature did indeed predispose
them against any idea of continuity between natural and supernatural mirth or folly, nevertheless, it is the social and political
upheavals of the sixteenth century, which affected all nations and
communities, Protestant and Catholic alike, that did most to
undermine the old tradition of folly. The fool, as Miss Welsford
has written, belongs to 'a society shaped by belief in Divine order,
human inadequacy, efficacious ritual'. Consequently, there is no
place for him 'in a world increasingly dominated by the notions of
the puritan, the scientist, and the captain of industry; for strange as
it may seem the fool in cap and bells can only flourish among people
who have sacraments, who value symbols as well as tools'.[59]

And yet the story of the holy fool does not end here. While it is true that the circumstances of a new age do not afford him as much protection as before, since there is less admiration for his voluntary poverty and very little compassion for anyone whose behaviour deviates from the norm, yet the holy fool survives. The tradition at the end of the sixteenth century has been transformed by the turmoils of history, but its vigour is undiminished. Indeed, it would seem that the experience of being 'marginalized' by cataclysmic events had a creative effect on the mystics of the period. Michel de Certeau has recently shown how the mystics of France in the sixteenth and seventeenth centuries are often drawn from oppressed cultural or social groups: 'They belong most often to regions and classes caught up in socio-economic recession, adversely affected by change, pushed to one side by progress or ruined by wars.'[60] They were haunted by a sense of loss. They are painfully aware that they are living in a time of decadence, an age of schism and religious conflict. They have witnessed the humiliation of a tradition and now experience a poignant sense of exile from their true home and resting-place. In the homeward pilgrimage, the journey to renewal, the holy fools will be in the vanguard.

The Last Laugh

It would be wrong to end this chapter on a note of pathos or tragedy. The holy fool embodies the gospel of good humour, the good news that Christ has conquered sin and death. Kingdoms may rise and fall, worldlings may persecute the saints, but Christ's fools will have the last laugh. Their godly mirth is irrepressible, their faith inextinguishable. For this reason Hans Urs von Balthasar would have us see Cervantes' Don Quixote as the epitome not only of the holy folly tradition but of Catholic theology: '[Don Quixote] is an article of dogmatics neglected by Catholic theologians, for dogmatics, on the Catholic side, can only be written with and through humour.'[61] The epitaph of 'Alonso Quixano the Good' belongs to all God's irregulars:

> Here lies the gentle knight and stout,
> Who to such height of valour got
> That, if you mark his deeds throughout,
> Death over his life triumphed not
> With bringing of his death about.

The world as nothing he did prize,
For as a scarecrow in men's eyes
He lived, and was their bugbear too;
And had the luck, with much ado,
To live a fool, and yet die wise. [62]

7

The School of Père Lallemant

'The secret power of the organization, and the casuistical principles maintained by many of its representatives, and generally ascribed to the body as a whole, have rendered its name odious not only in English but in French and other languages.' Thus begins the entry under 'Jesuit' in the *Oxford English Dictionary*. 'Jesuitical', we are told later, means 'deceitful, dissembling, practising equivocation or mental reservation; with cunningly dissembled policy'. In Russian the word 'Jesuit' achieved its greatest pejorative force in the writings of Dostoievsky, who saw the Jesuits as the epitome of Catholic absolutism and spiritual tyranny, that 'unity without freedom' so destructive of the human soul. In his novel *The Idiot* it is the saintly fool of the title, Prince Myshkin, who delivers a tirade against Catholicism and Jesuitry, which he regards as almost equivalent to atheism, far in spirit, in its arrogance and coerciveness, from his innocent folly for Christ's sake.

Dostoievsky's prejudices, while not wholly unjustified, exemplify that tragic ignorance of another tradition which has so vitiated the mutual understanding of Western and Eastern Christianity for many centuries, and which, despite the astounding ecumenical progress of our own times, continues to obstruct the path to reconciliation. Dostoievsky did not know that, within the Jesuit tradition he so despised, a spirituality had developed which more closely resembles his own vision of the compassionate folly of the cross than that of any of the other Western saints we have so far studied. At precisely the time when Pascal was anticipating Dostoievsky in his onslaught on the amorality of Jesuit casuistry, there were sons of St Ignatius engaged, as the Russian novelist would be later, in a spiritual descent into hell, in an exploration in faith of the very depths of human experience, even of madness itself. Just as Dostoievsky portrayed the ideal Christian as an 'idiot', so these Jesuits celebrated, both in literature and in life, the vocation to folly for Christ's sake, the wearing of the 'purple livery' of his humiliation. Gaspar Druzbicki (1590–1662), a Polish Jesuit (for Dostoievsky an unhappy combination of race and religious profession), boasted, when writing 'On the Sublimity of Religious Perfection', that

... The Society of Jesus professes JESUS, the very one who lived in this world despised, poor, suffering, crucified. Such a Jesus is folly, says St Paul, and to profess such a Jesus is therefore to profess folly. That is why the Society of Jesus, when it professes Jesus in this way, professes folly and is a society of fools. . . . "We are fools for Christ's sake", says St Paul, and so the profession of the Society of Jesus is the profession of folly; it is a society of fools for Christ's sake.[1]

The Jesuits we shall meet in the following chapters are representative of the authentic spirit of St Ignatius Loyola; they are not the happy exception that proves the general rule of the moral and theological turpitude of the Society in this period. It is they, far more truly than the Jesuit hacks of textbook moral theology, who embody the living Ignatian tradition, even though their numbers and overall influence on the Church may seem negligible. After Scripture and the Fathers, the inspiration of their folly was the life and teaching of their Father Founder.

St Ignatius Loyola (c.1491–1556)

St Ignatius is a 'cavalier for Christ's sake, *caballero de Christo*; like Pachomius and Martin before him, one who renounced the armed service of an earthly monarch for 'service through love' of the Kingdom of Christ. In employing military metaphors St Ignatius was not proposing to interpolate the values and behaviour of the profession of arms into religious life as the military orders of the Middle Ages had done. The Ignatian way means the total transformation of the military ideal: the replacement of armed struggle by spiritual combat under the standard of Christ. Ignatius takes up the militant language of the desert, and indeed of the New Testament itself, according to which our foes are not flesh and blood but 'the spiritual hosts of wickedness' (Eph. 6: 12). Such warfare fully recognizes the reality of the social conflicts of history; spiritual combat shows the struggles of classes and nations to be not unreal but superficial when compared with Christ's battle against Lucifer, the deadly enemy of 'our human nature'. The convert abandons the militaristic struggle in order to enter more deeply into the underlying conflict.

In certain respects the circumstances of Ignatius's conversion from military service to the *militia Christi* resembles the battle trauma of the Irish *gelta*. While serving with the Duke of Najera, he was wounded in the right leg at the siege of Pamplona (1521) and, after a long and agonizing convalescence during which he read the lives of Christ and the saints, he was converted to the Lord's service. He exchanged his clothes with a beggar and, like Suibne or Mac-dá-Cherda, went wild for the sake of Christ, letting his hair and nails grow, committing himself to a life of pilgrimage and penance. However, such 'cultivated wildness' of an Irish or Byzantine kind was not for long to be the Ignatian model of folly for Christ's sake. Through his mystical experiences at Manresa, where he spent a year of withdrawal from March 1522 to February 1523, Ignatius learnt the wisdom of *caritas discreta*, of a love generous and foolish and yet disciplined for the service of God and his Church. Ignatian folly, like that of St Bernard, is a 'sober game', a directed spiritual extremism: like everything else in the Christian life, it has as its aim the greater glory of God and the salvation of souls. This is the supreme contribution of Ignatius and his sons to the folly tradition: the reconciliation of enthusiasm and discipline; the ordering of folly for Christ's sake towards an active apostolate. After Manresa, Ignatius the penitent and pilgrim became Ignatius, man of the Church. The externals of a Byzantine style of folly—sackcloth, a diet of herbs, long hair—were rejected, but the essential ideal, as we shall see, remained the same, albeit now enriched with a strong doctrine of the Church and her mission.[2]

In the *Examen generale*, which precedes the Constitutions of the Society, Ignatius presents, for the benefit of aspirants, an outline of the fundamental spirit and orientation of the Society. It is a strategic programme for unlearning the world's wisdom. Foremost is the idea of wearing the 'livery of Christ'.

Just as the men of the world, who follow the world, love and seek with great diligence, honours, fame, and esteem for a great name on earth, as the world teaches them, so those who are progressing in the spiritual life and truly following Christ our Lord, love and intensely desire everything opposite. That is to say, they desire to clothe themselves with the same clothing and uniform of their Lord, because of the love and reverence which he deserves to such an extent that, where there would be no offence to his Divine Majesty and no imputation of sin to the neighbour, they would wish to suffer injuries, false accusations and affronts, and to be held and esteemed as fools (but without giving any occasion for this); because of their desire to resemble and imitate in some manner our Creator and Lord Jesus Christ, by putting on his clothing and uniform, since it was for our spiritual profit that he clothed himself as he did. For he gave us an example that in all things possible to us we might see, through the aid of his grace, how to imitate and follow him, since he is the way which leads men to life.[3]

In the *Spiritual Exercises* Ignatius makes folly for Christ's sake the third and 'most perfect' way of humility:

I desire and choose poverty along with the poor Christ rather than riches, insults along with the grossly insulted Christ rather than honours; and I would much rather be thought a fool and a madman for the sake of Christ who was treated thus than be thought clever and wise in this world.[4]

Early in the following century this particular aspect of Ignatian spirituality was highlighted in the teaching of a Jesuit, whose mystical doctrine, according to Bremond, is 'more unified, more original, twenty items more sublime and twenty times more austere, more toughminded than Port-Royal': Père Louis Lallemant (1587–1635).[5] For him, the wearing of Christ's 'purple livery' of shame and folly is the only guarantee of progress in humility.

We normally propose a false idea of humility to ourselves, conceiving of it as something which disparages us. In fact, it does just the opposite; since it gives us true knowledge of ourselves and is pure truth, it brings us close to God and as a result brings us true grandeur, which we seek in vain without God. Humiliation only disparages us in the esteem of men, which is nothing; but it exalts us in the esteem of God, and in that consists true glory. In those encounters that are so painful at a human level, we must appreciate that, if men see us despised (*méprisés*), decried and scoffed at, God sees us exalted to the utmost; through the very things which humiliate us in the eyes of men, Jesus Christ takes pleasure in seeing us wear his livery, and the angels envy us this honour.[6]

Ignatius had exchanged the proud panoply of an earthly army for the purple livery of Christ's fools, exposed to the mockery of the world. Lallemant was to reaffirm that doctrine and through his reaffirmation to inspire a whole mystical 'school', for which folly for Christ's sake was a major preoccupation. The next three chapters will trace the development of the Lallemant school of holy folly during the seventeenth century.

The Lallemant Tradition

Before speaking of Lallemant, however, we must confess a real difficulty attendant upon the study of his spiritual doctrine. Lallemant himself wrote very little; we know him only at third-hand, through the re-editing of his disciples' notes by a priest who had never known him. It is the latter with whom we must begin.

At the end of the seventeenth century, when the reaction against mysticism was at its height, Lallemant found his 'evangelist' in Père Pierre Champion SJ (1632–1701).[7] A native of Avranches, Champion entered the Society of Jesus in 1651 with the intention of becoming a missionary overseas. After a chapter of accidents, he found himself engaged instead in the home missions in Brittany where, as we shall see, the spiritual sons of Lallemant had considerable influence. His main encounter was with Père Vincent Huby (1608–1693), the disciple of Père Jean Rigoleuc (1596–1658), who in turn had been the disciple, during his Third Year at Rouen, of Lallemant. In 1686 Champion published Rigoleuc's *Traités de dévotion*, which was followed in 1694 by the publication, under his editorship, of Rigoleuc's notes of Lallemant's conferences. Just as the edition was going to press, Champion found the notes of Jean-Joseph Surin (1600–1665), who had been Rigoleuc's companion in the Third Year at Rouen under Lallemant. With the Surin material as an 'Addition', the *Doctrine spirituelle du P. Louis Lallemant* was finally published in Paris by 'Estienne Michalet, premier imprimeur du Roy'.

It is difficult to determine how much of the *Doctrine spirituelle* is Lallemant and how much Rigoleuc, Surin, or Champion. The latter's attempt at reassurance is somewhat alarming: 'With regard to the *Doctrine spirituelle*, it has been faithfully assembled by Père Jean Rigoleuc, who, far from depriving it of any of its vigour or authority, has rather added to it.'[8] However, what this remarkable work represents is 'Lallemant living *in* Rigoleuc *through* Champion'. We have no grounds for suspecting that the successors of Père Lallemant worked with anything but the highest motives, for their lives and writings give us abundant proof of their sanctity and integrity. There are, it must be admitted, *lacunae* in the *Doctrine*, but that is inevitable in a work of unsystematic mystical theology received third-hand.

The most important fact for us to grasp is that in Brittany, among

Jesuit missionaries engaged in an active apostolate, there flourished a theology of the spiritual life, which was at least partly inspired by Louis Lallemant, and which, through the labours of Père Champion, kept the flame of contemplative prayer and folly for Christ's sake burning at the end of the century, when mysticism was being rejected by the men of Enlightenment. The eighteenth century dawned in France with rich resources of Catholic spirituality available to a new generation. Beginning with Lallemant we shall meet in turn the great masters of his school—Surin, Huby, Maunoir, and the mystics of Brittany, and see the part played by folly for Christ's sake in their lives and teaching.

Who then was this obscure figure whose disciples, according to Bremond, are the spiritual giants of the seventeenth century, dwarfing, it would seem, the better-known spiritual writers and directors of the period? Louis Lallemant was born in Champagne, at Châlons-sur-Marne, the only son of a magistrate (*bailli*) of the *comté* of Vertus. His father sent him to be educated by the Jesuits at Bourges and he subsequently entered the Society in 1605, spending his novitiate at Nancy and continuing his studies at Pont-à-Mousson. He taught at various places before becoming Master of the Novices at Rouen. Just before his death in 1635 he became Rector of the College at Bourges. Champion describes him thus:

> He was tall in stature, of majestic bearing; he had a broad and serene brow, chestnut-brown hair, though already going bald, an oval, well-proportioned face, his complexion rather swarthy, and his cheeks usually aglow with the heavenly fire that burnt in his heart; his eyes, full of a pleasing gentleness, indicated the soundness of his judgement and the perfect equanimity of his spirit. I have heard it said by those who knew him, and were most capable of making a judgement, that one could not find a man better made in body, more composed in all his movements, more devout and recollected in outward manner, so that the mere sight of him won him the esteem and affection of everybody.[9]

Lallemant was clearly an attractive person, and his personal and spiritual gifts were recognized, at least in part, by his superiors, who entrusted him with posts of considerable responsibility. But in an important passage Champion admits that it was not always praise that Lallemant received from his brethren: 'God quite often allowed it to happen that some of those who ought to have shown him more kindness, such as his superiors, or more respect and submission, such as inferiors and disciples, forgot themselves

somewhat with regard to him and caused him pain.'[10] Bremond
rightly dismisses the idea that such trials were no more than the
stresses and strains of the common life, and hazards the guess that
Lallemant's teaching was thought to be 'too mystical' and not in
keeping with the spirit of the Society.[11] This intuition is somewhat
confirmed by Champion's enigmatic remark that 'among the Jesuits
of France, Père Louis Lallemant was what Père Álvarez was for
Spain'.[12] Baltasar Álvarez (1535–1580), for some time the director
of St Teresa of Avila, had been, like Lallemant, Novice-Master or
Rector of various houses and developed a spirituality which at the
time was not completely approved of by his superiors, even though
later it was seen to be in the classical tradition. It may be that,
among other things, what Lallemant and Álvarez had in common
was the experience of being persecuted for their witness to the place
and importance of contemplative prayer.[13]

Champion portrays Lallemant as an *autodidacte* with no director
but the Holy Spirit, with no literature save his breviary, Bible and
three or four other books. Bremond says that he 'cites only a very
small number of authors', including St Laurence Justinian and St
Vincent Ferrer. In fact, as Père Courel has pointed out, he quotes
the Fathers in great number, Gregory Nazianzen, Basil, Jerome,
Ambrose, Augustine, Pseudo-Dionysius, Isidore of Seville,
Richard of St Victor, Bernard, Bonaventure, Aquinas; and
moderns, such as St Teresa, St François de Sales, and many
others.[14] Pottier has also shown the traces of influence of those he
does not quote, especially Álvarez de Paz, and has argued that his
'original' doctrine of 'second conversion' comes from Rossignoli
or his predecessor as Instructor of the Third Year, Le Gaudier.[15]
According to Courel, there is only one name missing, a surprising
absentee, and yet one who has clearly left his impression on
Lallemant: St John of the Cross. Lallemant's first disciple,
Rigoleuc, obviously studied and made use of San Juan and wrote a
treatise on 'the dark night of the soul'; similarly, his master's
notions of the void (*vide*), the night, the desert, have a sanjuanist
flavour.

This possible influence of St John of the Cross is important to us,
because the tradition of the Jesuit fools in the seventeenth century,
of which Lallemant laid the foundations, gives the lie to the false
contrast between Ignatian and Carmelite spirituality, since it
happily synthesizes the teaching of both schools. In terms of the

doctrine of prayer, it is misleading to stereotype the Ignatian approach as absolutizing discursive, formal ,meditation and the Carmelite as speaking only of affective or contemplative prayer. In fact, the two schools have far more in common that this over-simplification suggests. In the *Spiritual Exercises*, while the first of Ignatius's Three Ways of Praying is schematic, discursive, and intellectual, the other two come closer to a simpler and more affective kind of prayer. In the Second Way, the one who prays, spending a whole hour dwelling on each word of the Our Father, is encouraged to hold himself open to be led into a deeper kind of prayer: 'If in dwelling on the Our Father he finds in one or two words abundant food for thought and a sense of spiritual comfort, he should not be anxious to move on, even if the end of the hour comes whilst he is still in that stage.'[16]

In the Third Way, this slow praying of each word of the Our Father is coupled with breathing, so that a rhythmic form of prayer is established. Here Ignatius is offering practical directives for a form of prayer which can prepare the soul for God's gift of contemplation. In many ways (for example, the breathing, the repetition of a single word) it resembles the Jesus Prayer of the East, which is certainly intended to lead the soul to contemplative union with God, from prayer of the lips or mind to prayer of the heart.[17] More striking, however, are the parallels between this section of the *Exercises* and the *Way of Perfection* where St Teresa, in describing the 'Prayer of Quiet', says that it is a sign of this state to be able to spend a whole hour on a single repetition of the Pater Noster.[18] Of course, it might be objected that, while Ignatius is concerned to offer practical directives as to *what to do* in praying, St Teresa is describing *what is received* from God in a supernatural state of prayer. In fact, this contrast, too, is oversimplified: Ignatius himself sees prayer as a gift, and Teresa has a thoroughly practical, incarnational approach to spiritual guidance. The 'Prayer of Quiet' is not subject to control; it is a supernatural gift that cannot be acquired, but there is much we can do to prepare ourselves for its reception and to respond fully and properly to it when it comes, to appropriate it to the full. St Teresa's instructions on affective repetition, using the imagery of breathing, afford a very close parallel both with Ignatius's Third Way and with Eastern hesychasm.

The most we should do is occasionally, and quite gently, to utter a single word, like a person giving a little puff to a candle, when he sees it has almost gone out, so as to make it burn again; though, if it were fully alight, I suppose the only result of blowing it would be to put it out. I think the puff should be a gentle one because, if we begin to tax our brains by making up long speeches, the will may be active again.[19]

What matters is the conforming of our wills to God, total unself-consciousness; that is the foundation of contemplative prayer. Not surprisingly, if those dispositions are present, God may well give contemplative union in and through vocal prayer: 'while you are repeating the Pater Noster or some other vocal prayer, it is quite possble for the Lord to grant you perfect contemplation'.[20]

It will be seen, then, at this level alone, that the Ignatian and Carmelite schools are not in a relationship of rivalry and competition, and so we need not be surprised at the synthesis of their teaching achieved by Lallemant and his successors. In fact, there are even deeper correspondences, particularly with regard to the motif of folly for Christ's sake. We have already mentioned Ignatius's third grade of humility and his stress in the Constitutions on the livery of Christ's humiliation and mockery. Padre Larrañaga has suggested that Ignatius's doctrine here closely matches that of St John of the Cross in the seventh chapter of the second book of the *Ascent of Mount Carmel*.[21] It will be remembered that Ignatius regarded the participation in the humiliation of Christ, the wearing of his purple livery of shame in the Praetorium, as the highest degree of humility. San Juan, likewise, throughout his writings, stresses that the only way to perfection, the narrow path to eternal life, involves nakedness and poverty of spirit, complete destitution and dispossession of self. Then, in the passage of the *Ascent* mentioned above, he says it means sharing in the 'reduction', 'annihilation,' and dereliction of Christ on the cross, when he endured the taunts and mockery of mankind.

It is certain that, at the moment of His death, He was likewise annihilated in His soul, and was deprived of any relief and consolation, since His Father left Him in the most intense aridity, according to the lower part of His nature. Wherefore He had perforce to cry out, saying: My God! My God! Why hast Thou forsaken Me? This was the greatest desolation, with respect to sense, that He had suffered in His life. And thus He wrought herein the greatest work that He had ever wrought, whether in miracles or in mighty works, during the whole of His life, either upon earth or in Heaven, which was the reconciliation and union of mankind, through grace, with God.

And this was, as I say, at the moment and the time when this Lord was most completely annihilated in everything. That is to say, with respect to human reputation; since, when they saw Him die, they mocked Him rather than esteemed Him; and also with respect to nature, since His nature was annihilated when He died; and with respect to the spiritual consolation and protection of the Father, since at that time He forsook Him, that He might pay the whole of man's debt and unite him with God, being thus annihilated and reduced as it were to nothing. Wherefore David says concerning Him: *Ad nihilum redactus sum, et nescivi.* This he said that the truly spiritual man may understand the mystery of the gate and of the way of Christ, in order to be united with God, and may know that, the more completely he is annihilated for God's sake, according to these two parts, the sensual and the spiritual, the more completely is he united to God and the greater is the work which he accomplishes. And when he comes to be reduced to nothing, which will be the greatest extreme of humility, spiritual union will be wrought between the soul and God which in this life is the greatest and the highest state attainable. This consists not, then, in refreshment and in consolations and spiritual feelings, but in a living death of the Cross, both as to sense and as to spirit—that is, both inwardly and outwardly.[22]

St John's mystical doctrine might almost be described as an elaboration of the gospel text: 'He who finds his life will lose it, and he who loses his life for my sake will find it' (Matt. 10: 39). He urges the most radical dispossession of self and poverty of spirit—renunciation not only of material possessions and security but of the more subtle spiritual buttresses of the ego: self-esteem, a sense of worldly reputation, the desire to cling to God's graces and consolations, rather than to God himself. Thus it is that purgation must precede union and that, as St Teresa teaches, God reserves the greatest trials for contemplatives.[23] Union with God through contemplation is but the practical realization of the apostle's words: 'it is no longer I who live, but Christ who lives in me' (Gal. 2: 20). Consequently, the contemplative way must involve the stripping of the last vestiges of the sinful, fleshly ego, which strives to live for itself and not for the Lord, which erects barricades of possessions, material and spiritual, against all challenges from outside. Readiness to be exposed to mockery with the naked Christ, humble submission to rejection by the world, and the loss of all respect and credibility—these are the marks of the true contemplative. As St Teresa says of Peter of Alcantara, 'Judging from the life he led, I think he is certainly a saint, yet those who heard him from time to time called him mad. Oh, what a blessed madness, sisters! If only

God would give it to us all!'[24] The contemplative way requires us fearlessly to renounce the world's wisdom and to endure accusations of folly and madness. The knowledge of God transforms our perception of the world; it certainly cannot encourage us in an uncritical acceptance of the world's prudence and maxims. As San Juan says:

> Hence the divinely wise and the worldly wise are ignorant in one another's estimation; for the latter cannot apprehend the wisdom and science of God, neither can the former apprehend those of the world; inasmuch as the wisdom of the world, as we have said, is ignorance with respect to the wisdom of God, and that of God with respect to that of the world.[25]

The mystical doctrine taught by the great Carmelites challenges the world. It is not surprising that St John of the Cross suffered persecution, for he questioned the conventional assumptions of conformity to the world and of peace at any price, which had overtaken the ideal of conformity to the will of God and the 'peace that passes understanding'. Kidnapped and confined in a dark cell in the monastery of the Toledo Carmelites, bleeding from the wounds inflicted by their floggings, starved and racked with pain, tormented by his religious superiors, this tiny friar nevertheless sang with ecstatic lyricism of the soul's union with God, of transformation in love for the Heavenly Bridegroom.

Ignatian and Carmelite traditions are in agreement, not competition, precisely in those aspects which stimulate and feed the spirituality of the holy fools. The teaching of the Carmelites on darkness, dereliction, and dispossession of self became a manifesto for the valiant Jesuits and others who in the seventeenth century experienced these at first hand and led others to God through the same austere and forbidding country. Louis Lallemant, following in the footsteps of Baltasar Álvarez, was perhaps the first in France to realize the unity of the two schools and provided his spiritual heirs with a firm theological basis for their practice of holy folly. To understand Lallemant aright, we must recall to whom his *Doctrine spirituelle* is addressed: Jesuit Fathers of the Third Year, priests who have finished their studies and now undertake a period of 'second novitiate' in retreat before their final vows. Ignatius envisaged it as a time for deeper conversion, for intensifying their conformity to Christ.[26] Lallemant's doctrine continues in this spirit:

There are normally two conversions for the majority of the saints and for those who become perfect: the first is the one through which they dedicate themselves to the service of God, the second by which they give themselves entirely to perfection. This is to be seen in the Apostles, when Our Lord called them, and when he sent them the Holy Spirit; in St Teresa and in her confessor Père Álvarez, and in several others. This second conversion does not happen to every religious, and that is through their own negligence. The time for this conversion in our case is commonly the Third Year of the novitiate.[27]

Lallemant encourages young priests to renew their commitment to Christ, as Christians and as religious, and to reject spiritual defeatism and half-heartedness. Nothing but perfection will do, for 'the salvation of a religious is inseparably bound up with his perfection'.[28] So he urges his hearers to 'take the leap', and to wrench themselves away from boring, cramped substitutes for living faith, and throw themselves completely into the hands of God.[29]

Inseparably connected with this second conversion is Lallemant's doctrine of guidance or direction by the Holy Spirit:

The end to which we should aspire, after we have trained ourselves for a long time in purity of heart, is to be so possessed and governed by the Holy Spirit, that it is he alone who guides all our faculties and senses, all our actions, both interior and exterior, and to whom we abandon ourselves entirely, through a spiritual renunciation of our wills and our own satisfactions. Thus we shall no longer live in ourselves, but in Jesus Christ, through faithful submission to the operations of his divine Spirit, and through a perfect subjection of all our rebellions to the power of his grace.[30]

The reason why people arrive at perfection very late, if at all, is that in almost everything they follow only nature and the way of men. They are led only a little, or not at all, by the Holy Spirit, whose special function is to enlighten, direct, and inflame. There is an almost 'Pentecostalist' quality about Lallemant's insistence on the Holy Spirit as the primary force and directing influence in our lives. It has much in common with the teaching of the Russian St Seraphim of Sarov (1759–1833), who in his famous discourse with Motovilov describes the 'true end of the Christian life' as 'the acquisition of the Holy Spirit'.[31] Now, if, as Lallemant stressed, the Holy Spirit is to possess and rule us, then our only wisdom can be his divine gift of wisdom. But that will mean that we are exposed as

fools in the eyes of the world. Lallemant offers a charter of holy folly
for his spiritual sons:

> There is a folly which is true wisdom in the eyes of God. To love poverty,
> contempt, crosses, persecutions, that is to be a fool according to the world.
> And yet the wisdom that is a gift of the Holy Spirit is nothing other than the
> folly which delights only in what Our Lord and the saints have delighted in.
> Now, in everything he touched during his mortal life, such as poverty or
> abasement, there is a sweet odour, a delicious savour. But few souls have a
> sensibility refined enough to smell this odour and to taste this savour, which
> are both supernatural. The saints 'have run after the odour of these
> perfumes'—like St Ignatius, who took pleasure in finding himself mocked;
> St Francis, who loved humiliation so much that he performed actions to
> become an object of ridicule; St Dominic, who was much happier to be at
> Carcassonne, where he was usually scoffed at, than at Toulouse, where he
> was honoured by everybody.[32]

It requires spiritual discernment to comprehend the true meaning of
folly for Christ's sake:

> To say that Our Lord could have redeemed us without suffering at all,
> could have won everything He has won for us without dying a death as
> sordid as that of the cross, and yet chose the death of the cross for our
> salvation—to say that is madness by the standards of human reason. But
> 'what seems folly in God is wiser than the wisdom of all men'. How different
> are the judgements of God from those of men! Divine wisdom is folly in the
> judgement of men, and human wisdom is folly in the judgement of God. *It is
> up to us to see to which of these two judgements we are going to conform our
> own.*[33]

The 'monstrous' fact against which Lallemant inveighs is the
capitulation of so many religious to the judgements of the world,
their aspiring after worldly wisdom, knowledge, and sanity, and,
most hideous of all, their desire for respect, reputation, and
grandeur in the eyes of the world. Lallemant overthrows the
bourgeois idol of respectability, normality and good sense, which so
often usurps the place of a religion on fire with the wild flame of the
Holy Spirit. According to Lallemant, there must be no defection;
we must wear the livery of Christ's humiliation before the world and
be prepared to be written off, derided, and laughed at, as he was.
That is the only road to glory. Seeking the respect of men is a denial
of our supernatural dignity as sons of God: 'through the very things
which humiliate us in the eyes of men, Jesus Christ takes pleasure in
seeing us wear his livery, and the angels envy us this honour'.[34]

'Contempt', 'the livery of Christ', 'folly'—these become the ideals of the spiritual heirs of Lallemant in the seventeenth century. Later in the century they will give strength and hope to priests and others in the face of mockery and misunderstanding, depression and despair. In the midst of their dark night, their descent into hell, these holy fools will be sustained not by stoical resolve but by a living faith in Christ, a desire to be thoroughly converted to him, and an experience of the healing wound of the Holy Spirit. This great tradition, expounded so magnificently by Père Lallemant, later tried and tested in his successors' own lives, will be transmitted to the many souls whom they direct and for whom they will write. And to us, too, their witness to the purple livery of Christ may still communicate its power and consolation across time and death.

8

Jean-Joseph Surin:
Schizophrenia or Spirituality

The first of Lallemant's disciples to be considered is an enigma. Jean-Joseph Surin (1600–1665) was one of the most prolific spiritual writers of the seventeenth century, but for twenty years he suffered a mental illness with many of the symptoms of catatonic schizophrenia.[1] The most promising Jesuit of his generation, he was brought to a condition of total mental collapse following his traumatic experiences as exorcist at Loudun. Then, later, restored to health, he became an indefatigable correspondent and author and, in his last years, an active apostle in the countryside round Bordeaux. Surin is a classical instance of a fool for Christ's sake. It is true that his madness was involuntary and caused him great pain; there was nothing simulated or 'mimic' about it. But by humbly enduring it, he became a witness and prophetic sign: *prodigium factus sum multis.* Here was one who, in the midst of mental breakdown, heard the word of the apostle: 'If any one among you thinks that he is wise in this age, let him become a fool that he may become wise' (1 Cor. 3: 18). Quoting this passage, his biographer, Boudon, offers a gloss which effectively describes the spiritual career of Surin:

> That is to say, let his spirit be humbled and annihilated before God; let no man, be he preacher or doctor, whatever wit he might possess, rely or dwell upon his natural abilities; let him not imagine he can do any great thing in the eyes of God, whatever prestige he might possess, by his own lights, in the eyes of men; let him renounce the wisdom of the age, which gives him esteem and approval in the world, and which all too easily convinces him that he is wise and prudent; let him follow and let him practise the maxims of the Gospel, which speak only of confusions, humiliations, poverty, annihilations, which seem like folly to noble spirits, but which are the real wisdom; for in becoming a fool in this way, he will be truly wise.[2]

The Child

Surin was born on 2 April 1600 in Bordeaux, the son of Jean de Seurin and Jeanne d'Arrerac. We know little of his childhood, but the evidence we have suggests that it was a *temps perdu*, 'the sweetest I could imagine', a time of freedom and spontaneity before 'they' began to take control of his life. At the age of eight, during a plague, his parents sent him out of town to stay in the country. There in beautiful surroundings he knew a peace and absence of fear which were not to be his again until he was an old man. Surin's later healing is, for him, a return to the bliss of childhood.

I seem to have returned to that sweet state of spirit which I enjoyed in my childhood, in my eighth year, when I feared nothing. At that time it happened that, while my parents were away in the country, I was left alone in my father's house with a few servants. Then the plague broke out in the house, which caused my parents to return and procure a place of quarantine for me—this time was the sweetest I could imagine. They took me to a country house, close to the town, in a very beautiful place, during the fairest season of the year, and here I was left alone with a governess whose only care was to obtain for me every pleasure. Each day I was visited by my family, who, one after the other, came to see me and bring me presents. My whole day was taken up with playing and going for walks, without fear of anyone. After that quarantine, they (*on*) made me begin my education, and my bad time began, Our Lord dealing with me, no doubt by his providence, in such a rough way, that since then, until four or five years ago, my ills have been very great and have increased to the limits of natural endurance.[3]

Surin records another incident of his childhood, or rather of his early adolescence, which is most important for the later development of his spirituality. In 1610 he entered the Jesuit college at Bordeaux, and while there he became acquainted with a spiritual daughter of St Teresa of Avila, Mère Isabelle des Anges, who had known the great saint and was now prioress of the Carmelite convent in Bordeaux. Surin began to visit her on his days off from school. In 1613 in her convent chapel he had an experience that he describes in his autobiographical *Science expérimentale:*

In their chapel, where there was no one but me, I was drawn to sit down in a confessional, for even though I was a child of little devotion and wisdom, Our Lord nonetheless gave me great graces. He then gave me a sign, for in addition to the very profound perceptions of himself . . . he gave me, that afternoon, a declaration of his principal attributes and made me savour them.[4]

This early experience, and its setting in a Carmelite chapel, proved to be of great significance for the priest and spiritual writer forty years later, for, as we shall see, the doctrine of Carmel was to be one of his chief resources in the long struggle that was to follow.

In 1616 Surin entered the Jesuit novitiate, completing his Third Year from 1629–1630 at Rouen under Père Lallemant. He was made a Bursar in the Society and thenceforth combined this duty with preaching, first at Bordeaux, later at the residence at Marennes in the district of Saintonge. During these years he acquired a reputation for being a man of great spiritual power and, in 1634, at the personal command of Cardinal Richelieu, he was sent with another priest as exorcist to Loudun where Urban Grandier, the parish priest, had lately been burnt as a sorcerer on the charge of bewitching the Ursuline nuns.[5]

Loudun radically altered the pattern of Surin's life. It would be nearly thirty years before he was able to take up again the preaching and catechizing which, at his ordination, he had expected to be his life's work.

The Exorcist

Loudun had become a crucible for all the obsessions, political as well as religious, of seventeenth-century France. For two years the convent had echoed with the screams and hideous laughter of the possessed nuns, and when Surin arrived it was a veritable hell on earth. The exorcisms were attended by every kind of ecclesiastical and political dignitary, visitors coming from all over France and from abroad to observe the macabre spectacle so that the convent was turned into 'a theatre to which all sorts of people flock'.[6] Attempting to put this extraordinary situation into perspective, de Certeau writes: 'The pathetic personal adventures of Mère Jeanne des Anges and Grandier were engulfed in a vaster drama: the religious war of Huguenots and Catholics, the political struggle between the provincial feudalities and the royal power, the crisis which disturbed the economic equilibrium, the social hierarchy and the fundamental attitudes of the age.'[7]

Whether or not this view is correct, it was certainly into a maelstrom of political intrigue, religious conflict, and demonic possession that Surin came in December 1634. His superiors had doubted his suitability for this work, having already noted his not over-strong constitution. Nonetheless, he began the exorcism on St Thomas's Day, 21 December. His particular charge was the

Prioress, Mère Jeanne des Anges. In contrast to the grotesque practices of Père Tranquille, his predecessor as exorcist, Surin's methods were those of patient counsel and prayer. The exorcisms were not long drawn-out displays of demonic pyrotechnics but short, quiet sessions in the presence of the Blessed Sacrament, when Surin would speak gently into the ear of the possessed woman of the spiritual life and its blessings.

Unlike his predecessor, Surin did not make Mère Jeanne 'perform' for the sake of the 'audience'; far from seeking to exploit her he ministered to his spiritual charge with selfless generosity. According to his own account in his *Triomphe de l'amour divin*, he was prepared to give his own soul in exchange for the deliverance of Mère Jeanne:

He begged God with tears to give him this handmaid, to make her a perfect religious, and found himself drawn to pray God for that cause with such ardour that one day he could not prevent himself offering himself to the divine Majesty to bear the burden of this wretched woman's affliction and to share in all her temptations and miseries, even to the extent of asking to be possessed by an evil spirit, provided that God would agree to give him the liberty of entering within her soul and devoting himself to her. From then on a paternal love towards this afflicted soul was engendered in the heart of this father . . . and he decided that his great happiness would be to imitate Jesus Christ, who, to lead souls from the captivity of Satan, had borne the burden of their infirmities and suffered death.[8]

Surin did not have to wait long to begin his journey along the way of substitution and exchange. On Good Friday 1635 he fell into an extraordinary state of mind and body, as he describes in a letter to Père Achille Doni d'Attichy in May of the same year:

For three and a half months I have never been without a devil at work beside me. Things are come to such a pass, permitted by God, I think for my sins, and never before seen in the Church, that in the exercise of my ministry the devil passes from the body of the person possessed and, entering my own, assaults me, knocks me down, agitates and visibly torments me, possessing me for several hours like an energumen. I could not explain to you what happens within me during this time, how that spirit unites itself with mine without depriving me of either consciousness or liberty of soul, becoming nevertheless like another self (*comme un autre moi-même*), as if I had two souls, one of which is dispossessed of its body and the use of its organs, and holds itself apart, observing the actions of this interloper in its body. These two spirits fight on the same field, the body; and the soul itself is, as it were, divided—in one part, subject to diabolical impressions, in the other, it has the motions proper to it, or those which God gives it. At the same time I feel a great peace under the good pleasure of God, and, without knowing how, an extreme rage and aversion to him, which produces a sort of vehemence to separate me from him—this astonishes those who see it; at the same time, I feel a great joy and sweetness and, on the other hand, a sadness showing itself in lamentations and cries like those of the damned. I feel the state of damnation and fear it, and feel myself, as it were, pierced by the arrows of despair in that stranger soul, which seems to be my own; and the other soul, which finds itself in perfect confidence, mocks at such sentiments and, in all freedom, curses the one who is their cause. Yes, I feel that the same cries which escape from my mouth come equally from these two souls, and I find it hard to discern whether it is joyousness which produces them, or the extreme fury that fills me. . . . When the other possessed see me in this state, it is a pleasure to see how they triumph and like devils they mock me: 'Physician, heal thyself! Now get up in the pulpit! How fine it will be to see him preach after he's been rolling on the ground!' *Temptaverunt me, susannaverunt me subsannatione. Frenduerunt super me dentibus suis* (Ps. 34: 16). What cause for blessing to see oneself the sport of devils, and divine justice taking account of my sins, but what a privilege to feel the condition from which Jesus Christ has delivered me and to feel how great is his redemption, no longer by hearsay, but by direct experience of that same condition! And how good to have together the capacity both to penetrate this adversity and also to give thanks to the loving kindness which has delivered us from it with so much labour. . . . The devil has said to me: 'I will rob you of everything, and you will need your faith to stand by you. I will make you become one devoid of his reason (*hébété*)'. He is in league with a sorceress to prevent me from speaking of God and to have the strength to hold my mind bridled; and this he carries out most faithfully, as he promised, and, in order to have any thought at all, I am constrained to hold the Holy Sacrament often on my head, thus using the Key of David to unlock my memory. [9]

This first trauma, which was the herald of a further twenty years torment, in many ways resembles schizophrenia: the sense of alienation from a part of oneself, of the 'stranger self' that inhabits the same body as one's true self, is commonly experienced by those diagnosed as schizophrenic. [10] It would be wrong however, to assume such a psychological description to be applicable in this case. For, seen in the full context of Surin's life, this breakdown should not lead us to interpret mystical experience in terms of abnormal psychology but rather to re-examine our tendency to account for human behaviour from a purely psychological standpoint. The folly tradition does not allow us to equate sanity with conformity to prevailing *mores*, and we should therefore beware of too quickly dismissing as mythological Surin's own analysis of his state as one of demonic possession; such an analysis is no more mythological than one that uses the language of *id* and *ego* or of stimulus and response. It is not sufficient to say, as some theologians would, that Surin had to use the language of demonic possession because of his cultural conditioning. On the contrary, Surin freely uses other terminology, often of considerable psychological precision, to speak of his own and others' behaviour, but finds it inadequate. One should not overlook the extent to which he *describes* what is happening, strives to be an impartial observer of his own divided self. There is the constant, repeated use of the verb *sentir*: '*Je sens . . . je sens*'; the insistence that what he describes he has experienced, felt, perceived. He does not tell a straightforward story of demonic possession, a saga or epic in which the only actors are devils and angels. On the contrary, his basic story is one of perceived experience, described with acute observation.[11] The account of the demonic possession is not a rival, if outmoded, explanation but the only valid interpretation, as Surin sees it, of what is happening to him. The language of faith, which speaks of the imitation of Christ, the participation in his humiliation, the struggle with Satan and his devils—this is the only *accurate* language at his disposal; it is the most refined, the most precise; it can offer the only truthful account of his experience. He is a man of the seventeenth century, concerned with the fate and destiny of the individual subject and has considerable psychological perception, but he stands ultimately as a Christian, one whose grasp of reality and the dynamics of human behaviour, while being greatly assisted by the resources of psychology and the sciences, draws its main power and resilience from revelation. Surin shows us early psychology and Christian spirituality interlocked and mutually illuminating, but the spirituality remains dominant and so the danger of determination by ephemeral ideology is averted. Surin sees that the wisdom of God, which looks like madness to the world, inevitably questions the comfortable assumptions we make about what counts as normality and sanity.

Enduring this intense spiritual and mental anguish, Surin continued in his combat against the devils of Mère Jeanne until October 1636, when he was replaced as exorcist by Père Antoine

Ressès, who believed in the educational value of admitting the faithful to the edifying spectacle of exorcisms. Nothing could have been more opposed to the prayerful approach of Surin. Mère Jeanne in any case remained possessed by the last and most pugnacious of the demons, Behemoth, who continued to make it a condition of his departure that Surin and Mère Jeanne go on pilgrimage to Annecy to the tomb of St François de Sales. At the same time there was mounting controversy in the Society about the exorcisms in general and the state of Mère Jeanne in particular. Her hand now bore the sacred names of Jesus, Mary, and Joseph, miraculously scored in the flesh as evidence of the devils' departure; tracts and rumours about this and the behaviour of the exorcists were circulating throughout France, while the Jesuit authorities, especially Père Vitelleschi, the Master General, anxiously looked on. It was eventually decided to send Surin back to Loudun to finish off the exorcisms as quickly as possible, but no longer in public. Finally, on 15 October 1637 (the feast of St Teresa of Avila) the last devil was exorcized from Jeanne, who then began to plan the pilgrimage to Annecy. Surin, however, was beginning his journey into darkness. For seven months he was in a state of almost total stupor:

> He could not say Mass, read, write, or make the slightest movement without suffering extreme pain. He could not even dress himself. All official activities were denied him. He could not make or respond to any appeal, which was the result not so much of fatigue following the exorcism, as of the strange operations of the demons and the traumatized state of his every faculty (*par des saisissements en ses facultés*) which rendered him incapable of almost anything. . . . He made great efforts against it, but all served only to increase his illness. He fell into an unknown malady which baffled the doctors.[12]

The Madman

This condition continued during the journey to Savoy, and after two years of remissions alternating with relapses, from 1640 to 1653 Surin became officially an *infirmus*, treated as a madman by his brethren, convinced in his own mind that he was damned. In 1645, while at Saint-Macaire, he even attempted to commit suicide by throwing himself out of the window; the consequent injuries left him with a permanent limp.[13] In 1655 the long process of convalescence and healing began. He was delivered not by a dramatic spiritual experience but by the simple words of a priest. It is true that a few days later the old feelings of despair returned with ferocity, but the first *guérison* of October 1655 marked the beginning of the end of Surin's personal hell; everything henceforth was to be progress. The story is movingly told in the *Science expérimentale*. The priest, Père Jean Ricard, came to his cell to hear his confession and prepare him for communion:

Although I was not in hell, I felt myself to be as damned as those who were there. That is why my most frightful crime was still to hope and to want to try to do good. . . . When I was seated, I began to accuse myself in this manner, because, quite honestly, all the other sins seemed nothing to me, mere bagatelles, in comparison with that. . . . And so I confessed as one who was damned, and not as a man living on earth, who still had hope. At this the father told me that he had great compassion for me, but that he had to let me into a secret. 'I am not,' he said, 'a man of revelation, nor one who trusts much to instinct. All the same, I must tell you that I have often had the conviction, which comes from neither my imagination nor my own consciousness, that, before you die, Our Lord will give you the grace to see that you are wrong and that you will come at the last to be like other men, and I hope you will die in peace.' These words made a great impression on me, and so I asked him if he really believed that I was capable of hoping in God and of using the remedies Our Lord has given to men in this life in order to be reconciled with him, such as the sacraments. He told me that, with all his heart, he believed so. The divine goodness willed that this entered my spirit, and then I confessed and received absolution. After that the father left me, and I remained alone in my room. Then I thought that it was quite possible that Our Lord might show me mercy and that I might possibly live with hope like other men and faithful Christians. Then I heard within my heart an utterance which was like those words of life, which Our Lord can pronounce and which he alone can say, words of life bearing their efficacy within them, so-called substantial words, '*Yes, it may be so*'. This utterance pronounced within me gave life to my soul and raised it up, in such a way that it produced a forceful and inexpressible response of tenderness and love. Afterwards, as if coming out of a deep sleep, I said again: 'Is it really possible that I am capable of returning to God and of hoping in him?' He replied to me in the same language of life: '*Do you doubt it may be so?*'[14]

The consolations Surin experienced during his healing provoked a controversy between him and his spiritual father, Bastide, who had shown him considerable kindness. Bastide warned him not to rely on mystical graces, which may be illusory, to reject all sensible

favours, along the lines of St John of the Cross's teaching in the
Ascent of Mount Carmel, where he teaches detachment from all
consoling religious experiences and is insistent that visions and
locutions, even when from God, may mislead us.[15] Surin's reply was
that he was aware of the dangers and saw that, even if such
experiences were genuine, an attitude of possessiveness towards
them was spiritually harmful. Nevertheless, he believed quite
simply that this was the way God had chosen to heal and restore
him. An appeal was made to the guardian angel of Jeanne des
Anges, who replied ambiguously to the question whether Surin or
his director were right. The matter was finally resolved by an
important experience on 9 June 1656, which saw the final defeat of
the devil in Surin. While standing by the bed in his room in the
infirmary of the Bordeaux college, he was suddenly seized with the
thought that had haunted him so long: '*Mais pourtant tu es damné.*'
This time, however, he did not descend further into despair:

This began to reduce me to a state of great anguish, and I felt a very strong
stirring of the heart, which made me resign myself to it, if it were the will of
God, and I said these words: 'I desire it, if God desires it', and I threw myself
face down on my bed to submit and abandon myself totally to the divine
will. At that moment I felt in spirit as if a second wave were covering and
drowning me, bringing peace to my soul, and it was as if, at the height of this
self-abandonment, my soul were saying, *Fiat voluntas tua*. And Our Lord
made me see then that abandonment to the divine will must take the soul to
the point where, without so much as discerning what or how, it just accepts
for eternity, by submission to the power of God, what pleases him. And
that brought me into a state of such peace that never again could despair
rule within me, and this was the last blow the enemy struck against my soul. I
have never since relapsed, for although he has not ceased, from time to
time, to approach my territory and still makes efforts to attack my defences,
nevertheless, since that day I have never again experienced any penetrating
wound from that cruel enemy of the human heart, and Our Lord has given
me the grace of holding myself just so far removed from mistrust and
despair.[16]

Life now changed for Surin. The episode of 9 June was, in one
sense, no different from the nightmares of the previous twenty
years. The difference was in his response. He accepted humbly and
submissively and abandoned himself to God's will. De Certeau puts
it well:

This acceptance is not something purely passive, it is an offering of self, and stems from something more radical than despair. His indomitable desire to remain united to God, whatever the cost, gives the lie to the apparent acceptance of his loss. It transforms the whole psychological situation and reduces what seemed a fixed decree to the state of hypothesis. The soul is open to the mystical 'flood'; the divine presence within him takes possession of a soul that is thus intent on appointing no limits to the gift of himself. From now on the powerful wave welling up from the depths of the Godhead will gradually wear away the superficial split in his personality which is the outward sign of his madness. [17]

Surin journeyed through the darkest of nights; he descended into hell and, according to his own account, suffered something of the pain of the damned. As in every classical experience of hell, his agony was made the more exquisite by the certainty of God's reality; what made his suffering the more intense was his conviction that, as one of the damned, not even his faith could help him. The reality of the divine presence was beyond question; all that was lacking was his own creative response. This unspeakable torment finally ended when the night was found to be a dazzling darkness illuminating the soul at a level deeper than that of sensory perception. Surin discovered that there is no depth of unmeaning to which a man may sink which has not already been explored and evacuated of its horror by the risen Christ, triumphant over Hades: 'If I go down to hell, thou art there also.' Surin joins that blessed company of men and women who have suffered martyrdom, not just at the hands of earthly rulers, but through the activity of the powers of evil in the depths of the soul.

The only fully adequate commentary on the madness and final healing of Père Surin is to be found in a revelation of Our Lord to an obscure Russian monk living on Mount Athos nearly three hundred years later. Staretz Silouan (d. 1936) was told by God in prayer: 'Keep thy mind in hell, and despair not.' His biographer writes:

At first the experience brings little but personal suffering caused by dwelling in 'outer darkness'. At this stage the ascetic, too, finds himself more or less in the power of hell. But when he sees in himself the light of deliverance from sin there awakens in his soul a mighty compassion for all who 'come short of the glory of God', and 'prayer for the whole Adam' fills his being. Man's consciousness that he is unworthy of God, and his condemnation of himself for every sin, in strange fashion makes him kin with the Spirit of Truth, and sets his heart free for divine love. And with the increase of love and the light of truth comes revelation of the mystery of the redeeming descent into hell of the Son of God. Man himself becomes fully like Christ; and through this likeness to Christ in the 'impoverishment' (*kenosis*) of His earthly being he becomes like to Him also in the fulness of Eternal Life. God embraces all things, even the bottomless abysses of hell, for there is no domain outside His reach, and the Saints behold and abide in hell, but it has no power over them, and the manner of their abiding differs from the abiding of those who constitute hell. The Lord's bidding to the Staretz—*Keep thy mind in hell and despair not*—reveals the unique path to complete purification and divine love. This is the unmysterious mystery of the Saints. [18]

Not every man, thank God, will experience this infernal whirligig of confusion, split personality and sense of damnation; it is good to remind ourselves of the Cistercian school already mentioned, with its almost unmitigated emphasis on the divine light. Nevertheless, it is the experience of some, and in our own time, the age of Auschwitz and Gulag , it is the experience of many. Surin faced the mystery of iniquity in all its horrific power to confuse and disorientate the soul; he bore its full onslaught and, without despairing, finally found peace and joy in God. He was dragged into Hades and knew its torments, but responded finally, not by giving in and sinking into its depths, but by courageously witnessing to Christ.

The Spiritual Writer

From 1657 Surin began an extensive correspondence in which he recounted his adventures, like an explorer returned from strange and distant lands. Spiritual treatises and poetry poured from his pen, and then finally, in the last three years of his life, with the greatest enthusiasm and devotion, he took up again the active ministry to which he had been assigned thirty years before. In the evening of his life, after twenty debilitating years of madness, this indomitable little man limped along the country lanes, seeking out the least of Christ's brethren, preaching to all and sundry of the mystery of God's love and of his amazing grace.

What, then, are we to make of Surin: is he mystic or madman, schizophrenic or man of the Spirit? Put like this, the question begs many others; we have already said that the importance of the folly tradition is that it forces us to reconsider our simplistic equation of Christian wholeness with conventional 'normality'. On the other hand, we have not claimed, as have some,[19] that mental illness is a 'myth', a construct of late capitalism or any other repressive society; there is much real madness about, and it destroys. We would be untrue to his own Ignatian tradition if we simply accepted Père Surin's account of his experiences on trust without discerning the spirits. At the end of the seventeenth century, when there was a debate in the Society about the insertion of Surin's name into the Menology, Père Jacques Nau (1618–1710), who had known Surin personally for a time, attempted such discernment and wrote a vituperative letter to the Father General:

Père Surin, whom I myself knew for twenty years or more, led so deranged and shameful a life that one hardly dares speak of it. In the end it reached the point where the most wise attributed it all, quite correctly I believe, to madness; others regarded it as diabolical possession, but wrongly so it seems to me, for there was nothing about it to suggest more than ordinary mental illness, or that could prove or demonstrate the intervention of a spirit from outside. As far as I know, he was never exorcized. There were four or five Fathers of this province, including Père Babinet, at present Spiritual Father in this College (Poitiers), prepared to say that these abominable and impious attitudes were mystical revelations from God, that they were compatible with the purest love of God and the highest perfection. I do not doubt that the Quietists say as much and would defend this Père Surin as one of theirs, this man whom I have often seen blaspheme the name of God and walk about naked in the College, soiled with excrement—I would then take him by the hand into the infirmary. I have seen him lashing out with his fists and for years perform a hundred other insanities, even to the point of trying to trample on the Sacrament of the Eucharist—I did not see this myself but learnt it the next day from witnesses. He lived like this for several years. For the rest of his life, he never fulfilled any function within the Society. When he recovered self-control, he wrote books and letters, visited his neighbour and spoke very well about God, but he never said his prayers, or read his Breviary, said Mass rarely and to his dying day jumped about and gesticulated in a ridiculous and absurd fashion. During the last year of his life, while at dinner with M. Du Sault in the company of a large gathering, he threw a full cup of wine at the serving-girl's head. Of course, his devotees went ecstatic at that and found it all divine![20]

Père Nau admits, finally, that Surin was 'a good religious' (a surprising admission after all his criticisms), but 'deprived of good sense and above all melancholic'. He then rather gives the game away: '*Excessive reading of certain mystical authors threw him into confusion.*'[21] It may be that the good father's own judgement was somewhat clouded by the residual Jesuit prejudice against the Alvarez-Lallemant emphasis on contemplation shared by Surin. Surin's spiritual doctrine was often contested, during and after his lifetime, but he can never be fairly accused of Quietism. There is, it must be confessed, an extremism of expression which loses him the sympathy of his reader on several occasions, but, as we shall see, the main tenets of his doctrine are thoroughly orthodox. Moreover, it would seem that Nau was something of a martinet, notorious for his 'excessive and inquisitorial curiosity, more inclined to condemn than to praise'.[22] He was in no position to make judgements about Surin's devotional life after his healing; the evidence we have suggests that he was utterly faithful to prayer and the Sacraments. Likewise, Nau never considers the possibility that, like Louis du Néant, whom we shall consider below, Surin maintained the appearance of folly on occasions, even after his healing, for the purposes of prophetic sign and witness.

'By their fruits . . .' Generalized denunciations, from the perspective of late seventeenth- or twentieth-century 'normality', will not assist us in making a final judgement about Surin. Bearing in mind all the time the possibility of delusion and self-deception, we must allow Surin to speak for himself and judge from our knowledge of the workings of his mind and of the spiritual quality of his life whether or not he was called to be a fool for Christ's sake. We are in a particularly fortunate position in the first respect, since Surin's literary output was enormous. In addition to the many treatises and much poetry, there is a voluminous correspondence, which in its modern critical edition consists of nearly 1800 tightly packed pages. Here are rich, autobiographical resources for the understanding of folly for Christ's sake. In what follows, we shall listen to Surin's voice and attempt to discern whether its timbre is that of the gospel.

The Sources of Surin's Spiritual Doctrine

What were the main influences on Surin, and what were the sources of his inspiration? Like his master Lallemant, Surin was indebted to both the Ignatian and Carmelite traditions. He says of St Teresa: 'The doctrine [of this saint] is infinitely dear to me, and I associate it with that of the holy founder of the Company of Jesus.'[23] We have already noted the importance of his boyhood experience in the Carmelite chapel in Bordeaux and of his relationship with the Prioress, Isabelle des Anges, who had known St Teresa and introduced the young Surin to Teresian mysticism. Writing in September 1660 to the Carmelite prioress Mère Jeanne de la Croix, who shared with Surin the 'same spiritual mother, to wit, Mère Isabelle des Anges', he encouraged her to do no more than renew within her the spiritual doctrine taught her when young by that great religious.

I do not think I can give you better advice than to renew in your own mind the ideas that lived in the spirit of that good Mother and to root yourself firmly in them, so that they are never removed from your memory. It seems to me that her example and her words had the effect of bestowing an inestimable grace, impressing upon hearts the vivacity of faith, raising them up to eternal things and withdrawing them from the affections of present existence, so that nothing temporal, on whatever pretext, might lead the soul away from finding release in God alone and repose in the bosom of his providence.[24]

There is also clear evidence of the influence of St John of the Cross. It has been shown recently that much of Surin's mystical vocabulary is derived from the French translation of St John by René Gaultier, published in 1622, and, moreover, that the dialectical relation of poetry and prose, of enigma and elucidation, which we see in the work of San Juan, has its equivalent in the canticles and prose treatises of Surin, who has a sanjuanist style and way of speaking.[25] The exegesis of the Carmelite doctor was a decisive issue in the controversy over Surin's mystical graces: while it is hard to see how Surin's attachment to his consolations can be squared with the severe doctrine of the second book of *The Ascent of Mount Carmel* it should not be forgotten that he never consciously repudiated that doctrine; the difference of opinion with his director was over its correct interpretation.

It is above all the teaching of St Teresa on which Surin leans. In a letter of 1662, written on her feast day, which always had special associations for him, being the anniversary to the day of Mother Jeanne's exorcism and close to the date of his own healing in 1655, Surin says that St Teresa is an essential guide in the spiritual life:

We must not pass by the feast of St Teresa and its octave without reflecting on the grace which heaven presents to us in the examples and merits of such a great saint, devotion to whom is essential, I believe, for all those who wish to give themselves to the love of Our Lord.[26]

It is not hard to detect Teresian influence in many places in Surin's writings, especially with regard to prayer, where he defends 'prayer of silence' (corresponding to Teresian 'prayer of quiet') against its critics. Indeed, Alphonse Vermeylen, in his study of the influence of St Teresa in seventeenth-century France, sees Surin as one of the most faithful Teresians in that period.[27]

Writing shortly after her feast in 1662, Surin cites Teresa's revelation of the meaning of true virtue as one of her greatest achievements:

True virtue is not forming great designs, carrying out great undertakings, performing great austerities or great works of charity, having a sweet recollection, feeling emotions of great tenderness and consolation in prayer. It means throwing off entirely the old man, mortifying his disordered passions and inclinations, combating his humour, tearing off even the smallest fibres of self-love from his heart, dying to self. It is to cleave with all one's might to Jesus Christ, to his doctrine, to his maxims, to love and imitation of him. God only approves of this kind of virtue. As he is a God of truth, indeed truth itself, he takes pleasure only in the truth, which is to be found only in purity of faith and the practice of the solid virtues. His spirit only abides constantly in a soul that is mortified, pure, and which enjoys a complete liberty. Such was the virtue of St Teresa. Solidity is so characteristic of her spirit and conduct that it seems to distinguish her among the favoured spouses of Jesus Christ.[28]

Conformity to Christ and non-conformity, in word, action, and thought, to the world—these are the prerequisites for advance in the virtues, according to St Teresa. Boudon, in his study of Surin, believes that it is this aspect of Teresian doctrine which left the most lasting impression on Surin. From the saint of Avila he learnt the basic axiom of the folly tradition, a doctrine which held him in good stead in the trials he endured: there can be no genuine spirituality in a soul seeking worldly respect, reputation and wisdom. Boudon writes: 'St Teresa teaches in a vigorous way the evils and injuries resulting from the "point of honour"; she declares that "the point of honour makes ravages in the ways of God. . . ." '[29] He then quotes from the sixteenth chapter of St Teresa's autobiography:

Why is it that there are so few people who are led by sermons to abstain from public sin? Do you know what I think? It is because preachers have too much worldly wisdom. They do not fling all restraint aside and burn with the great fire of God, as the Apostles did; and so their flames do not throw out much heat. I do not say that their fire could be as great as the Apostles', but I wish they had more than I see they have. Do you know, Father, what our chief care ought to be? *To hold our life in abhorrence and despise reputation.* So long as we speak the truth and uphold it to the glory of God, we should not care whether we lose or gain everything. For he who is truly bold in God's service bears loss and gain alike with equanimity. I do not say I am one of these, but I should like to be.[30]

In the same chapter St Teresa had spoken rapturously of the wild folly of the third stage of prayer:

The soul does not know what to do; it cannot tell whether to speak or be silent, whether to laugh or weep. It is a glorious bewilderment, a heavenly madness, in which true wisdom is acquired, and to the soul a fulfilment most full of delight. . . . Since as I write this I am still under the power of that heavenly madness, the effect of your goodness and mercy, O my King, and a favour that you grant me for no merits of my own, I implore you that all those with whom I converse may also become mad through your love, or let me have to do with none.[31]

For St Teresa contemplative prayer is not compatible with modes of thought and feeling encouraged by the world; rather it enables the praying man to discern its true nature. The passionate and forthright expression of this theme in St Teresa's autobiography and her other writings, especially in her poetry, must have made a great impression on Surin, who, from his childhood, felt himself to be a stranger in this world, in search of 'elsewhere', like an Irish or Russian wanderer. In the saint of Avila he found theological confirmation of his childhood's intuition. The pursuit of spiritual perfection requires a radical departure from the prudence, wisdom, and maxims of this world, a glorious journey of adventure through the madness of this age to the homeland of divine wisdom in heaven. St Teresa finishes her chapter on heavenly madness with a flourish:

O what a grand freedom it is, to look upon the need to live and behave according to the world's laws as a captivity! When this comes as a gift from the Lord, there is no slave who would not risk everything to earn his ransom and return to his own country. Since this is the true road, there is no reason to linger on it.[32]

Surin's fundamental doctrine is the pure love of God alone, *Dieu seul*—which becomes the motto of his spiritual heirs, especially, as we shall see, Boudon and Montfort. In one of his longest letters, written in 1661 to Père Louis Tillac, he explains that all the powers of the soul must be given over to love of God alone. He cites the scriptural text about loving the Lord your God 'with all your heart, and with all your soul, and with all your strength and with all your mind' (Luke 10: 27) and Jesus' words about the impossibility of serving two masters (Matt. 6: 24). He then considers the other Dominical command to love our neighbour and asks: is there a contradiction? Not at all, says Surin:

> Just as the law of love of neighbour obliges us to love him for the love of God, so the motive which makes us love God makes us also love the neighbour. From which it follows that, in only loving the neighbour for the love of God, in loving the neighbour we love God more than the neighbour himself, or rather we love only God in the neighbour, the love of neighbour being in no way different from love of God.[33]

The Incarnation makes this a reality, for manhood has been assumed by God; God now dwells among men; and the Incarnate Word takes up his dwelling and waits to be loved and honoured in men:

> It is God's will that, in all our good works for one another, we always have him before our eyes, even in the actions which seem to have the least to do with him, such as the help of the poor and the sick. That is why Jesus Christ says in the Gospel: 'Whenever you do these works of charity to the least of my brethren you do it to me.' And this incarnate God, who intended as one of the ends of the Incarnation to provide us with the means of referring all things to him, goes so far as to say: 'I was hungry and you gave me to eat', etc. He makes himself indigent and weak in the person of the poor and the sick, and it is his will that we should see him only in the wretched who have need of our help, so jealous is he to draw to himself all our duties and to enjoy all the fruits of our existence, without letting us do anything whatsoever out of consideration for any creature. He wants everything for himself, without reserve. It is not only our acts of homage, our adoration, our love, our service, he requires. He even asks for our compassion, our help, and our alms, and he accepts them as if he had need of them.[34]

If we make any human love independent of our love of God, if we stress the 'horizontal' to the neglect of the 'vertical', if we see love of God and love of neighbour in competition, then we may delude ourselves that we are acting selflessly or disinterestedly, but in fact the tares of self, pride, and glory will choke our love. Surin exposes the illusions which mislead us whenever we seek a love which pretends to independence of the love of God. Far from denigrating love of neighbour, Surin is in fact defending its rightful dignity. For the pure love of God alone liberates the other loves and protects them from disfigurement by self-will.

The Holy Idiot

At several points in this story of holy folly mention has been made of the closely related, but not identical, theme of the holy idiot, the 'enlightened illiterate'. We shall discover that during the seventeenth century the interest in such figures became almost a cult, and perhaps no single account of such a person was more influential than that contained in a letter of Surin, written from Bordeaux in 1630, to his *confrères* at the College of La Flèche.[35] Its literary form is epistolary, but it reads more like a manifesto. Surin's correspondents shared it with others, made copies and distributed it widely, eventually circulating it throughout France. It was printed, and editions soon multiplied. The incident it recounts took place during a coach journey from Rouen to Paris, presumably at the end of Surin's Third Year.

> I found placed beside me in the coach a young man, aged about eighteen or nineteen, simple and extremely coarse in his speech, quite illiterate, having passed his life in the service of a priest. He was nevertheless filled with all kinds of graces and with such exalted interior gifts that I have never yet seen his equal. He has never been instructed by anybody but God in the spiritual life, and yet he spoke of it to me with such sublimity and solidity that all that I have read or heard is nothing in comparison with what he told me.[36]

On the journey the young man was continually in prayer, apart from the times of conversation when he spoke profoundly to Surin of the spiritual life. At every point he manifested a deep humility and confessed that he believed himself to be one of the great sinners of the world and asked Surin to pray for him. Surin asked if he had a devotion to St Joseph and he replied that for six years the saint had been his special protector: 'He told me that St Joseph had been a man of great silence; that in Our Lord's home he spoke very little, but Our Lady even less, and Our Lord less than either; that his eyes taught him quite enough, so there was no need for our Saviour to speak'.[37]

De Certeau regards the letter as the reworking of the traditional theme of holy idiocy, especially of its classical reinterpretation within the fourteenth-century *Gottesfreunde* movement. Boudon, Surin's biographer, tells us this story of Johannes Tauler (*c.*1300–1361), who was closely associated with that movement.

You know what happened to Tauler, one of the most famous preachers of his time. He preached well-prepared sermons, which contained all you would think necessary. He was greatly appreciated, and the intelligentsia of the time gave him their applause. . . . It happened that a poor man, ignorant of all these necessary things, but most wise in the science of the saints, advised him not to preach any more, and made him lead a life which was ridiculous in the eyes of the intellectuals who had held him in such high esteem. See how this learned idiot, full of the spirit of God, advised him to do what the humanly learned and wise would have prohibited! Nevertheless, after such a humiliating experience, the idiot advised Tauler to go back into the pulpit; and that is what happened. But as there was still a little of the purely human in him, the Spirit of God made him dumb, this man who before had spoken with such eloquence and ease on those occasions when he had spoken through his own spirit: He blocked his speech, because there was still in him something that wanted to speak, and he intended that it should no longer be him who did the speaking: *Non enim vos estis qui loquimini*. This last action made him look completely insane— and in the presence of the other preachers, too; and so, being thus completely ruined of all reputation, performing no longer for either men or himself, the Spirit of God took possession of him and spoke through him: *Spiritus Patris vestri loquitur in vobis* (Matt. 10: 20).[39]

The fact that this tradition is alive at the end of the seventeenth century in the writings of one of Surin's spiritual disciples is adequate testimony to what his letter achieved as a 'reappearance and new departure' for the tradition of the illiterate saint.[40]

The Holy Fool

Explicit discussion of holy folly appears first in Surin's writings at the beginning of his trials at Loudun and re-emerges twenty years later after his healing when he is able to reflect on his illness. He never contradicted the accusation that he was possessed, like the Ursuline nuns of Loudun; indeed, an absence of self-defensiveness is essential, he claimed, to spirituality, for being scorned is a precious privilege which joins us closer to the Jesus of the Praetorium. In April 1635, after his first experience of derangement, he wrote thus to Mère Anne d'Arrerac of Poitiers:

When they tell me I am possessed by the devil, I can only say that I find great benefit in a state so contemptible that it could bring me, if it so happened, the opprobrium of the world, like those poor Ursulines who go up to Calvary every day to be immolated in the full view of all France. Blessed maidens, who, while in one sense the devil's prisoners, triumph over him in another way, by their patience and humility, happy to be called by the world witches, deceivers, vicious and mad: these are the names of their spouse Jesus Christ, who has honoured them with his livery, and who, by the very same means by which the devil has tried to separate them from him, has united himself to them more generously. You can be sure that there is no one in this world so despised, rejected, hated, maltreated, and cursed as Jesus Christ and his disciples.[41]

Writing only two years later to another religious in Poitiers, Surin says: 'Be a fool for God, if you want to be holy.'[42] Shortly after being delivered from his illness, in a letter to Mère Jeanne, he compares himself to Nebuchadnezzar and says that when Our Lord appeared to him in a wrathful manner, he was reduced to a state of such weakness that 'without losing my judgement, I performed the actions of a madman and was treated as such for two years'.[43] More systematically, elsewhere, he relates his own experience to the classical tradition of holy folly and to the Pauline texts. In his *Catéchisme spirituel* (written between 1654–1655), he describes the true and secret wisdom of the saints:

Question Give us an example of this secret wisdom.
Answer The practice of St Francis and the very great instinct St Ignatius had to be reckoned a fool and even to do the actions that will lead to our acquiring such a title—this is the result of that secret wisdom of Jesus Christ which the saints regard as a precious stage in the spiritual life, although they say one must not express such instincts lightly or without the ultimate goal of the glory of God.[44]

It is again in a letter to a religious of Poitiers that Surin expands his comments on holy folly:

I have always believed that the things of God are folly where human judgement is concerned. When I am told of somebody's excellent attributes, that he preaches well, that he does good works, that he has great ability, and even that he is drawn to what pertains to virtue, if I do not see at work in him that docility to grace which might make him believe that he must, out of an abundance of devotion and submission to God, become a child and not use any of his subtlety, whether natural or habitual, I am not satisfied.[45]

Surin, following his master Lallemant, insists that this holy folly is
the true spirit of the Society of Jesus. Thus, to Père Léonard Frizon
on the occasion of his profession:

> This [Ignatian] spirit consists in two admirable dispositions. The first is a
> perfect abnegation, a true and solid humility, a sincere hatred for every-
> thing that might be called the 'elements of the world', even to the extent of
> discovering an exquisite taste in abjection and contempt (*mépris*), of seeing
> oneself rebuffed, hated and persecuted, passing for a fool in the minds of
> men and becoming an object of abomination before the whole world,
> finding in that one's glory, out of respect for Jesus Christ and in view of his
> shame and his cross.[46]

To Mère Jeanne de la Conception, a Carmelite at Bordeaux, on
the feast of the Annunciation in 1662, he says that the amazing love
of God revealed in the Incarnation should carry us away in a flight of
holy folly:

> Dear daughters of an infant God, brides of a crucified God, how can you
> not be transported by his love to the point of folly, since he lets you kiss him
> with the very same liberty with which a mother kisses her child, and since he
> takes pleasure in your caresses and your heart is made to love the sovereign
> goodness, . . . So, now being beside herself in holy inebriation from the
> love which possesses her, being a fool of heavenly wisdom, she will find
> nothing beautiful or good except in Jesus, she will be able to think only of
> Jesus, speak only of Jesus; and coming to herself once more, she will have
> no other design than the perfect service of Jesus.[47]

One of the most striking images Surin uses to describe holy folly is
that of a savage: the holy man, the one who pursues virtue and
union with God, must appear a wild and confusing alien, a savage,
whose *mores* are in conflict with the world. He expresses it
forcefully in the canticle, *De l'abandon à la divine providence*:

> To this world I want to appear as a savage
> Who defies its most severe laws.
> I wish only to imitate the folly
> Of that Jesus who once upon the cross
> Freely lost honour and life,
> Abandoning all to save his Love.[48]

Again, on the same day in 1635 that he wrote to a religious in
Poitiers of the 'benefit' of being written off as a madman and
demoniac, he also wrote to a Benedictine nun: 'You ought to
become a savage in the eyes of the world, pass for a fool in the
judgement of human prudence; you ought to be lost to yourself, no

longer conscious of yourself; you ought to behave like a person with an alienated spirit, no longer in possession of yourself, your spirit having been seized from you.'[49] Occasionally, the image is reversed and true recollection is compared to that state of detachment forced upon a man who lives among savages: 'St Laurence Justinian lived in his monastery with his religious, as if he were living, so he said, among savages, and . . . Fr Baltasar Álvarez maintained the same recollection as though he had been, he said, in the deserts of Africa.'[50]

This image is important because Surin was writing at a time when explorers were still discovering new territory, when, for many Jesuits, missionary endeavour and life among the savages remained the ultimate dream and ambition. This nostalgia for life among the savages was not a species of religious imperialism but the outcome of a genuine spiritual ideal, a desire to live a Christian life without the materialistic pressures and temptations of Western Europe.[51]

Surin also reinterprets the tradition of the wanderer. On his view, true detachment means a permanent condition of being an alien or 'odd man out', of not belonging. At the height of his illness he was unable to speak and knew at first hand the powerlessness of the savage among the civilized, of the foreigner who cannot speak the language of the land in which he has settled. He does not seek such alienation for its own sake but as a means of mortifying the last vestige of possessiveness, of grasping, self-protective pride, which obstructs that death to self essential for eternal life. Surin uses violent imagery in order to raise spiritual direction above the level of cliché and platitude, to demonstrate that 'dying with Christ' is more than a pretty phrase. He calls upon the religious to unlearn the world, to exorcize the consensus view of reality from their minds and hearts: in manners and in mind, the religious must be uncon-formed to the present age. Indeed, says Surin, he must shock the world, not with the excesses of licentious behaviour, but with the wild truth, purity, and holiness of his baptismal identity. The inebriating love of God subverts the world and its laws.

> But when the man, drunk on divine Love,
> Has learned its language and the manners of its court,
> Caring no more for the world's fashion,
> He seeks profound wisdom from God alone.
> He tramples everything under foot and, in daring combat,
> Shocks the sentiments of this crazy world.[52]

In a letter of October 1634, Surin describes how at Marennes, 'among a population of heretics and boorish persons', he discovered

> . . . to what a state of mendicity God wants to reduce us and to what a desert he wants to lead us to attain the purity of his grace. . . . God has cut out our work for us, enjoining us to imitate his Son and to live in a way that goes against the grain of the world, shocking everyone with whom we live by manners, sentiments, and maxims contrary to theirs, being rejected by them, treated as fools and eccentrics (*extravagants*), so that by this turning away from all creatures and by utter deprivation of all solace, we should be obliged to seek our refuge in him and find our consolation in familiarity with him, and our strength and stay in his guidance, having an abstracted, solitary, strange heart, a heart incapable of accommodating or conforming itself to the customs of this country we regard as a place of exile.[53]

In the Praetorium

We have seen how a succession of Jesuit divines, beginning with St Ignatius himself and continuing in his disciple Lallemant, regarded the condition of Jesus in a purple robe of shame, mocked and treated as a fool, as the paradigm of true holiness. In Surin's case it is significant that the theme receives its most detailed treatment in letters to fellow Jesuits; the purple livery is part of their common inheritance as members of the Company. The image recurs frequently in a letter of 1659 to Père Frizon, to whom Surin says: 'I take the liberty of telling you what might be useful in your spiritual advancement and what I usually say to souls of the same profession as myself who are specially dear to me.'[54] Throughout the letter Surin cites the teaching of Ignatius and other Jesuit authorities on what is essential for growth in union with Jesus Christ:

> The third disposition, which immediately joins us to Our Lord and makes us enjoy the closest embrace of his love, is that which St Ignatius recommends so much and which he calls a precious stage in the spiritual life: to be able to long with all our might for the state in which Jesus Christ appeared in the Praetorium, when Pilate showed him to the people, his body lacerated and his face quite disfigured, his head crowned with thorns, a reed in his hand, an old purple cloak round his shoulders, put alongside Barabbas, ranked below this notorious ruffian and judged more worthy of death than he. This state embraced by the Son of God out of love for us, to provide us with an example, was a state of complete loss of everything that could render him illustrious in the eyes of men; the loss of honour, reputation, esteem, authority, comfort, peace, life; a state of hatred,

rejection, contempt, abandonment; a state where he reserved for himself only the will of the Father and perfect obedience; a state which he has ennobled for us to love and desire, as one might love and desire the baton of a Marshal of France, a Cardinal's hat, and the highest offices and dignities of the age. . . .[55]

To Père Huby Surin writes that Christ in his livery in the Praetorium is the model of every penitent.

Let us contemplate the mirror of all the penitent saints: Jesus Christ in the Praetorium of Pilate and upon the cross. In the Praetorium he appears as an object of abomination before the whole people, in the ludicrous regalia of a mock king (*l'équipage ridicule d'un roi de farce*). . . . For since an Incarnate God was willing to appear in that state in which Pilate showed him to the people, what point would it have if not to say to men, through his example, what St Ignatius says in his *Constitutions*, that 'out of gratitude and love for him, we should desire to be reckoned fools and glory in wearing his livery'. Now the livery of Jesus Christ is the state of a crucified man, that is, of a victim of every kind of suffering. Penitence, to be solid, must be exercised through love, and love is founded upon what I have just been talking about.[56]

Elsewhere, in a Holy Week letter of 1661 to Mère Anne Buignon, he says that this whole 'apparel' of mockery and humiliation had no other purpose than to be a 'striking lesson in the way God wants to save men'.[57]

Connected in the thought of both St Ignatius and Père Lallemant with the Praetorium is contempt of the world, *mépris du monde*, which the Ignatian tradition commends in both its active and passive forms: passively accepting the world's contempt of a truly evangelical life and actively despising all that the world delights in. Surin says bluntly that this is not just an option: 'The love of Jesus Christ and the love of contempt (*mépris*) are inseparable. The latter is the closest bond of union of souls with their Saviour and the distinctive character of the spirit of the Society of Jesus.'[58]

This contempt of the world should not be misconstrued. For Surin, as for classical Christian asceticism, 'world' does not mean 'mankind'. As we have already noted, Surin is no misanthropist; he teaches the absolute necessity of love of neighbour, especially of the poor, for the sake of God, and in his own ministry he showed his obedience to the new command of Christ. Nor does 'world' mean 'the created order'. There is in his thinking no trace of a

Manichaean contempt for material reality. Surin's theology is incarnational: there is constant reference to 'an Incarnate God' and a thoroughly Catholic view of the dignity of matter. There are examples, such as his account of his childhood sojourn in the country, of his poetic delight in the beauties of creation. The 'world' for Surin is equivalent to the *kosmos* of St John's Gospel or the *aiōn* of St Paul; indeed, he uses the terms *monde* and *siècle* interchangeably. By 'world' Surin means his own cultural epoch, 'the present age', the world as it is now governed, organized, and understood. Such concrete reference does not imply, though, a naively sociological analysis; 'world' is a theological, eschatological concept. There is much specific, historical reference in what Surin says about *mépris du monde*, but it is more than revulsion at the moral failures of seventeenth-century French society. What Surin argues against is the refusal to look beyond the maxims, precepts and sensibility of our present world; that is the height of folly, for the pattern of this present world is passing away. It is in the collision of two wisdoms, the abiding wisdom of God and the ephemeral wisdom of the age, that we should seek to understand *mépris du monde*. This is made clear by what Surin says about the apostles' preaching against the world after Pentecost: they had come with the sword of the gospel to set men free from 'the degrading slavery of being a child of the age',[59] from complacent or fearful but, in either case, self-indulgent capitulation to the *status quo*:

> They felt themselves filled with courage to proclaim to the world a doctrine which only the authority of God can urge on those who are docile to his word, to preach to men those truths which are so opposed to the inclinations of corrupted nature: that the true poor are blessed; that those who are afflicted, those who suffer persecution for the truth, must reckon themselves blessed; that, to be saved, one must renounce oneself, mortify oneself, humble oneself to the point of becoming a child; that one must despise what the world esteems, flee what it seeks; that the wisdom of men is folly to God; that we should live on earth like pilgrims who aspire to life eternal, without attaching ourselves to transitory things.[60]

The 'inclinations of corrupted nature' are such that fallen man is constantly tempted to play safe, to seek his own good rather than that of others, to proclaim his own rather than God's glory, to seek immediate gratification of his sensual appetites instead of long-term fulfilment of his deepest desire. The 'world', the 'present age', with its inflated sense of its own wisdom and values, inevitably panders to the safety-first mentality of fallen man. 'Here and now', it says to each one of us, 'you may settle down, adjust yourself, and find peace'. Surin, and with him all the prophets, urges us to despise that mentality and to look beyond, to journey on, as wayfarers satisfied with no homeland but heaven, fools for now in quest of the eternal wisdom of God.

The Little Way

Mention in the last quotation of 'becoming a child' introduces us to another frequent motif in Surin's later correspondence: spiritual infancy. We have already quoted his letter of March 1661 to Mère Jeanne when he expressed his belief that his healing had restored him to the state of untroubled peace he had known last as a little boy. He repeats this claim in several places, speaking freely of spiritual rejuvenation. Thus, in November 1661, to Mère Jeanne:

As for me, it seems that my youth has been renewed and that Our Lord has put me back into the state I was in at the age of only eight. In his providence he has willed that I should spend almost all of this autumn, which is perfectly lovely, in the country. . . . Our Lord has seen to it that I am without anxiety or any bodily indisposition.[61]

On the same day, in similar terms, he writes to the Marquise d'Ars:

My natural vigour has been, by the grace of God, so renewed that I have nearly forgotten the ills of the past, and this year, which is my sixty-second, seems to be joined directly to my eighth, which I remember as a time when I enjoyed in peace the blessings God gives to children. This autumn, which has been so lovely, I have spent in the country. I have only just come, and I think I will not return until Advent. For some time I have been sleeping all night a tranquil and uninterrupted slumber. Quite sincerely, it seems to me that I am like a child on the heart of Our Lord, with as little anxiety as if I were eight. My only cross is the sight of the miseries of my neighbour and the extreme poverty of the people, which I cannot see without sorrow. It is for you to say whether 'our youth has been renewed like an eagle's' (Ps. 102: 5), after all the ills they thought were incurable. Pray Our Lord to give me the grace to put no trust in this present age but to live always on earth like a stranger occupied only with the thought and desire of his homeland.[62]

The serenity of these letters, their gentle mingling of the themes of spiritual childhood and pilgrimage, of holy folly and non-conformity, scarcely supports Nau's suspicion that Surin's deliverance was illusory. The childlikeness is not feigned but breathes spontaneously out of all his writing. As he says in a *cantique*, quoted also in a letter:

> In His presence I want to be
> A child without fear,
> A child who understands nothing,
> Who seeks no other blessing
> Than to be on his mother's lap,
> And living on His milk,
> To seek to delight
> Only in what pleases Him. [63]

There is nothing sentimental about this childlikeness. It is a state attained only through those crosses which Surin has endured. It is, moreover, linked with the folly theme. Surin inveighs against the worldly wise, those who reckon themselves 'grown up' or, as has been claimed in our own day, 'come of age'. Here he takes Mère Françoise Daviau de Relay to task for being too much taken up with contemporary trends and fashions:

> The Reverend Father N. a little time ago read me one of your letters. *Mon Dieu*, what a fashionable style you have! You speak better than the Academy. You've got a strong character and every qualification to be the secretary of a prince. Abandon this style of self-communication. Speak as a daughter, speak as a good child. I think your prayer to God is very different from what it was when you were more simple. It's already many years since you lost that spirit. Alas, for that lost time! Think about it. Go back over those years, and if you'll believe me, begin to become small. Learn p-a-p-a, and then you will call God your *papa*, and not only *My Lord*; both of these titles belong to him. The apostle Paul tells us that the Spirit of God within us cries out 'Abba, Pater', a tender name, which only little children say to their father. . . . Go a little mad (*Devenez un peu sotte*), and remember what St Paul said: 'If anyone of you wants to become wise, let him become a fool to be wise'; that means, be a little bit of an idiot. [64]

Surin's writing in the 1660s has a marvellously relaxed quality. No longer does he see God menacing him with the words, 'You're damned'; now he speaks of God as *papa* and, like St Paul, encourages his disciples to address the Father in familiar, intimate terms, with the 'boldness' (*parrēsia*, Eph. 3: 12) of infants.

> You'll find prayer easy when you see it, not as an exhausting exercise, as a spiritual labour, but rather as an agreeable diversion. To do that, we must

approach God in a familiar way and use the sacred liberty bestowed on us by our status as children of God. He is our creator, our Father. We can go to him, then, without any breach of decorum, with the same freshness and simplicity with which children go to their father and mother. A little child goes up to his father without ceremony, through an instinct of filial love, through a feeling of his natural good, and perhaps through the attraction of his father's goodness, which gives him that assurance. He goes into his room without knocking and places himself beside his father. He remains there intending only to be very quiet and not to make any noise. He is happy to be close to his father and to stay there in respect and love. I believe that when a soul is pure and untroubled in conscience by any grievous sin, the grace of divine adoption gives us free access to the presence of God. 'We are', says St Paul, 'members of the household of God'; 'he has sent into our hearts the Spirit of his Son crying: my Father, my Father'. We can, then, take the liberty not only of conversing with him, but still more of doing it in a familiar way, like a son talking with his father, a friend with a friend.[65]

Contrary, then, to the impression Père Nau gives us, the Surin of these last years is one for whom the evangelical virtues are uppermost in his thoughts. Likewise, we can make little sense of Nau's claim that he rarely celebrated Mass. Writing from Saint Macaire in January 1664, he rejoices in the privilege of finding Our Lord in the Mass, that 'banquet in the sight of all paradise'.[66] There is no suspicion at all of one who profaned the Blessed Sacrament, but rather every indication of a profound eucharistic piety. It is commonly alleged that eucharistic thought in this Baroque age is Calvary-centred, with little reference to the Resurrection. For Surin, however, it is the living Lord we receive in the Sacrament: '. . . in the Holy Sacrament Jesus Christ is symbolically (*en figure*) dead and crucified and nevertheless effectively (*effectivement*) glorious; when I receive him at the holy table, I take him both as one dead or dying on the cross and as one living and life-giving.'[67]

Peace at the Last

Père Surin's secret is known only in heaven, where he knows 'as he is known'. His firm progress from 'real' to feigned madness can never be exactly determined. All we can say is that Surin made his madness, real or feigned, a witness to the humiliated Christ of the Praetorium. We see him now as he was in his final years, when the 'Pentecostalism' he learnt from Père Lallemant comes to the fore, and he returns time after time to the activity of the Spirit and the urgent necessity of fully acquiring, and being led by, him. The old man has gone through the blackness of despair and now is bathed in the warm light of Pentecost. The writing of his last years, centred as it is on the Holy Spirit, provides us with a perfect synthesis of his thought and a fitting point at which to take our leave of him. Here he is, writing to a Carmelite shortly before Pentecost 1661:

If we have just a little share in the grace of the mystery we are about to celebrate, the truths preached by the apostles, which are the object of our faith, will produce in us the same effects. They will make us love abjection and humiliations, find pleasure in mortification and sufferings, overcome our sloth and natural timidity, direct ourselves with fervour towards every sort of perfection, reach out to God with a holy impetuosity, burn with love for Jesus Christ to the point of wearing ourselves out in his service. Miserable Christian soul, so beguiled by the pleasures and vanities of the age, languishing in its weakness, depressed under the weight of self-interest, that it cannot experience these great effects of the coming of the Holy Spirit! Let us dispose ourselves, my dear sister, to receive this divine fire which Jesus Christ desires to send us. . . . Remain constantly on the mountain where Elias [the patron of Carmel] has placed you, that man of fire, who, having poured out his flames on the heart of your holy mother [St Teresa], teaches you through her to be likewise all aflame, like burning torches or lamps alight, to shine within the Church and to burn before Jesus Christ to the glory of his name and the edification of the faithful.[68]

9

Bretons, Bards, and Buffoons

In the sixteenth and seventeenth centuries mystics frequently emerged among racial and cultural minorities, and in the France of this period many of the centres of spirituality appeared at the geographical periphery. This is certainly so in the case of holy folly. In this chapter we shall be concerned with the resurgence of this phenomenon, and the continuing influence of the school of Père Lallemant, in the Celtic north-west of France.

La Bretagne mystique produced many of the outstanding spiritual writers of the century. Through its re-evangelization by a group of priests trained in the Lallemant tradition, Brittany became a centre of spiritual renewal, 'a land where tnere is a miracle every hour, where each village has its ecstatic'.[1] Above all, it produced saints, who were generally not priests or religious but laymen, humble country folk, 'idiots' in the classical sense. One of them, a poor housemaid, was regarded in her own lifetime by the Breton Jesuits 'as realizing, better than anyone, the mystical ideal of their [Lallemant] school'.[2]

Jean Rigoleuc (1595–1658)

The first Breton Jesuit to be considered, Père Rigoleuc, was born at Quintin in the diocese of Saint-Brieuc and spent most of his priestly ministry as a missionary in the dioceses of Quimper, Vannes, and Orléans, although he ended his life as a teacher of moral theology at Vannes.[3] His importance for us is threefold. First of all, he is an intermediary in the continuation of the Lallemant tradition, especially in its transmission to Brittany. He was a fellow student of Surin during their Third Year under Lallemant, and it was from Rigoleuc's notes that Champion compiled his *Vie et Doctrine spirituelle du P. Louis Lallemant.* Moreover, he was the teacher of Père Huby, who kept alive the distinctive doctrines of Lallemant at the end of the century.

Secondly, like Surin, he continued his master's work of synthesizing Carmelite and Ignatian teaching on prayer. He makes extensive use of such sanjuanist concepts as the dark night of the soul and the active mortification of the senses, and he warns those whom God is leading towards the prayer of simple union against encumbering their souls with formal meditations, which none the less are excellent for those less advanced.[4]

Thirdly, Rigoleuc discovered the truth of these doctrines in his own experience. Like Surin, he confirmed at first hand St Teresa's dictum that God reserves the worst trials for contemplatives. Three years after his Third Year we are told that Rigoleuc received from God the gift of infused prayer and entered into 'that state mystics call passive'.[5] For him, as for Surin, the accompanying purification of his soul involved a veritable descent into hell: for six years he believed himself to be damned. It was a 'folly' far more excruciating than even that painful state of being despised by the world, and yet in this darkness Rigoleuc persevered in prayer and the practice of Christian virtue. Speaking of himself in the third person, he wrote: 'I know someone who in this state of affliction singlemindedly set about schooling himself in purity of heart, dedicating himself to works of charity and throwing himself into the service of God.'[6]

Rigoleuc suffered hell without self-pity and was finally rewarded with peace of soul.

Vincent Huby (1608–1693)

Rigoleuc's disciple, Père Huby, was a Breton, born in Hennebont in the diocese of Vannes, the youngest child of Jacques Huby, seneschal of the fiefs of Léon and Plouhinec. At the age of fourteen he was sent to the Jesuit College at Rennes, where he was taught humanities by Rigoleuc and was a fellow student of Blessed Julien Maunoir. After some initial parental opposition, he entered the novitiate in 1625 and continued his studies and formation at Rennes, La Flèche, Vannes, and Paris. After his Third Year at Rouen, under Jacques Grandamy, he was appointed Prefect of Studies at Orléans. During a further period at Vannes he began to take part in the Breton missions. As Rector of the College at Quimper from 1650 to 1654, he had to face serious administrative and pastoral problems. It was during this time that he instituted perpetual adoration of the Blessed Sacrament, a practice which rapidly spread through France and ultimately throughout the Church. He returned to Vannes, which was his base until his death, and found Rigoleuc established there as a colleague. At Vannes, in co-operation with the Abbé Louis Eudo de Kerlivio (d. 1685), Huby established a retreat house for the laity, of which he was superior until his death;[7] he also assisted Catherine de Francheville (1620–1689) in founding the first retreat house for women, also in Vannes.[8]

The ministry of the last forty years of his life was taken up almost exclusively with the promotion of retreats, and his literary projects were largely concerned with providing suitable material for retreatants. He established other houses in Brittany and in the rest of France; he helped too in the recruitment of religious dedicated to this ministry. The nature of this work inevitably influenced Huby's writing. Like Rigoleuc, he shows obvious signs of standing in the Lallemant tradition: there is stress on docility to the Holy Spirit, *mépris*, purification of the heart, and so on. The difference is that whereas Lallemant and indeed Surin are largely concerned with religious at a particularly impressionable stage of their formation, Huby is concerned with all types of Christians, of every age and background and with varying intellectual and spiritual needs. Consequently he simplifies and streamlines his teaching, but in a way which, while it facilitates reading, does not diminish its spiritual depth.

According to one of Père Huby's biographers, 'all that breathed in him was the love of God'.[9] He manifests true fervour when he speaks of his favourite theme, the love of God, which he understands in a fully trinitarian way, a love drawing us into the love and life of Father, Son, and Holy Spirit: 'Eternal Father, love. Eternal Word, love. Divine Spirit, love. Father, Son, Holy Spirit, Adorable Trinity, love, love, love.'[10] God's love in Christ is a wonder, an amazing love that baffles men's understanding by its unreserved generosity, its going to the limits of the cross and the descent into hell:

> *Cum dilexisset suos, in finem dilexit eos*, says St John. Jesus, having loved his own, loved them to the end. 'To the end'—that is to say, to the extremity of great calamities, humiliations, shame, pain, right to the end of his life, in death ignominious and grievous beyond human understanding.[11]

According to Huby, his love—incomprehensible, humanly speaking—is what makes the Eucharist the sacrament of the richness and profusion of the love of Christ. This belief underlies all he says of the 'adorable Sacrament of the Eucharist', and especially of the cult of perpetual adoration:

> Yes, he is there; he is on earth in the consecrated hosts as truly as he is in heaven at the right hand of the Father. . . . And he is on earth with such an abundance of testimonies of his love for us, that while in heaven he is in only one place, on earth he is in more than a hundred thousand places, in every consecrated host, as much in the poor churches as in the beautiful, as much in the country as in the town, as much for the little as for the great, as much for the poor as for the rich, as much for sinners as for the righteous, finally, universally for all. [12]

The universality of Christ's love was the inspiration of Huby's work in the retreat movement. Like the other Breton missionaries, he had a passionate concern to preach good news to the poor, to win the vast multitudes of the rural population of Brittany for Christ, Thus, following a practice already established in the Breton missions, he used every available aid, visual and imaginative, to teach and encourage the people in the ways of the Spirit. His own particular concern was with the 'images or moral paintings otherwise called tableaux'—the holy cartoons, which taught basic truths of the gospel. In his treatise justifying the use of such visual aids, Huby cites the Fathers and develops a theology of images, based on the Incarnation, not dissimilar to that elaborated in the East by the iconodules. [13] The typical Huby image, usually exhibited in front of the retreatants in a large room, shows a head surmounting a heart. The 'Image of True Penitence' shows Our Lord on the cross surrounded by the various instruments of his Passion, the whole covered with tears of compunction. In contrast there are images depicting the disorder of sin, in which the heart is full of devils and the symbols of hell. [14] The teaching is basic and obvious, but the underlying symbolism of the head and heart is an example of the developing psychological sophistication of seventeenth-century spiritual writers. It is not sufficiently realized that the cultus of the Sacred Heart, which develops so much in the period, is not an irrational or sentimental devotion but is closely allied to a deepening sense of the heart as the centre of man, and of the need, in healing or spiritual growth, for the reconciliation of head and heart—a reconciliation which, in the wisdom of the Desert Fathers and the hesychasts, is a primary work in the life of prayer.

> From the heart issue all the sins we commit, says Jesus Christ. Thence also

arise all good desires and good works. We think a lot, if not too much, about external appearance. We look at ourselves in a mirror one hundred times. . . . But how often do we think about the interior?[15]

Devotion to the Sacred Heart of Jesus is intended to lead to the transformation of our own hearts into the likeness of his, so that what we think we truly are: 'Grant, then, if it pleases you, my adorable Redeemer, that my heart may be made to be like yours. Your heart is pure, let mine be pure. *Cor mundum crea in me Deus.*'[16]

But what of doctrines specifically associated with Père Lallemant and the holy folly tradition? Most important of all for Père Huby is openness to the Holy Spirit: everything in the spiritual life depends on his activity within us:

All the mysteries of Our Lord, his Incarnation, his Birth, his Life, his Passion, his Death, his Body and his Blood, which he has given us in the Blessed Sacrament, and which we receive in our hearts in Communion; none of this will sanctify us if we do not receive the Holy Spirit. That is what the Saviour made the Apostles understand, when he told them that it was to their advantage that he was leaving them, in order to send them the Comforter Spirit; to teach them, and us too, that it was better for men to possess the Holy Spirit than to enjoy the visible presence of his sacred Humanity.[17]

Huby has a vivid sense of the activity of the Spirit in the hearts of all and teaches the necessity of a personal Pentecost for each believer, who must appropriate daily the gift bestowed in Confirmation. 'Oh! Divine Spirit, come in, come in, dwell here, and drive away sin for ever. O happy day! O day of Pentecost for us! O day of the receiving of the Holy Spirit and his graces!'[18]

Huby speaks of the 'Incarnation' of the Spirit within us, an honour conferred on Christians alone.

The Incarnation is a general and universal blessing, given to the whole world, without exception. But the real presence of the Holy Spirit in our hearts, the fruit of the glorious Ascension of Jesus Christ, according to St Luke, is a privilege reserved to Christians alone, or rather to the just in the law of grace. Consider the glory to which this kind of incarnation of the Holy Spirit exalts us! It is the principle of our adoption; it makes us truly children of God, brothers of God, living animate temples of the Adorable Trinity; it makes us spiritual men and, to some degree, deifies us.[19]

Huby tell us that the Spirit desires to contract a 'spiritual marriage'

with our souls and thereby to come and abide within us. The section
dedicated to the Holy Spirit on the seventh day of the 'Retreat on
the Love of God' ends with a great invocation of the Spirit to indwell
the soul.

> Come then, Holy Spirit, come down into us, draw us to yourself. Come to
> us in the time of our exile. You are our good, and the heritage promised by
> Jesus Christ to sanctify those he has redeemed, and to fulfil the great work
> he began. Come to us. Is our heart too narrow for you to possess? Enlarge it
> by the ardour of charity. Save it from the inclinations and attachments
> which offend the delicacy of your eyes. You are a consuming fire, change
> our heart into a sanctuary worthy of you; it is only fitting that a God should
> make ready his dwelling place.[20]

But for such a union to be a reality, our co-operation is necessary;
the Spirit takes up his abode in souls prepared by prayer, purity of
heart, and great *courage*. This latter is necessary, because the Spirit,
in possessing us, crucifies, pierces, wounds, in order to heal and
purify us.[21]

Courage to receive the Spirit, and to be sanctified by him, is itself
the gift of the Spirit. It is necessary because the spiritual life is a
deepening of our conformity to Christ, a participation in, and
imitation of, the Incarnate Word of God. As we have observed so
often, the *rationale* of holy folly is: as for God, so for us. Huby
contemplates the *excès* of God's love in the Incarnation, in the crib
and on the cross, and is moved to share in it. In his retreat he
presents vivid images of God's 'mad love' to stir a reciprocally wild
and foolish love for God in the hearts of the retreatants. Above all,
he makes us contemplate Jesus in his purple livery, the joke king of
kings. He prays thus to Jesus in a litany:

> Jesus, mocked, scoffed at and slapped on the face, have mercy on us;
> Jesus, robed in a mantle of shame, and treated like a fool in the court
>   of Herod, have mercy on us;
> Jesus, whipped, lashed to ribbons, and swimming in your own blood,
>   have mercy on us;
> Jesus, crowned with piercing thorns, have mercy on us;
> Jesus, treated like a joke king (*un roi de théâtre*), have mercy on us.[22]

From the self-abasement of the Incarnate Son of God Huby learns
that humiliation is the only way to humility and thus to glory. On the
eighth day of the retreat, he describes the 'infinite, substantial,
eternal humility' of God in becoming man, in suffering for us, and

being present, in total vulnerability, in the Blessed Sacrament. There can be only one response to such humility—the desire for humility.

> The first virtue that I want to imitate in you is humility of heart; the second is still humility; and the third—yes, humility. It is the key to your most precious treasures and the root of all the virtues. I want to seek you, my Jesus, where you truly are, that is to say, in abandonment. That is where I want to live and die with you.[23]

Similarly, the poverty and weakness of the God-child in the crib proves to us the radical necessity of embracing poverty and the impossibility of a Christian life amidst wealth:

> The Child we see is God, the absolute master of heaven and earth, and in consequence the sovereign arbiter of his own destiny. What did he choose for his lot? Riches? No. In despising and rejecting them, he has imprinted upon them the character of baseness, which renders them despicable and odious to every truly Christian spirit. He has consecrated poverty, in a sense he has divinized it, by choosing it as his inseparable companion in every circumstance of his life. . . . But, alas, what difference does the example of a poor God make to my spirit and my heart? Ah! If I desire the ease and comforts of life; if I complain when I lack even the necessities of life, can I tell you, O my Jesus, that you are my only treasure, that you are my God and my all? From now on I want to be able to use such language with sincerity. Would I be a true Christian if I despised what my God has esteemed, if I fled from what he has loved and cherished? Poor and destitute, I desire to follow Jesus, poor and destitute of everything for love for me.[24]

Poverty, humility, self-abandonment, the perennial themes that cluster round holy folly at every point of its development in Christian history, reassemble in the teaching of this great Breton missionary. From such strong convictions about the 'marginality' of God Incarnate, it is but a short step to a critique of worldly wisdom and an exhortation to holy folly. According to Huby, there is a conflict of opinion between Jesus and the world on these subjects of poverty and humility. The teaching of Jesus collides with the wisdom of the world. For this reason there need be no fear in being written off as a fool by the world:

> Either Jesus is wrong, says St Bernard, or the world is in error, since the one and the other pronounce contradictory judgements on the same subjects—poverty, humiliation, suffering etc. But it is impossible that Jesus

Christ is wrong; he is the Wisdom of God, the brightness of the eternal and uncreated light, who cannot be obscured even by the thickest cloud. So the world is in error, its wisdom is a folly reproved by God, and we, if we firmly believe in the divinity and thus the absolute infallibility of Jesus Christ, are the children of light, and we see things as God himself sees them.[25]

We must rejoice, then, when the world laughs at us and scorns us for our senseless folly in following the Lord Jesus. We must rejoice 'to be reckoned without wisdom, without power, to have in fact no prestige, no authority; to love dependence like an empire; to be so detached that I am not myself with myself but God alone is with me'.[26]

Thus it is that the highest point of spiritual perfection is to have the innocent trust, poverty, dependence, and lack of worldly wisdom which belong to children:

The innocence, simplicity, candour of children is the ideal of the humility of Jesus and his saints. Whoever sets himself up by devious tricks is not a child. Whoever can no longer follow the opinion and inclination of others is no longer a child. Whoever is easily upset by little annoyances, and whoever unceasingly broods over little humiliations, is as far away from the Kingdom of Jesus Christ as he is lacking in the simplicity of children.[27]

The Breton Missions

Rigoleuc and Huby were close collaborators in the Breton missions, but it is not their names which spring to the lips of Bretons when they recall the evangelization of their country in the seventeenth century. The veritable giants, not only of the missions but of Breton history of this period, are Michel Le Nobletz (b. 1577) and Blessed Julien Maunoir (1606–1683), both still greatly revered in the land of their birth and apostolate. It is natural to link the two together since the older man appointed the younger as his successor, and the methods and approaches of the two, despite important differences, are substantially the same.

At a time when Jesuit missionaries and others were travelling to every part of the globe, especially to the Americas and the Far East, to preach the gospel, why was it that there should have been missions to such a solidly Catholic province of France as Brittany? It could hardly have been to convert Protestants, for the Reformation had hardly touched Brittany. There were only eighteen Protestant churches in the region in our period, all near the French border.

According to Père Maunoir, the man was still to be born who had seen a *breton bretonnant* (a Breton-speaking Breton) preach any religion but Catholicism.[28] Nevertheless, the missionaries came, preached, and converted as if they were in Canada or Japan. To understand this puzzle, we must consider the immediate historical background.

Brittany had known relative peace and internal stability for a long time, from the Treaty of Guérande (1365) to the Wars of Religion in the second half of the sixteenth century.[29] At the beginning of this period the great Dominican preacher, St Vincent Ferrer (*c.* 1350–1419), undertook missionary travels throughout Brittany and had considerable success in renewing the faith and devotion of the people. During the sixteenth century Breton sailors travelled all over the world, bringing prestige and not a little financial profit to their homeland. At the end of the century economic and political stability were disrupted when the Spanish and English disputed their claims to the territory. The province was torn apart by the conflicts of *ligueurs* and royalists; bandits and highwaymen made every country road dangerous; famine and plague decimated the population. Church buildings, including the great Abbey of Landévennec, were sacked and looted. Meanwhile, the Church seemed unable to offer the necessary spiritual resources to deal with the turmoil. Corruption was rife, and most of the lower clergy were ill-educated. In addition, the nominal Catholicism of a large section of the population scarcely concealed a virulent paganism, the old religion of the Celtic world practised darkly in groves and on hillsides. By the end of our period, however, Brittany was transformed. Mystics and visionaries of the greatest sanctity were to be found among the common people, while many of the nobility were converted from a life of indolence and immorality to asceticism and holiness. There was a revival of the eremitical life; religious houses were founded everywhere; the retreat movement began; calvaries were built in the major towns and villages. The people's devotion and life of prayer became fervent. Pilgrimages and *pardons* in honour of Our Lady and St Anne were occasions of deep penitence and prayer. The Breton language and culture were integrated deeply within Catholic liturgy and spirituality: the missionaries established a tradition of canticles in the Breton tongue, which still flourishes; a grammar and lexicon of the language were produced, and the Catholic Church stood as the stout champion of the

language and culture of the people. All this was the fruit of less than
a century of apostolic labour, and much of it is still in evidence in
Brittany today. Who, then, were these men who, through God's
grace, worked such a miracle? A modern author describes them
thus:

> They were idealists who led souls to the summit, artists who used nature,
> the visual images of life, in their teaching, realists who saw ascesis enough in
> daily labour, psychologists who could make the best of the deepest feelings
> bequeathed by race. . . . Their story presents them to us as mystics at odds
> with politicians, defenders of the purest Christian tradition, in conflict with
> men on whom the spirit of the Renaissance had breathed, confessors of
> Christ crucified in constant struggle with the followers of sects attached to
> subversive and destructive ideas.[30]

'Psychologists who could make the best of the deepest feelings
bequeathed by race.' Our missionaries were above all Bretons, men
who spoke the people's language. In Maunoir's case knowledge of
the language was bestowed miraculously, which gives his commitment to the Celtic culture of his people an added poignancy.[31] Both
Maunoir and Le Nobletz communicated Catholic truth in a style
and manner which touched the people's souls and, probably un-
consciously, drew on the ancient wellsprings of Celtic Christianity.
Not least in this connection is the theme of folly for Christ's sake,
which we have already examined in early Ireland, and which now
reappears in seventeenth-century Brittany—in Michel Le Nobletz
and in the disciples and followers of Père Maunoir—although,
interestingly, not in the same way in the 'perfect missionary'
himself.

Ar belec fol

Michel Le Nobletz was born on 29 September 1577 at Plouguerneau
in the diocese of Léon.[32] His father was one of the public notaries of
Léon, and his mother was from the ancient house of Coatmanach,
said to be descended from St Fragan and St Guen, parents of St
Gwénolé, the fifth-century founder of the Abbey of Landévennec.
After studying in Bordeaux Michel went to the Jesuit College at
Agen, where he met Pierre Quintin, who was to be his companion in
the missions. It was at Agen, too, that he first met opposition and
hostility, vilification and accusations of madness and eccentricity,
which were to recur throughout his life. On this first occasion, Our

Lady appeared to him and said, in Breton: 'My little Michael, do not fear, my Son will defend and I myself will help you.'[33] She then presented him with three crowns symbolizing virginity, mastery of the spiritual life, and contempt of the world (*mépris du monde*), the last of which is very characteristic of Le Nobletz and has already been noted as a feature of the spiritual doctrine of the Lallemant school. He expressed this new-found vision by refusing a benefice, which his father very much desired for him. The result was that he was thrown out of the family home. He then took refuge with his old nurse and celebrated his first Mass at Plouguerneau.

Before beginning his missionary endeavours, Le Nobletz spent a year in complete withdrawal from the world on the beach at Tréménach, near Plouguerneau. He practised the most austere eremitism. Père Maunoir, in his biography, writes as follows:

> He lived in this lonely place for the space of a year, clad in a hair-shirt from neck to knees, without linen, except for a simple collar. His bed was the earth, his pillow a stone. He took the discipline every day, very often to the point of drawing blood. . . . His silence was so rigorous that he forgot his mother tongue, that is the Breton language, which he had to learn afresh to help the simple people of Armorica, who spoke a language other than French.[34]

In a doctoral thesis M. Sainsaulieu has recently shown how popular such eremitical life became in France after about 1594, the year of the dissolution of the League. Old *ligueurs*, frustrated by the apparent compromise of Catholic principle, left the world rather than the Church.[35] It would be incorrect to see Le Nobletz's decision in this context, for he was a young man, too young to have been personally involved in the religious wars. What is, however, significant in Sainsaulieu's work is that it shows a widespread movement of protest against a Church set on compromise with the world, concerned not with authentic peace and stability, but with peace at any price. The eremitical movement was not simply one of despairing reaction but expressed a prophetic longing to wrest the Church from submergence beneath bourgeois moderation and political expediency.

Michel's year of withdrawal was spent in continual silence, broken only when he went to Tréménach to say Mass, and in daily prayer, meditation and study. It was at this time that he composed his famous 'spiritual parables, paintings, and enigmas'. Here was

perhaps the most truly original feature of his later apostolate, which
he bequeathed to his Jesuit successors in the missions. He used
painted charts, like those of sailors, painted in bright colours on
wood or parchment, to illustrate spiritual teaching. One of these
was *Les cinq portes*. At the top of the 'map' were depicted the joys
of heaven, while below were the pains of hell. To the right were the
five doors of salvation leading to heaven, and to the left the five
doors of perdition, which led straight to hell. On one occasion,
when he was expounding the tableau with great enthusiasm, a
woman remonstrated with him for wasting so much energy on a
catechetical technique that would die with him. Le Nobletz replied
that this was not so, that Jesuit fathers would come and continue the
work of explaining the tableaux.

In addition to his use of visual means of instruction, Le Nobletz
also composed canticles in Breton, songs that would be sung, with
those of Père Maunoir, for many generations in Brittany. Many of
these sing the praises of contempt of the world. According to one
biographer he spent day and night in the study of this disposition
and indeed wrote a treatise and catechism on it. He refused to wear
fine priestly clothes, because this would conflict with his ideal and
because he wished to be 'a poor priest, honouring in his person the
One whom he had to honour daily, to receive and bear in his hands
in the holy sacrifice of the Mass'. Contempt of the world is, he saw,
inseparable from contempt of self, for the two, the age and the ego,
are linked in an unholy alliance against holiness. Le Nobletz taught
a radical non-conformity to the world and its values, which he
regarded as 'insane', writing to it a series of vehement *adieux*, the
manifesto of a spiritual rebel:

Adieu, World, I detest you with all my heart, and I declare an everlasting
war against you, for it was you who first declared war against my God, and
you are known to be the chief of his enemies. . . . You are more barbaric
than the most savage races, since you have neither God nor faith nor king
nor law; or if you do acknowledge any of these, you make the vain desire for
ephemeral honour your god, money your king; the continual wandering of
your thoughts serves you as a law; you have false prosperity as queen, the
spirit of falsehood as father, the flesh, that cruel stepmother, as mother, the
behaviour of your passions as master. . . . So unjust and unfaithful are you
that your conduct is always totally full of extravagance and iniquity. You
exalt the wicked to humble and annihilate good men, you plunder the poor
to give to the undeserving rich, you absolve every criminal and condemn the

innocent, you embrace those you want to smother, you kiss those you wish to stab, you stretch out your hand to those you mean to slaughter.[36]

And again he writes:

Just as you reverse all things, so also you call nothing by its proper name; the timid you call courageous, cowards are peace-makers, spendthrifts are generous, the sluggish and melancholic are moderate, the indiscreet are fervent, the immodest are pleasant and agreeable, the cruel are just, sluggards are wise, the avaricious are prudent and good stewards, deceivers are modest, impostors are eloquent, the vindictive are men of honour, and the biggest liars are the most circumspect.[37]

Le Nobletz goes on to proclaim his defiance of this disordered 'wisdom' and to pledge his loyalty to Christ:

I swear, in the face of heaven and in the presence of Jesus Christ my Saviour and your conqueror, of his blessed and ever-virgin Mother, of all the angels and saints in heaven, that from now on and for the whole of my life I intend to break all ties with you, to live in a manner totally opposed to your maxims, to detest your counsels, and to hold your examples in horror, to choose my dwelling-place far from your supporters, never to see your friends, so that they might acknowledge your injustice and their blindness. I place myself at your feet, Word Incarnate, who during your life and at the time of your Passion, and above all when you were stretched out upon the cross, unfurled the standard of contempt of the world: I desire to live and die by the help of your grace in the shade of this banner: my resolution is henceforth to love and to desire ardently what the world abhors, and to fly from and to hold in horror what it seeks out passionately. I take your poverty for my inheritance, your shame and ignominy for my only glory, your crown of thorns and your Cross for the delight of my heart, your Crib and Calvary for my everlasting home.[38]

After a year of retreat Michel was compelled to reinterpret his *mépris du monde*. The interfering ways of an inquisitive woman made eremitical protest at Tréménach impossible, and so he began a ministry of public preaching, catechizing and confessing in the villages and hamlets around Plouguerneau. The poor villagers heard him gladly. For many, it was the first Christian instruction they had ever received. For others, this unrestrained preaching of Christian non-conformity to the world seemed dangerous insanity. His style of life was also profoundly shocking in its austerity. Michel never associated with the nobility and spent all his time with the rural poor. Each day, after Mass in the Chapel of St Claude, he would prepare his breakfast—bread crumbled in a wooden bowl,

covered with soup, the only kind of meal he would allow himself.
In complete contempt for money and all material possessions, 'he
defied the customs and opinion of the world with a holy audacity.
Nobody had ever seen a priest live like this in the diocese of Léon.'[39]

His father despaired of him: so many years of education wasted
in a life of mendicancy. His brothers and sisters lamented: 'Alas!
Sickness has taken hold of our brother; look how he goes running
through the fields.'[40] His father was greatly angered by his son's
refusal to accept payment for Masses, sermons, and confessions,
and by his contempt for benefice or ecclesiastical office. So great
was his fury that, on one occasion, he struck him in church with
his stick.

Such trials did not deter Michel; indeed, they were a source of joy
and confirmed his belief that God was calling him to the service of
the forgotten rural poor of Brittany, sunk beneath the appalling
weight of paganism and ignorance. In company with Père Pierre
Quintin OP he began to catechize and preach in Morlaix, and then
undertook missions to the islands of Ouessant and Molène. It was
on these storm-swept isles especially that his painted allegorical
charts came into their own. The sailors and fishermen there
depended for their survival on accurate maps and reliable naviga-
tion, so they were held spellbound when the language of seafaring
was applied to the soul's voyage to heaven. Never before had they
heard the gospel preached so vividly in words they could understand.

Equally influential on the missions was Michel's use of the
canticles he composed in Breton. Here the missionary of seventeenth-century Brittany takes his stand with the monastic bards of
early Ireland and the preacher-poets of Wales. The words used by
a modern Welsh poet to describe Pantycelyn (that is, William
Williams, one of the major figures in the Welsh Methodist revival of
the eighteenth century), apply directly to the apostle of Brittany:

> You took your course through the land, minstrel of heaven,
> And in your pack the Holy Ghost's credentials,
> You were the chief bard of His Eisteddfod
> And the certified teacher of minstrels . . .
> To the peasants, yoked to their lot for life,
> You sang, in their patois, the song of faith
> That you heard from the unbranched tree of the Cross,
> And lifted them high above bog and rock and hill
> And placed them at round tables laden with God's gifts.[41]

Like the bard-evangelists of Ireland and Wales, Michel Le
Nobletz wandered from remote islands to lonely hills, through the
streets of towns of which he was never to be a citizen; like Columba,
he was an exile and pilgrim, long before he was a missionary. Like
the Irish, too, he was called a fool for his sanctity and rejoiced to be
disowned by the worldly wise. In the midst of this restless spiritual
pilgrimage, Michel Le Nobletz is a classic Celtic saint—first hermit,
then wandering ascetic, a mad priest, the bard of God. His canticles
were soon sung and loved by all the Catholic people of Brittany.
They were taken up by Père Maunoir on his missions; indeed, the
Jesuit successor of Le Nobletz added his own compositions to the
repertory. They are still loved by Breton Catholics. We cannot be
sure of the authorship of all the hymns ascribed to Le Nobletz,
but the following is most certainly his. It deals once again with the
theme of *mépris du monde*:

> Every morning, when the sun rises,
>> I thank you, my God,
> For inspiring me to wrench my heart away from the world.
>> If my heart had belonged to the world,
> My soul would have been damned.
>> Lord God, look upon me,
> And grant me what I desire.
>> Give me the grace of contempt of the world
> And the grace of loving you perfectly . . .
>
>> Although I am dressed poorly
> And despised by so many in the world,
>> I have hope and I believe
> That I will be pleasing to the Saviour of the world.[42]

Like the hymns of the Wesleys in eighteenth-century England,
these canticles were greeted with the utmost suspicion in certain
quarters. In his defence Le Nobletz cited the precedents of St
Francis Xavier, who in the Indies had taught religion and Christian
duty through the medium of song; of St Athanasius, who made the
people sing of the faith; of St Jerome, who wrote joyfully to Rome
of his arrival in Palestine, where he found the people singing the
praises of the Trinity in the vernacular. Like General Booth, Le
Nobletz was convinced that the devil should not have all the good
tunes, and in consecrating popular song, its melodies and metrical
patterns, to the worship of God, he continued to undermine the
influence of pagan religion, especially potent in song and dance.

→

With his songs and his pictures, his exuberance and vivacity, Michel Le Nobletz was loved by the children. He would instruct them by means of ingenious stories and anecdotes drawn from everyday life and reward them with little presents—images, Agnuses, sweets. But if the simple and the little loved him, the great ones continued to mock him. When the grandees saw this poorly dressed priest singing songs and exhibiting colourful pictures and giving away sweets, they thought he was mad. This could not be catechism; it was far too enjoyable! This man, they said, is *ar belec fol*, 'the mad priest'. What is more, Le Nobletz performed symbolic actions of a foolish and shocking nature to startle the people out of their half-heartedness and complacency. On one occasion, he rang the tocsin in the middle of the afternoon. The people came running from their homes and places of work, thinking there was a fire. No, said Le Nobletz, something worse had happened: they were not listening to the word of God.

Equally scandalous in the eyes of some, certainly as reckless and foolish in its social implications, was Michel's determination not only to preach good news to the poor, not only to share their life and hardship, but also to treat them as brothers and sisters, without a trace of paternalism; above all, to make use of the poor as teachers and instructors of their own people, to treat them as equals and fellow workers. Michel's great achievement was to involve the laity, above all women, in mission—poor, semi-literate 'idiots' were enlisted for the task of catechism and instruction. One of these was Claudine Le Belec, a widow of Douarnenez. Le Nobletz converted her from a worldly life, and a Jesuit became her spiritual director. According to Père Maunoir, she was quite illiterate but received great spiritual graces. He writes about her as follows:

Not being able to devote working days to prayer, as she would have liked, she got up every night at midnight for mental prayer. She had a little parchment book with a picture on every page designating the meditation her director wanted her to make. A Father of our Society, who was staying with her one day, asked her how she said her prayers. She showed him her book and said: 'When I have adored the presence of God, and offered my prayer to his greater glory, I open my book and look at the pictures which show me the subject of my meditation'. The Father asked to see the page with her last meditation. She showed him. At the centre was the eternal Father and opposite him a sun. Underneath it were ten paths, all leading to this sun. She said that the image in the middle represented the divine majesty, that she applied herself to consider his power, goodness, wisdom, beauty, and holiness, and her conception of his perfections, that she made an act of faith about these truths, that she adored her God, his power, goodness, and other perfections. Afterwards, she thanked him for being powerful, wise, holy, and infinitely perfect. With regard to the sun, she considered that this sun represented to her the end for which she had been created in this world, which is the knowledge and love of God in this life, and the vision of his blessed face in the next. With regard to the ten paths, she paused a little, and considered that she had been led astray from the path which leads to eternal life, by such and such sins; finally, she made acts of contrition and resolved, with the grace of God, to abandon similar offences. The Father was greatly astonished to see an illiterate woman (*femme idiote*) thus enlightened in prayer and the ways of the Spirit, as if she had been used to it from the age of seven. All day long her spirit was taken up with God. As the mouth speaks from the abundance of the heart, she ordinarily spoke only of God, and of what concerned his glory: in this she had a special grace, a particular unction of the Holy Spirit, such a fecundity and force of spirit that one day, urging a Father of the Company to commence the conversion of the souls of Douarnenez, she suggested ten arguments to him, suitable to the time and place of his preaching, which he used to compose a sermon, abandoning the one he had prepared.[43]

As we shall see, the place of women in the missions was carefully preserved and defended by Père Maunoir, and in the later part of the seventeenth century there are further instances from Brittany of the holy 'idiot woman'.

What, then, shall we say of this extraordinary man, whose work began the spiritual transformation of a whole province of France? Père Renard, a recent biographer, describes the 'mad priest' well.

Ar belec fol, the foolish priest—that was the judgment of the respectable, the people already familiar to us from the gospel. These are the worthies who keep their place in church with a great sense of propriety, the place of the distinguished, the leading citizens. They pay their tithes, they observe fasting and abstinence, they are not as other men. In this portrait we recognize those who regarded Dom Michel as a poor fool. They are the ones whom the Lord denounced as a generation of vipers and as whited sepulchres. And yet they were right: Dom Michel was indeed *ar belec fol*, the foolish priest. But his folly is the folly of the cross, of which St Paul tells us that it is a scandal to Jews, ignominy to pagans. . . . Dom Michel will not make religion a compromise between the cares of the world and the demands of divine life. Between heaven and earth, he has made his choice: he has chosen heaven; between the shortness of days and blessed eternity, he has made his choice: he has chosen eternity.[44]

The John Wesley of Armorican Cornwall

Michel Le Nobletz chose as his successor in the Breton missions
Blessed Julien Maunoir (1606–1683), recognizing in him an answer
to prayer. According to their biographers, Père Michel had prayed
for a successor on three occasions: first, at exactly the time of
Blessed Julien's birth, seven years later at Landerneau, and finally
a little later at Douarnenez, when he knew miraculously that his
successor had been born, that he was aged seven, and that he
would be a Jesuit.[45] Moreover, Père Michel was later to hand on
personally some of his own missionary techniques and ideals,
including the canticles, the 'visual aids', the use of the laity, and
(possibly) the *Malleus maleficarum* as a handbook in the war
against demonism.[46]

It would be expanding our concept of holy folly beyond the
bounds of credibility to include Blessed Julien, *an mad tad*, 'the
good father', as an example. Temperamentally, he could not have
differed more from Dom Michel, who has all the marks of a *salos*
with his delight in contempt, strange symbolic acts and eccentric
behaviour, his excessive poverty and austerity, social prophecy, and
so on. Maunoir is altogether a more restrained figure: his politics
are conservative and royalist,[47] he is much more of a Frenchman
than Le Nobletz, despite his enormous achievements in the field of
Breton lexicography. His true greatness lies in his synthesis of the
Lallemant tradition of spirituality with indigenous Celtic religion. It
is out of this synthesis that folly for Christ's sake begins to manifest
itself in mid-seventeenth century Brittany.

Maunoir was born into a *petit bourgeois* family on 1 October 1606
at Saint Georges-de-Reintembault in the diocese of Rennes, close
to the border of Normandy. After a school education at Rennes, he
entered the Jesuit novitiate on 16 September 1625 and proceeded to
the scholasticate at La Flèche. Among his fellow students were
Vincent Huby, St Isaac Jogues (the future martyr of North
America) and Jean Pinette (future Provincial). He eventually
became regent of the fifth class at the new college at Quimper,
where his *confrère*, Pierre Bernard, became so convinced that
Maunoir was destined to be the evangelist of Brittany and successor
of Père Michel, that he advised the young man to learn Breton.
Maunoir was aghast; like many other Jesuit novices of his day, his
heart was set on being a missionary to Canada. However, he went

on pilgrimage to the chapel of Ty Mam Doue ('The House of the Mother of God') near Quimper and asked Our Lady's help to learn Breton. Six months later at Pentecost he received authorization from the Provincial to learn the language, and on the Tuesday after Pentecost he was able to conduct a catechism class in perfect Breton.[48] He was now convinced that God, Our Lady, and St Corentin, the patron saint of Quimper, were determined that he should be the apostle of the Bretons. Maunoir completed his theological studies at Bourges, where he came under the influence of Père Lallemant, who was then Rector. He spent his Third Year at Rouen under Père Ayrault. Before beginning his missionary endeavours, however, Maunoir was commissioned by Père Michel, who gave him his little bell, 'enigmatic paintings', and advice on the pastoral problems that awaited him. The old man was particularly insistent on the continued use of the paintings and the canticles.

Now began forty years of missionary activity, which has won Maunoir the title of 'The John Wesley of Armorican Cornwall'.[49] It is estimated that in forty-three years Maunoir instructed and formed two and a half million souls, converted 300,000 public sinners, and reconciled 200,000 hostile families. One of his earliest missions was to the islands of Ouessant, Molène and Sein. In the first two the people's welcome was so enthusiastic that Maunoir began hearing confessions at three o'clock in the morning and did not finish until eight or nine o'clock at night. In August 1641 he visited the Île de Sein, an island of wild beauty with a flat terrain fully exposed to the onslaught of wind and rain. At that time, the small squat houses of the islanders were half buried in the ground for protection. The people were a hardy breed and had the reputation of being savages, 'les démons de la mer'. They had first been evangelized by Le Nobletz and since then had been maintained in the faith by a seaman and leader of the island, François Guilcher, alias Le Su. Maunoir was convinced that Le Su should be made parish priest of the island and sent him off to the mainland to be examined by the chapter of Quimper. The reverend fathers were not impressed by this rough and ready fisherman and turned him down. However, after persuasion from a Dominican, they relented, and Le Su was ordained priest.

Maunoir's missions employed various means of communication. In addition to the use of canticles and paintings, great importance was attached to a procession of the Blessed Sacrament, which had

elements of what today would be called 'street theatre'. At the front
of the procession would be large numbers of the faithful dressed in
costume to represent saints or scenes from the Life of Our Lord.
Men with muskets marched beside the company and let off salvos
from time to time. In the shadow of a great cross carried at the head
came a barefoot company, representing the apostles, the evangelists, and the seventy-two disciples. After them came the patriarchs
and prophets, the Baptist, three martyr deacons and four doctors of
the Church; tableaux depicting Our Lady and St Gabriel at the
Annunciation, the Nativity, the flight into Egypt, Gethsemane,
Christ before Pilate, Our Lord carrying his cross; then a great
number of priests vested magnificently, and, last of all, the *Sanctis-
simum* carried by the Rector of the parish. They sang the Breton
canticles of Le Nobletz and Maunoir *en route* and, when assembled
in an open space, *Pange lingua*. Maunoir would then preach
fervently on the Passion, on conversion to Christ and repentance.
Attractive and vivid though it was, this procession was more than a
mere show; no one could take part in it who had not been to
confession. At the time of the missions young people could be seen
in great numbers, keeping vigil right through the night outside the
churches, singing canticles and praying. There were conversions
from lives of iniquity and immorality, reconciliation of families and
individuals. And, at the end of it all, Maunoir preached with all the
intensity of a revivalist: 'You would have to be completely hard-
hearted not to love a God so good. . . . To win your love he was
made a small child; having created you, he redeemed you; he died
for you upon the cross; and yet you would not love him, this same
God who will soon give you his body and blood.' Moved to tears by
this passionate proclamation of God's love for unloving mankind,
the congregation would shout back, 'Yes, we love him!'[50]

   While it is true, as we have said, that Maunoir was not known as a
belec fol, his life nevertheless exhibits an exhilarating enthusiasm
and zest for God and his glory. Maunoir recklessly combined activities and concerns more moderate men would hesitate to juxtapose.
He was missionary, preacher, confessor, catechist, but he was also
Breton bard. He expounded the enigmatic tableaux to the rural
poor, but he also wrote spiritual books and hagiography. He translated basic prayers, a catechism, and other devotional works into
Breton, and compiled a manual of Christian instruction 'with a
lexicon, grammar and syntax in the same language'.[51] Maunoir's

work as lexicographer and grammarian contributed greatly to the preservation and development of the Breton language and is comparable to the achievement of William Morgan (*c*.1547–1604), who translated the Bible into Welsh, and Richard Davies (1501–1581), who translated the *Book of Common Prayer*. It is conceivable that, if 'Great Cornwall' had had a Maunoir or a Morgan in the sixteenth or seventeenth century, the Cornish language would have proved more resilient. So significant was Maunoir's achievement that a translation of his lexicon was included by Edward Lhuyd in his *Archaeologia Britannica*.

The question of the Breton language is not irrelevant to the subject of this book. For Maunoir's dedicated service of the language and culture of the Bretons meant a commitment to a people who had long been a joke, an anomaly in an increasingly centralized state, in a culture where the French language was assuming almost divine status. Here was a Frenchman who, only shortly after the foundation of the *Académie*, attempted what was to some the ludicrous task of preserving an archaeological relic, one of 'the fourteen languages of the children of Japhet'.[52] He did so, not simply out of philological interest, but because he saw it as the only way to preach Christ to the people. In a prayer to St Corentin, the patron of Quimper, he says: 'Considering then, Great Apostle [of Cornouaille], that by a special providence of God, I find myself in a place which has always held on to the language you spoke and the faith you established, I feel obliged to give to the public some instructions for preserving the one and the other.'[53]

Maunoir identified himself with a cultural minority despised by the rest of France. The apostles of Brittany were truly men of the people, not religious colonialists implanting a foreign way of life alongside the Catholic Faith. Maunoir's was a foolish and reckless vision of 'becoming all things to all men', but it was foolishly and recklessly successful.

'Idiots' and Converts of Brittany

The greatest achievement of the missions of Blessed Julien and Michel Le Nobletz was to further the spirituality and apostolate of lay people. We have already mentioned Père Michel's use of laywomen as instructors. Maunoir continued and extended the practice. Many of these laymen and women became famous in their own lifetime for their sanctity, and we have many lives of Breton lay saints of the period. What is more, the theme of folly for Christ's sake figures largely in these lives. Most of the saints are simple, semi-literate 'idiots', despised by the grandees but endowed with heavenly wisdom. There is another form of hagiography in which the theme emerges: the lives of *converts*, usually noblemen converted from decadence and immorality to holiness and asceticism. We shall consider the lives of the 'idiots' first.

These last few chapters have centred round the influence of the mystical school of Père Lallemant, for which folly for Christ and the 'purple livery' of Christ's humiliation were major preoccupations. We have discussed the theme as it appears in the writings and lives of several Jesuits of this school. For these priests themselves, the mystical ideal of the Lallemant tradition was embodied not in one of their own number but in a Breton laywoman, whose life was one of drudgery, contempt and hiddenness: Armelle Nicolas (1606–1671), 'la bonne Armelle'.

At the age of twenty, Armelle left her poor family and work in the country to seek domestic employment in Ploërmel. This was not to her liking, and soon she was wandering from job to job, restless and dissatisfied. A Carmelite nun in Ploërmel came to her rescue and found her a post as a nursery maid to the children of her sister, Mme Le Charpentier du Tertre. It was the custom of this lady's household to have readings from the lives of the saints every night after supper. On one of these occasions Armelle was filled with an ardent desire to imitate the saints and for days and nights afterwards she could think of nothing else. This ecstasy, however, was only the first sign of a deeper, more solid experience of God's call. The readings from the lives did not satisfy the young peasant girl, and so she asked one of the daughters to read her something else. The young lady agreed and read from a book about the Passion of Our Lord. 'This served as a kind of bait', her biographer, Jeanne de la Nativité, observes:

Her soul remained so wounded and inflamed with love, that she was quite beside herself, and at the same moment all idea or thought of anything whatsoever was banished from her spirit; she was left with no other object of thought than the sufferings of her Saviour. . . . So much so that she did not know what to do or become, for the ardour and interior distress were so great that it seemed to her that she was in a consuming fire, which day by day grew more intense. . . . There was also, in addition to these visions of the torments of Our Saviour, another very particular and sensible vision of his precious blood, so that, wherever she went, or whatever she did, she saw herself always bathed and saturated with this precious blood. . . . Whenever she had anything to eat, it seemed to her that all the morsels were soaked in the divine blood; when she drank, it was as if she had swallowed that precious liquor. . . . She could not look upon blood or the colour red without pain of such intensity that it almost made her lose the power of speech; the streets, when she was walking along them, often seemed to her completely painted with blood, like those of Jerusalem at the time of the Passion—which seized her heart in such a manner that she was more dead than alive.[54]

Armelle admitted later that these experiences were not wholly supernatural, and she was well served by the counsel of a Carmelite priest who, with the discerning common sense associated with the mystical doctors of that Order, gave her no encouragement to assume that such phenomena were of God. In fact, these first experiences soon gave way to others, even darker. Armelle, like Surin, became convinced that she was damned, indeed already in hell, and was constantly tempted to suicide. Sleep at night became impossible because of the diabolical images continuously passing before her imagination. One one occasion a friend, another serving-maid in the house, found Armelle in this state, manifesting every sign of demonic possession, speechless and gesticulating wildly. While the friend looked on, she suddenly saw the figure of Our Lord:

Sweetly and lovingly, he approached his dear bride and covered her with the mantle he was wearing, as a sign that he was keeping her in his sacred protection; whereupon he disappeared. At the same time the one who beheld the incident cried to [Armelle]: 'Courage, my dear sister, do not be afraid, for I have just seen Our Lord, who has taken you into His safekeeping. . . .' Armelle was aware of none of this, but at the very moment when Our Lord bestowed this grace upon her, her heart was purified.[55]

This condition lasted seven months. It proved too much for Mme Le Charpentier, who regarded Armelle as a half-witted peasant, and subjected her to the harshest treatment, much to the disgust of her good-natured husband. Armelle bore it all without complaint.

Three years were spent in illness, travail, fatigue, contempt, humiliation and rejection . . . and several other experiences that I shall pass over in silence, in all of which Armelle persevered, always undisturbed and content, in the practice of exalted and heroic virtue, which won her the strength to withstand the trials.[56]

At last her mistress's heart softened. After three years of cruelty, on a summer's day, by the water's edge, Madame had a vision of her servant's sanctity:

> She caught sight of [Armelle] all at once completely recollected and enclosed within herself, not speaking a word. Reproving her for it, [Madame] said to her: 'Well, you great scatter-brain, what are you still dreaming about?' And as if woken from a deep sleep, she replied, with great sweetness and simplicity, that she was thinking of the extreme anguish . . . which had penetrated the heart of the Son of God when he passed over the brook Kedron, which this stretch of water reminded her of. [Madame] replied: 'Who taught you that the Son of God passed over the brook of Kedron?'—'I do not know,' she said to her, 'but I am sure it is so.' And saying these words her face was inflamed with great ardour and her eyes poured out tears in great abundance. This touched the heart of her mistress, who thenceforth changed her opinion. . . .[57]

Somewhat later, the eldest daughter of the family, Françoise, married Gabriel du Bois de la Salle, equerry and seigneur of Roguédas, in the parish of Arradon. Françoise asked if she could take Armelle with her as her maid. Armelle agreed to go, and for the next thirty years the manor of Roguédas was her home. Roguédas was close to Vannes and, as a result Armelle soon came under the influence of the Jesuits in that town, notably Pères Rigoleuc and Huby. She placed herself entirely under their guidance and imbibed the mystical theology of the Lallemant school. For a short time she was prevailed upon by her confessor to leave her employers and become a doorkeeper at the Ursuline convent in Vannes, but this served only to impede her spiritual progress, and so Rigoleuc advised her to return to Roguédas, where Armelle combined quiet, efficient domestic labour with a simple but powerful exercise of spiritual motherhood. It is deeply moving to read in her biography of the way she cheerfully applied herself to household tasks while at the same time enduring the most harrowing spiritual trials. However, on occasion her mystical participation in the Passion of Our Lord was manifested in an outward demeanour the world only too readily identified as madness. During Holy Week each year she was reduced almost to immobility: 'She found herself in a state of stupidity, no longer knowing where she was, so greatly had possession by God enraptured her; she was so withdrawn within herself, that even her breathing was impeded, and she

felt as if she were suspended in the air, like a person being choked or
strangled.'[58]

On Good Friday the suffering increased and she underwent 'a
kind of mystical and spiritual death'. Finally, at Pentecost, the Spirit
came with his grace to comfort and restore her. She discussed this
experience with some priests. '"At last he will come, yes,
. . . fathers, my Love and my All will come." Then one of them
said, "Do you not possess him already?" "Of course, I do; I could
not doubt it", she replied, "but no matter, I am certain that he will
come anew, with an even greater abundance of graces."'[59] This last
comment shows how, like Lallemant himself, Armelle preserved a
strong sense of the continuing activity of the Holy Spirit in the soul.
The Spirit is to be acquired or possessed not in the sense of being
trapped or confined in our souls but as the source and medium of
our renewal and transformation into the very likeness of Christ. The
Spirit who dwells for ever in our hearts is also to be invoked
unceasingly to transfigure us from glory to glory. Transfiguration,
indeed, is the secret of saints such as Armelle. She witnessed to the
triumph of divine love, to God's grace fulfilling and perfecting the
human soul, to the completion of the 'good work' begun at Baptism
(cf. Phil. 1: 6). Armelle, according to her biographers, became
quite transparent to the Spirit, transforming and deifying her
from within. The mark of such growth in deifying grace was the gift
of unceasing prayer, 'a clause' making 'drudgery divine'. Her
biographer writes:

I shall not pause further to give proof of the special character of her
prayer. For one would have to go over all the details of her life, which was
but a very faithful practice of Our Lord's express command in the gospel,
namely, that we ought always to pray; and since the end of all prayer is
nothing less than the union of our souls with God, which gives rise to an
intimate familiarity with his divine Majesty and finally makes us, in some
way, like him and participators in his divine perfections, from what has been
said it may easily be deduced that her life was a continual prayer, and so
fervent and aglow, that in the end she was, as it were, transformed into him
who made her, that she might be the temple of his glory, the dwelling-place
of his delights, a perfect imitation of his virtues, and the triumph of his
love.[60]

The appeal of 'la bonne Armelle' transcends the bounds of
culture and ecclesial communion. In the eighteenth century John
Wesley translated her life under the title *Life of Armelle Nicolas,*

Commonly Called The Good Armelle; A Poor Maid Servant in France Who could not read a Letter in a Book, and yet a noble and happy servant of the King of Kings.[61] Armelle exemplifies the truth of St Paul's words about God 'choosing what is low and despised in the world, even things that are not, to bring to nothing things that are' (1 Cor. 1: 28). Armelle is a holy innocent, a spiritual child, a holy 'idiot', an ignorant doctor of the true faith. The subtitle of the 1704 edition of her life puts it well: 'The school of pure love of God opened up to both the Wise and the Ignorant in the marvellous life of a poor idiot girl.'

Another illiterate peasant mystic was Marie-Amice Picard who greatly assisted Père Maunoir in the region of St Pol-de-Léon. She also suffered the pains endured by Our Lord and the martyrs at the time of liturgical feasts: her agony began when the bell rang for the first Vespers of the feasts of martyrs. Opinion was strongly divided as to the genuineness of Marie-Amice's sanctity, and an eighteenth-century biographer, writing in the uncongenial atmosphere of the Age of Reason, felt constrained to offer precise criteria for deciding on the authentiticy of extraordinary experiences such as those of Armelle and Marie-Amice: experiences mean nothing, he rightly stressed, in the absence of solid Christian virtues.[62]

Breton sanctity is remarkably homogeneous in this period. Catherine Daniélou, whose life was written by Père Maunoir, underwent similar torment on Fridays and the feasts of martyrs.[63] It would not be hard to explain such experiences simply in patho-logical terms—the psychotic terror of hysterical women exploited by unscrupulous priests. Certainly, it would be dangerous to advocate uncritical acceptance of the lives as they stand. The objectivity of the Carmelite tradition needs to be vigorously applied to this exotic world, where sensible religious experience sometimes seems to be an end in itself. And yet the hagiographical tradition of seventeenth-century Brittany does preserve essential aspects of Christian spirituality: simplicity, humility, the 'little way', folly for Christ's sake. Moreover, before we dismiss the com-passion of these women, it should not be forgotten that Christians have been given the awesome task of truly 'making up in their bodies the afflictions of Christ' (Col. 1: 24), of bearing his stigmata visibly in their flesh or spiritually in their souls. But it was not only women who emerged as the saintly fruit of the re-evangelization of Brittany. There were also male 'idiots', such as Yves Nicolazic, a monoglot 'breton bretonnant', whose devotion to St Anne led him to rebuild a chapel dedicated to her, which had been ruined for '924 years and six months', and on its site to found a great shrine 'in honour of the Grandmother of God'.[63]

In a different but related category were the aristocratic converts, those who abandoned worldly excess to embrace a vigorous asceticism, a spiritual 'excess' for the sake of Christ. Louis Eudo de Kerlivio (b. 1621), the friend and colleague of Père Huby, was one such who gave up the life of a young *chevalier* and became a priest, 'modest, recollected, solitary, reflecting in his speech and deportment, in his whole bearing, a mind totally opposed to that of the world, a man entirely unencumbered by the things of the earth, and dead to himself'.[64] Then, too, there is Monsieur de Trémaria (1619–1674), a country gentleman who became a priest-missionary, a fellow worker of Père Maunoir, and the passionate advocate of 'prayer of the heart'.[65] Perhaps most colourful of all is Pierre de Queriolet (b. 1602), a murderer, duellist, and debauchee, who became 'the great converted sinner', a priest of the utmost austerity and purity of life. Before his conversion he was 'totally earthly, totally animal, and totally brutal'; his last years were 'totally heavenly and divine'.[66] So incredible was his conversion to the mass of the population, who had held him in terror hitherto, that he was treated as a madman. Finally, though, his sanctity was acknowledged. At the centre of his spirituality was the prayer of the publican, which he recited repetitively like the Jesus prayer:

He usually presented himself before the Majesty of God in the posture of that poor publican, remaining at the back of the church on his knees, and striking his breast, having only this as his prayer, expressed more in his heart than in his lips, 'Lord, forgive me, please, because I am a great sinner'. He continued that prayer to the last breath of his life.[67]

Like the holy fools of Russia, he shared the poverty of down-and-outs and vagrants and wandered perpetually. His social doctrine was clear and militant:

He said that we were very far removed from the spirit of the first Christians who were of one heart and one soul, according to the Acts of the Apostles, and that this lack of charity and compassion for the poor was one of the most deplorable aspects of our religion. Those who knew the opinion of St Gregory in his Morals, of St Chrysostom in his homilies, and other holy fathers and doctors of the Church on this subject, will testify that those of M. de Queriolet were in complete conformity to them.[68]

Francois Guilloré and Louise du Néant

We have spoken of the holy idiot, Armelle Nicolas, as the embodiment of the Lallemant mystical ideal. Armelle was much more, however, than a mere 'product' of the school, a mystical Eliza Doolittle made saintly by a Jesuit Higgins; she also made an active contribution of her own to the development of Jesuit spirituality towards the end of the century, primarily through her influence on Père François Guilloré (1615–1684). Guilloré was born on the very edge of Brittany at Croisic, in the diocese of Nantes, on Christmas Day 1615. Of his family or early life we know nothing except that he was sent to the Jesuit college at La Flèche where he proved to be an excellent pupil and showed an inclination towards a life of solitude, silence, and prayer.[69] At one stage he considered becoming a Benedictine, but finally entered the Jesuit novitiate in Paris, where his master of novices was the wise and holy Père Julien Hayneufve (1588–1663). He made the conventional progress through the Society: philosophy at La Flèche, regency at Caen, theology at Bourges, ordination to the priesthood in 1647. From 1648 to 1651 he taught in the College at Vannes, where he came under the influence of Père Huby and possibly also of Père Rigoleuc. He completed his Third Year under Père Hayneufve at Rouen and then took to teaching again. While lecturing in rhetoric at La Flèche, in November 1654 he wrote to the Master General, Goswin Nickel, asking to be sent on the missions to peasants in the French countryside. The request seems to have been granted, for by 1656 he is described in the catalogues as an *operarius* in the houses at Blois and Alençon, as superior of the Dieppe house (which was concerned with the missions), and then again as *operarius* at La Flèche, Bourges, and Nantes. For his final years from 1673 to 1684, Guilloré lived at the novitiate in Paris, exercising a varied ministry as spiritual director, confessor, preacher, retreat conductor, and visitor of religious congregations. During this period he wrote most of his spiritual works.

Before discussing the theme of holy folly in Guilloré's writing, we should consider two episodes in his life which are essential to a full appreciation of his mystical theology. The first is his endurance of spiritual darkness and mental anguish, during the course of which he was much aided by 'la bonne Armelle'. The second is his direction, while in Paris, of Louise du Néant, the holy lunatic who had been incarcerated in the Salpêtrière. These experiences add weight and authority to Guilloré's theological reflections on folly for Christ's sake and his attempt, perhaps one of the earliest, to apply a rudimentary psychology (in the modern sense) to spiritual direction. Père Guilloré knew at first hand the meaning of *mépris* and *folie*; he had descended into that hell himself.

The first episode concerns Guilloré and Armelle Nicolas. Guilloré is unnamed in the account of it given in the life of Armelle, but we may deduce that it refers to him from an insertion in the second edition of Jeanne de la Nativité's *Triomphe*. It would seem that throughout his life Guilloré was tormented both externally and internally: '. . . despised, insulted and ridiculed to such an extent that there were times when it seemed that every creature had conspired to crush him with the most horrible persecutions of every kind'.[70] While at Vannes Guilloré had to suffer calumny and the loss of all worldly respect. We do not know the details, but it would seem that Guilloré was being laughed at by all and sundry. It was then that little Armelle came to his aid and encouraged him to suffer these trials without complaint. Guilloré descended into such an abyss of depression and melancholy that he believed himself 'utterly lost and reprobate'. In a dream Armelle was told that Guilloré was suffering 'like a damned soul'; she later discovered he was at that precise moment experiencing the pains of hell. At nine in the morning they suddenly ceased—just when Armelle was receiving Holy Communion for him. As long as this state lasted, 'he had no other support or relief than that which he received from the words and advice of this holy maid'.

As a young man, then, Guilloré was aided in his spiritual and mental darkness by a woman, a veritable 'spiritual mother'; in his later years he himself directed a woman similarly plunged into madness and dereliction who clung tenaciously to her faith and became 'Love's Martyr': Louise du Néant, 'Louise of the Nothingness'.[71] Louise de Bellère was born into a noble family in the Château of Tronchay near Angers in September 1639. She was a weak and sickly child, rather picked on by her parents, but endowed with a precocious piety. In her teens she was sent off to a lady in Angers to learn to dance, sing, and play musical instruments, and returned an accomplished and beautiful young woman. However, she expressed a desire to enter a religious house, which provoked her mother into sending her to live with a very worldly woman in

Poitou. For a time she turned away from religion and was courted by young men, but this was short-lived and soon she was seeking God's will for her through the Eucharist and the sacrament of Penance. She decided that she must give her life to the care of the poor and went off to the Hôtel-Dieu in Poitiers, but the authorities were reluctant to admit her without the express permission of her father, who would not give it. Thrown back on her own resources, Louise began to withdraw from the world as much as she could while remaining in the family home. She constructed a little cabin of twigs and leaves in a copse quite close to the château and there spent her time contemplating the four ends of man and eternal punishment and reading St Augustine's *Confessions* and *Soliloquies*; although she had no place in a religious choir, the singing of the birds, we are told, helped her to raise her heart to God.

Louise was eventually admitted to Guilloré's recently founded community, the *Union Chrétienne* at Tours, where Mlle de Meuvrèze was Superior. She took St Mary Magdalene as her patroness and devoted herself to great penitential austerity. After only a short time she became ill. She suffered convulsions and screamed like one of the damned. Her own community soon came to the conclusion that she was bewitched and put her into the hands of the Daughters of Providence, who judged her to be a notorious sinner now justly being subjected to the extreme wrath of God. Her biographer reports that Louise was not responsible for her own behaviour, that it was the work of the devil, who acted upon her without her consent. Demons taunted her: 'No more God for you; go to the everlasting flames.' In this extremity of suffering Louise prayed: 'O my God, I ask to suffer in this life pains like those of hell as a penance for my sins and to pass for a fool: if you are gracious to grant it to me, I shall be content.'[72]

Her constant screaming proved too much for the Daughters of Providence, who put her into lodgings with the local squire, but he too could not endure her infernal shrieks and handed her over to 'Messieurs les Administrateurs de l'Hôpital Général', to confine her in the Salpêtrière (the former saltpetre works which now functioned as an asylum). Bremond has described it as the 'antechamber of hell', and with justice.[73] Not only was it part of that harsh and repressive movement we have described in Chapter Six; it had also become a macabre theatre for the amusement of the nobility, who frequented it as later generations might visit the zoo.

In the Salpêtrière Louise was put in a dungeon with an old hag covered in sores and vermin and soon became infected herself. She was treated as just another madwoman and was not spared the spite and fury of her fellow inmates. After a little time she began to show some improvement and was given into the spiritual care of M. Guilloire (not to be confused with Guilloré), a Doctor of the Sorbonne, who heard her confession and assured her that she was not damned. Having received absolution and Holy Communion, Louise ceased to scream and was filled with joy and peace. She was given the grace of infused contemplation and devoted herself to prayer and the dedicated care of the wretched madwomen, whom she called 'mistresses' or 'princesses'. Here is her rule of life:

I shall rise at midnight to pray for an hour; I shall rise at three and say my prayers until four. I shall say my Little Hours from four until five; then I shall clean the cells of my Mistresses, that is to say, the madwomen and paupers, and I shall empty their pots; at six I shall assist at Prayers in the Dormitory, and then I shall go to Holy Mass; at seven-thirty I shall return to help carry my Mistresses to breakfast; at eight I shall bring them to pray to God; at nine I shall retire to my cell, to write or read; at ten I shall have dinner and shall remain for a time with my companions the fools to allow them a little recreation; at eleven I shall wait on my Mistresses, at noon I shall go to church to say my vocal prayers; at one I shall read or write; at three I shall pray; at four I shall catechize twenty girls they have given me to instruct; at five I shall wait on my Mistresses and my companions the fools; at seven, prayer; after which I shall undress my Mistresses and put them to bed; and at eight I shall put my beast [body] to bed. [74]

Louise then lists her mortifications which, even by the standards of the seventeenth century, are extreme:

I shall take the discipline three times a week; every day I shall wear my wedding garment [hair shirt]; on Wednesdays and Fridays I shall lick ulcers; I shall eat raw herbs whenever I utter unnecessary words; I shall drink from a skull; I shall always eat on the floor, and not at table; and, like an animal, I shall scrape up with my tongue the morsels that fall to the ground. [75]

Her biographer is insistent that by this time Louise, whose suffering had hitherto been involuntary, was now *simulating* madness: 'They continued to treat her like a madwoman, and she pretended to be one, so that she could remain humiliated in the eyes of men and could better conceal her intercourse with God.'[76]

Her motive in serving the poor was neither philanthropy nor

mortification; it was simply her belief that these madwomen were 'the least of Christ's brethren' and that he was present in them to be served or neglected.

Her admirable courage and charity derived from the faith she had that it was Jesus Christ himself whom she helped in these sick persons; and her usual practice was to say to herself before she began: Louise, what are you going to do? You are going to serve your Jesus. But how, my Jesus, she continued, how can it be you? Yes, I believe it. Oh, then, with what respect must I serve these poor women who are your members. [77]

She was discharged from the Salpêtrière in 1681 but continued to wear the clothes of an inmate. At first she lived with the Daughters of Providence, where she had her own room and began to give spiritual direction to the pious women who called on her. M. Briard, who was not her director, put her with one of his penitents, a blind woman, with whom Louise was much happier, treating her as her new 'Mistress'. She continued to feel drawn to serve the poor and asked permission of the Superior of the Hôtel-Dieu to nurse the sick but she was driven away from the hospital as a thief. At first she sought refuge with the Religious of the Blessed Sacrament but then took to wandering in the streets of Paris, working among the poor, and living as a beggar woman.

Guilloré, who by now was her spiritual guide, took pity on her and let her live with the community he directed. It must be said that Guilloré's treatment of Louise was extremely cruel. After years of pain and humiliation, she received precious little kindness from her confessor. As we shall see, he probably treated her thus only because he was convinced of her sanctity and anxious to protect her from the dangers of spiritual pride. At the end, however, after the death of Guilloré, Louise came to live a more normal life, helping her cousin in a community concerned with charitable work at the hospital at Loudun. From then until her death her correspondence testifies to a perfect peace and joy in the Holy Spirit.

Louise de Néant is a fool for Christ's sake in the classical Eastern sense. After recovering from a mental illness she simulated madness as a means of growing in humility and conformity to Christ. We must resist the temptation to psychologize, for to protest that she was *really* mad is to make the mistake of those who confined her. It is clear that for a time she was either mentally ill or demonically possessed (or both), but she emerged from that madness, 'broke through', and ceased to be enslaved by it, without, nevertheless, wishing to become 'normal', to adjust herself to society. It is important to remember that the real madman or possessed person is a slave, unfree, whereas the saints of God are on fire with the Spirit, which is freedom (2 Cor. 3: 17). In Louise's case, we see holy folly embraced freely after humble endurance of involuntary madness. Of course, it could be argued by some that all schizophrenia is a kind of theatrical madness, a 'playing at being mad'.[78] But, most commonly, such simulation is a 'cry for help', articulated in despair and fear, while the madness of the saints is joyfully and lovingly feigned.

With such a convoluted pattern of sanity and insanity, feigned and genuine, spiritual discernment is essential. Nothing is more susceptible of fraud than holy madness; the phenomenon only has meaning when it is undergirded by spiritual discipline and carefully guided by a spiritual father. Because the vocation is so dangerous, perhaps we can better understand, if not approve, Guilloré's harsh direction of Louise. Guilloré was probably the most acute psychologist among the Jesuit masters we have considered; no one was more aware of self-deception, illusion, and delusion, which can corrupt even the sincerest spirituality. One of his most important works is *Les Secrets de la vie spirituelle qui en découvrent les illusions*, which lists and analyses every possible falsification of spiritual truths, every travesty of virtue and holiness.[79] Book 1 lists the illusions of austerity, fasting, mortification of the senses; Book 2, illusions of the virtues; Book 3, illusions of the Spirit. In each case, Guilloré seeks to vindicate the authentic virtue and unmask the impostor. More than two hundred years before Freud, Guilloré sought to unravel the mystery of human motivation, the complex interweaving of desires and intentions, honourable and dishonourable, godly and sinful, involved in any human decision or action. In this he was following a great Jesuit tradition and consciously emulated the example and teaching of St Ignatius himself. He dedicated *Les Secrets* to his Father Founder and addressed him thus: 'Was it not you who taught us to exercise discernment between good and evil spirits and also provided us with rules for avoiding the illusions daily encountered in the spiritual life?'[80]

Guilloré distinguishes between two kinds of illusions: the *innocent* and the *affected*. The latter is hypocrisy, the intentional deception of other people in religious matters, whether out of

vanity or for material gain. There is a probable reference to
Molière's *Tartuffe*, who was, of course, guilty of such deception:
'Our age, alas! is only too infected by Spiritual Persons of this kind,
whom one sees very well set up in business in a short time, and who
accept huge alms from pious people, for public charities, believing
that they can equally well bestow charity on themselves.'[81] Such
'illusion', while greatly harmful, is not the primary concern of
Guilloré's book. He deals, rather, with the involuntary illusions
afflicting even the best-intentioned Christian, and his general
remedy is the opening of the conscience to a spiritual director,
together with purity and simplicity of heart. He is also particularly
insistent on *mépris du monde*, on the repudiation of the world's
'maxims', which are nothing but folly and will delude the soul. As he
says in another work:

> I would go further and make her see the folly of all the maxims the world
> habitually follows, insofar as these maxims are in direct conflict with those
> of the cross and Jesus Christ, for ordinarily [the world's maxims] teach only
> totally ridiculous things, as much against good sense as good morals; . . .
> through impious and profane behaviour, they make us act contrary to the
> profession we have made as Christians at the sacred font of Baptism.[82]

The conflict, however, between the world, its maxims and
wisdom, and the maxims and wisdom of the spiritual life, is only the
outward expression of a battle between two 'depths' (*fonds*) within:
the divine depth—the divine spark, the image of God; and the
demonic depth—the radical egoism of fallen man, his self-love.[83]
The aim of the spiritual life is to allow God to increase and reign
within the soul and that the bloated ego should die. Essential to this
death to self and growth in God is participation in the ignominy
and folly of Jesus in the Praetorium, the purple livery of Christ's
humiliation, where there is no vaunting of self but only naked trust
and obedience.

In his *Conférences spirituelles* Guilloré gives us an exegesis of the
Passion narrative in terms of a sacred tragi-comedy: we must share
the shame of the divine joke-king. In Herod's palace Guilloré sees
'the theatre where I find five scenes of this ignominious tragedy'.[84]
He then lists the five characteristics of the fool, each of which is
found in Jesus: (1) the fool does not reply to the questions he is
asked; (2) the fool is in no position to resent the sting and outrage of
what is being said and done to him; (3) the fool is dressed in a white

garment to show he is an innocent and an idiot; (4) the fool lets himself be dressed and undressed and hardly notices what is happening to him; (5) when the fool has been mocked in one place (Herod's court), he is then sent out to be mocked by all the world.

Jesus, the Word Incarnate, is the eternal wisdom of the Father, and yet in Herod's court he is treated as a stupid man. But in this mockery the folly of the world's carnal wisdom stands judged.

> This worldly and political wisdom is . . . very abominable in the eyes of God, since it is proud, in conflict with every maxim of the gospel, opposed to the Holy Spirit at every point, and the cause of a deplorable incapacity for sincere conversion . . . Oh, have nothing to do with these wise men of the world . . . but let the wise and holy folly of the crucifix be the rule of your actions, preferring much more to pass for a fool in your relationship with Jesus, the only and eternal wisdom, than to appear wise according to the flesh, following the maxims of the world which, in truth, are nothing but pure folly.[85]

The two conflicting wisdoms accuse each other of folly. The foolishness of God, however, is wiser than men, and the folly of the cross, which Jesus consecrated and sanctified in his person, will triumph. The Word 'emptied himself', a *kenosis* which Guilloré sees, as did the Fathers before him, not as the casting off of the divine attributes, but as the experience by the impassible and immutable Word of the extremities of our condition—not just physical pain, but the agony of Gethsemane, the 'interior anni-hilations' of dereliction and mockery as a fool. For the Christian, joined to Christ in his mystical Body, there can be no descent from the cross, no exemption from this hard and demanding way. This way, however, leads to heavenly joy, the only true joy.

Guilloré personally faced disgrace and shame; we know too, of his severe direction of Louise, whose following of Christ involved the endurance of madness and abandonment. Guilloré's literary exposition of holy folly begins, perhaps, to place this severity in perspective. He did not intend to torment Louise but was aware, *from his own experience*, of the corrosive effects of the world's esteem and reputation. That is a danger for any Christian soul, but for one who has experienced the total absence of such esteem, who has been treated as a madman, the temptation to revert to a 'carnal' or 'secular' normality or wisdom is particularly strong. Precisely because Louise came to be respected as a spiritual woman in and through her assumption of folly, the dangers of worldly wisdom were so much greater. Detachment from self is made complete only by death and the fires of purgatory; and reversion to egoism must mean spiritual death.

In this chapter we have seen the spirituality of Père Lallemant extending its influence to Brittany, where it mingled with the native culture and produced a reawakening of the gospel virtues of simplicity and holy folly. We have seen a priest-psychologist, formed in the Breton school, struggling to illuminate his own and others' darkness from the resources of the Ignatian tradition. We leave the 'bards and buffoons' at the dawn of a new era, the century of 'enlightenment', when there will be even less toleration of the holy fool than there was at the end of the 'Golden Age'.

Excursus: Henri-Marie Boudon

Before we take our leave of the seventeenth century, mention should be made of one who was neither Jesuit nor Breton but nevertheless of great importance in continuing the tradition of the holy fool. Henri-Marie Boudon (1624–1702), Archdeacon of Evreux, was the first biographer of Surin and, as we saw above, explictly described the latter as a fool for Christ's sake. Moreover, Boudon himself was mocked in the Praetorium: he was accused of immorality and replied not with protestations of innocence but with silence, humbly accepting the time of scorn as a trial sent by God for his purification and spiritual growth.[1] The charges against him were finally withdrawn; his principal accuser confessed that he was lying and repented. Meanwhile, Boudon had suffered ten years of harassment and ridicule.

The basic idea of his spirituality can be summarized in two words: 'God alone' (*Dieu seul*), which, as we have already noted, was also a motto of Surin. It appears at the head of every one of Boudon's letters: 'God alone, God alone in Three Persons, and for ever God alone in the blessed union of the Sacred Heart of our good Saviour Jesus Christ, the Saviour of all men.'[2]

Boudon frequently reflects on the significance of this *leitmotif*. In a letter to a Carmelite nun he explains that it was this unshakeable conviction that 'alone God suffices' which gave him the strength to withstand unpopularity and derision.

Long ago I first said these words: *Dieu seul*. And long ago it pleased him in his ineffable mercy, which makes me tremble (and with good reason since I have used that mercy so ill), to make known to me that, strictly speaking, there is none but he; that all other things are like shadows, figures—in fact, in his presence they are nothing. But I must confess to you that never until now have I had so powerful a sense (thanks to the abundant mercies of our kind Saviour) of what it is to enjoy the inestimable grace of having no part in these shadows, these figures, this nothing. Oh, who would ever think to find the gift of God in being deprived of all creatures, particularly of their esteem and friendship! Oh, who would ever think to find the gift of God in being cut off, snubbed, despised, rejected and shoved to one side as the scum of the earth! Oh, who would ever think to find the gift of God in being entirely abased in spirit and in heart, and in having no place of one's own save in the heart of God alone![3]

Such detachment from worldly esteem and from all creatures, such singleminded devotion to God alone, does not, however, make for a narrow and ungenerous heart. On the contrary, in its very exclusiveness the love of God alone draws others into its scope. The one who loves God comes to love others for the sake of God alone. Thus, one of Boudon's treatises has the *prima facie* perplexing title, *Dieu seul, ou Le Saint Esclavage de l'admirable Mère de Dieu*, 'God Alone, or Holy Enslavement to the Wonderful Mother of God'.[4] Surely, it might be protested, if Boudon meant what he said, he could not for one moment have tolerated 'enslavement' to anyone or anything except God alone. But, Boudon replies, 'God alone is the foundation of slavery to the Blessed Virgin'. It is precisely because, in comparison with God alone, all creatures are 'shadows, figures, nothing', that we find ourselves lost in wonder, in speechless adoration, when we consider that this very God, 'the sovereign lord of all things', has been subject to a creature, to Mary. She is a 'new heaven and a new earth, an earth bearing only the God-man, a heaven containing nothing but him'. 'God alone', he says, 'is the source and unique cause' of the greatness of Our Lady, and the service we render her, our enslavement to her, 'must have as their end his honour and glory'.

According to a contemporary Life, Boudon was a master of 'wise folly'.[5] And indeed there are many references in his writings to the Pauline texts concerned with folly. Boudon was driven by his own experience of being despised and laughed at to reconsider the relation between the rival wisdoms—of God and of the world. He was convinced that there was a head-on conflict between the two:

'If anyone among you thinks that he is wise in this age, let him become a

fool that he may become wise' (1 Cor. 3: 18). He refers to that folly which is
a wisdom far greater than all the prudence of men: does he not affirm that he
is himself one of the fools for Jesus Christ? If we are to believe the book, *The
Imitation of Christ*, we must embrace this folly to lead a holy and religious
life. Just think how many actions performed by saints seemed pure folly to
human prudence, which scoffed at them, censured them during their life,
contradicted them. Just think how many practices used by the Desert
Fathers to mortify the judgement and reason of their disciples were
ridiculous to human prudence! Was it not a laughable thing in the eyes of the
worldly wise to see St Teresa crawling along the ground carrying a pack-
saddle full of stones, like some beast? . . . But what could human prudence
say to what Jesus Christ commended and performed? But these things are
hidden from it; they are revealed only to the little ones (Matt. 11: 25). These
sages, these prudent men—said a servant of God—see absurdity and darkness where the saints discern only great wisdom and divine light, because
they (the worldly wise) are destitute of the light of piety, which is the science
of the saints and is given to holy doctors.[6]

Boudon speaks explicitly of a *tradition* of holy folly. In the
chapter from which we have just quoted, he cites other examples
of holy fools, among them the disciples of Baltasar Álvarez,
St Dominic, and the sixteenth-century holy fool, St John of God, for
whom he had a particular devotion. Of him he says in a letter:

I am writing to you, Monsieur, on the 8th March, the feast of St John of
God, the founder of the Order of Charity, who spent several years performing actions which made him look like a man who has lost his wits, and yet
here he is now raised up to a state so glorious that the pulpits are full of
preachers proclaiming his greatness, while his relics are venerated by the
highest in the land.[7]

In another letter, a year later, close to the feast, he speaks of 'St
John of God, who, playing the fool before men, arrived at true
wisdom before God'. He continues: 'I have a singular devotion to
states which seem like weakness, abjection and folly to human
prudence.'[8]

At the beginning of the eighteenth century, then, the flame of
holy folly still burnt brightly. The Archdeacon of Evreux, in both
his life and letters, demonstrated the triumph of God's love over
human prudence and passed on the ideals of the Praetorium to a
new generation.

10

The Love of Eternal Wisdom

The school of Lallemant, which we have studied in the last three chapters, is only one small detail in the huge canvas of French religion in the seventeenth century. It was an age of extraordinary spiritual vitality. Never before, not even in the Middle Ages, had so much preaching and teaching been directed at such a wide cross-section of the population. Missionaries and evangelists worked among all classes and as actively in the country as in the city, in contrast to the preachers of the fourteenth and fifteenth centuries, who had concentrated on the urban population.[1] It was also a time of unprecedented development and expansion in church building and religious publishing. In the city of Angers, for example, ten abbeys and other religious houses were founded before 1596, but no less than eighteen between 1598 and 1698. Likewise, H. J. Martin has demonstrated the dominance of the religious book over all other forms of literature. It was the era of Racine and Corneille, and yet from the 1640s onwards nearly half of the books published in Paris were in some way directly concerned with the Christian faith.[2] It was also, of course, a period of religious conflict—of continuing tension between Catholics and Huguenots, culminating in the revocation of the Edict of Nantes in 1685, and of the running battle between Jansenists and Jesuits.[3] It was the century of the political Cardinals, of Richelieu, Mazarin, and de Retz, an era of absolutism in Church and State. It was the age of the Baroque, of triumphalism, opulence, and glory.

In such a period it is remarkable that there should be so much emphasis on the gospel virtues of simplicity, humility, childlikeness, and holy folly. A cynic might, with some justice, point out that a religious body in the ascendant can 'afford' to experiment with the rhetoric of ascetical extremism. Certainly, holy folly in France in the seventeenth century confirms the general principle already noted in the case of Russia and Byzantium, namely, that the fools appear during the Peace of the Church, when Christians are conformed to the world. However, we can absolve our fools, clad in Christ's scarlet motley, from the charge of merely playing with

words. Surin in his catatonic stupor, Louise du Néant amid the
rats and vermin of the Salpêtrière, Guilloré and Rigoleuc in their
dereliction, La Bonne Armelle in her sanctified idiocy, Boudon in
his disgrace, Lallemant, father of them all, rejected and harassed
for his teaching on prayer—all of these, some more dramatically
than others, explored the mystery of Christ's humiliation through
direct personal experience of mockery by the world.

But what of the continuing tradition? Does the holy fool die out
during the eighteenth century, the age of 'dechristianization'? Is the
historian of folly for Christ's sake to join Dean Swift in his lament
for the dead buffoon?

> Here lies the Earl of Suffolk's fool,
> Men called him Dicky Pearce,
> His folly served to make men laugh,
> When wit and mirth were scarce.[4]

St Louis-Marie Grignion de Montfort

In the eighteenth century there are certainly fewer saints whose
lives contain traces of holy folly, but those there are stand out with
even greater clarity. Pre-eminent among them are St Louis-Marie
Grignion de Montfort (1673–1716), who bridges the gap between
the two centuries, and St Benedict-Joseph Labre (1748–1783), the
beggar and wanderer for Christ, whom we shall consider in the next
chapter.

Montfort is of interest to us because he is another Breton bard,
the heir of Surin and Boudon, and a successor to Père Maunoir in
the Brittany missions; above all, because 'his entire life was such an
exhibition of the holy folly of the Cross, that his biographers unite in
always classing him with St Simeon Salos and St Philip Neri'.[5] Everything we know of him supports the comparison, beginning with his
remarkable journey from Brittany to St Sulpice, his seminary in
Paris. Having given his coat to the first beggar he met, he knelt
down and vowed that he would never possess anything again; he
gave his money to the next beggar and exchanged his remaining
clothes with the third. For the rest of the way to Paris he begged
bread and shelter and shared the humiliating lot of the vagabonds,
barked at by dogs and shunned by the country people. Throughout
his life, whether as a seminarian, hospital chaplain or mission priest,
Montfort had a special ministry to the poor and destitute. He saw

every poor man as a shrine of Jesus Christ; in the twisted limbs and
sores of the wretched of the earth he saw the incarnate Son of God
bearing our miseries and bowed beneath our shame. On one famous
occasion in Dinan the missioners with whom he was lodging heard a
banging on the door and the powerful voice of Montfort crying,
'Open, open for Jesus Christ'. On opening the door they found
Louis-Marie with a diseased and filthy old tramp in his arms.[6]

Montfort's writings also reflect the traditional theology and
spirituality of the holy fool. Like Surin and Boudon, all is rooted in a
pure love of God alone (*Dieu seul*), which knows no limits. The love
of God in Montfort's heart is a generous love, which overflows from
God to the neighbour, to all men for God's sake, even to enemies.
The absolute primacy, the utter exclusiveness, of love for God
alone, is miraculously inclusive and draws others into its orbit.

> Oh what a great master he is!
> He has been from all eternity,
> He will never cease to be.
> Let us for ever adore
> The Lord in what he is.
>   GOD ALONE.[7]

And, for the sake of 'God alone', out of love for Jesus, the Christian
loves Our Lady:

> I love only Jesus
> I love only Mary.
> Let no one speak to me any longer
> Of any other love in life.
>   Love.
> Jesus is my love
> Night and day.
>   Love.
> Mary is my love
> Night and day.
>   GOD ALONE.[8]

Another aspect of Montfort's spirituality, with obvious relevance
to holy folly, is his mystical theology of Wisdom. Indeed, so central
is this concept in Montfort's thinking that we might almost speak of
his 'sophiology'. He dedicated a whole treatise to the subject of
'The Love of Eternal Wisdom' and founded a religious congregation, the Daughters of Wisdom, under its patronage. Wisdom, for

Montfort, is a christological and trinitarian concept, the Second Person of the Holy Trinity under one description. Jesus Christ is 'Wisdom made flesh'. To know true Wisdom is to know Christ.

> To know Jesus Christ, incarnate Wisdom, is sufficient knowledge; to know everything and not to know him is no knowledge at all. . . . What use are all the other sciences necessary for salvation if we do not know that of Jesus Christ, who is the one thing necessary and the centre to which all things tend?[9]

But what is this 'science' of Jesus Christ? It is, says Montfort, the Cross, 'the greatest mystery of Eternal Wisdom'. 'Although the great Apostle knew so many things and was so well versed in human learning, nevertheless he said that he decided to know only Jesus Christ crucified' (1 Cor. 2: 2). Such learning, such 'science of the Cross', is seen differently by the world; a religion centred on a sacrificial death is consummate folly. But not only to the world, says Montfort, for the Cross remains a scandal and a folly to many who devoutly sing its praises. At the level of intellect they profess their faith in the Cross but they will not suffer or endure even the smallest trials for the sake of Christ.

> Oh how humble, little, mortified, inferior, and despised by the world, must one be to know the mystery of the Cross, which is still today a subject of scandal, an object of folly, contempt and evasion, not only among Jews and pagans, Turks and heretics, the worldly wise and lapsed Catholics, but even among people they call devout, very devout: not at a speculative level, for there has never been so much talk and writing about the beauty and excellence of the Cross as we have at present; but at a practical level, where there are fears, complaints, excuses, avoidance, whenever it is a case of suffering something.[10]

In a canticle entitled 'Adieu to the insane world' Montfort offers a succinct definition of the world's wisdom. It is, first of all, a wisdom that encourages self-preservation and regards vengeance and anger as the ideal, and love of enemies as weak-kneed folly:

> Suffer, says Jesus Christ,
> If men persecute you,
> If everybody curses you,
> Maltreats or rebuffs you.
> You say those who respond thus are fools.
> Oh arrant cowards, take vengeance, take vengeance!
> As men of spirit, men of honour,
> Avenge this insolence!

The madness of the world also manifests itself in oppression of the poor:

> For your neighbour
> You have only a merciless heart.
> You have only disdain
> For the poor man in his wretchedness.
> If he approaches you for anything,
> You answer him,
> 'Go away and work, rogue.
> Who inflicted this nuisance on me?
> I have neither doubloon nor farthing'.

In truth, of course, the world worships Mammon:

> Your money is your King.
> The Devil is your father.
> Your pleasure is your law,
> And your flesh is your mother.
> But what is your favoured learning?
> Vanity, iniquity, crime.
> Those who do it most artfully
> Are greatest in your esteem.

Against such a world, the Christian is committed to vigilance and unceasing warfare:

> O Lord, we want
> To march under your flag
> Against this enchanter,
> Even though he grumbles and growls.
> Oh how glorious,
> Oh how sweet, how sweet, it is, good Master,
> To have you as our leader
> To fight against this traitor.
> Wretched world, adieu.
> More evil than an atheist
> Without faith or God,
> More changeable than Proteus,
> More cunning than a serpent;
> Adieu, wretch, adieu, impious wretch,
> We despise you, we detest you,
> We condemn your manner of living. [11]

Such contempt of the world is mandatory for Montfort's

Missionaries of the Company of Mary and is included explicitly
in their Rule, and in terms which his Quaker contemporaries in
England would have approved:

> They do not have the world's thoughts in their mind, nor its maxims
> in their hearts, nor its customs in their conduct. Their motto is: *nolite
> conformari huic saeculo.* That is why they avoid, as much as possible,
> without offence to charity or obedience, whatever manifests the spirit of the
> world, such as wigs and skull caps, muffs and gloves, flowing sashes, dainty
> shoes, precious fabrics, glossy hats, tobacco in powder or any other form,
> etc. [12]

Like others we have considered, Montfort demands not only active
contempt of the world and its values but also the absolute necessity
of being condemned by the world. He has left us several vigorous
canticles against those who seek 'human respect'.

> What an insult to the Creator
> To have more fear for the creature,
> To have less respect for his greatness
> Than for a babbling earthworm,
> And to prefer a sheer nothing (*rien*)
> To the one and only sovereign Good (*bien*). [13]

We have several times commented on holy folly as an important
area of common ground between the spirituality of the Christian
East and West and have noted how hagiographical details apparently
more characteristic of an Eastern saint are found in a thoroughly
Latin *milieu*. This is true of Grignion de Montfort. For example, his
love of wandering resembles the Russian (and, of course, Irish)
vocation to pilgrimage. One of his canticles is a hearty marching
song in praise of 'The Holy Journey'.

> We're searching for life,
> Glory and peace
> Which lasts for ever.
> Is that what you long for?
> Then come with us,
> And we shall all have it . . .
> The worldling goes to the dance,
> The drinker to good wine,
> The glutton to the feast,
> To delights and revels.
> As for us, so very joyful,
> We're going to Heaven . . .

We're seeking Mary,
We're seeking Jesus,
Jesus and nothing else.
This is glory and life.
Come, follow us,
And we shall have it. [14]

Again, like St Seraphim of Sarov, he was transfigured in the un-created light, a grace sometimes alleged to be peculiar to the East.

It came to pass that as he was speaking, there shone down upon him, as of old on the face of St Stephen, a reflection of the glory of his transfigured Lord. Of a sudden his worn and wasted face, from which all the ruddy glow of health had passed away, became luminous. Rays of glory seemed to go forth from it, and it was so transfigured in the light of God that even those who were most in the habit of seeing him knew him no more save by his voice. [15]

It is as a writer on Our Lady that St Louis-Marie is best remembered. The *Treatise of True Devotion of the Blessed Virgin* is his masterpiece and remains a much loved classic of Marian spirituality. There are some who would see this cultus as a decadent feature of Baroque piety, in which Mary takes over from Jesus all his divine prerogatives and titles. But a reading of the *True Devotion* will show its firm christological foundation. The first basic principle upon which devotion to Mary is said to rest is that 'Jesus, our Saviour, true God and true man, must be the ultimate end of all our other devotions; otherwise they would be false and misleading. He is Alpha and Omega, the beginning and end of everything. "We labour", says St Paul, "only to make all men perfect in Jesus Christ"'. Montfort then addresses Our Lord on the subject of those who say that love of Mary stands in the way of love of Jesus. Can they really be serious, he asks?

Does devotion to your holy Mother hinder devotion to you? Does Mary keep for herself any honour we pay her? Is she a rival of yours? Is she a stranger having no kinship with you? Does pleasing her imply displeasing you? Does the gift of oneself to her constitute a deprivation for you? Is love for her a lessening of our love for you? [16]

To these questions Montfort replies with a firm negative and provides us with a rich theological justification for devotion to Our Lady. In so doing he makes use of ideas closely associated with folly for Christ's sake: specifically, childlikeness and the real presence of Christ in the poor.

Montfort stresses that the gospel is preached first and foremost as good news to the poor, the humble, the little ones. In 'The Love of Eternal Wisdom' he says that 'the poor and the little children followed Wisdom everywhere as their equal'. He says, too, that the mystery of the Cross, the heart of Wisdom, is comprehended only by the little ones unseduced by the world's adult propaganda. 'One day Incarnate Wisdom, seeing the beauty of the Cross, said in a transport of joy: "My Father, I thank you that you have hidden the treasures and wonders of my Cross from the wise and prudent and revealed them to the humble and to little ones."'[17] But, for Montfort, even more persuasive than the formal teaching of Our Lord on childlikeness, is the fact of the divine childhood, the God-child of Bethlehem.

> The Most High, the Incomprehensible,
> The Eternal and All-Powerful
> Has just now been born.
>   Is it possible?
> The Eternal is a day old, the Word is in silence,
> The All-Powerful has become a child.
>   Let us acknowledge,
>   Adore, praise,
>   Praise, love
>   And acknowledge
> Our God reduced to infancy.[18]

He devotes a whole canticle to the call to spiritual infancy implied in the infancy of God: 'The Great Lesson of Children, Whom We must Resemble If We Are to Enter Heaven.'

> Whoever wants to be
> An all-powerful King,
> According to our Master,
> Must be a child.
> Let us then listen to
> A little baby;
> Let us then learn
> His sweet lesson.[19]

Let us, he says, learn from children, above all, learn from *the* child, of whom every child is an image.

Do you see his face
Full of sweetness.
Do you see the image
Of our Saviour?

But, as we gaze at the baby in his cradle and place ourselves humbly beside him as our spiritual master, what do we learn?

Without answering back he does
What he is told,
He believes without criticism
And without contradiction . . .

He is without malice,
Without guile,
Without any artifice,
Without obstinacy;

He never thinks
Ill of his neighbour,
He is without vengeance,
He is without spite.

And yet Montfort reminds us that true spiritual infancy has a sternly prophetic quality; it challenges a world puffed up by 'maturity' and 'grown up' wisdom. 'For you, little child, shall be called a prophet of God the Most High.'

Listen, worldlings:
Do you desire heaven?
Then without reluctance
Abandon your proud air.
Become, by grace,
Like this child,
And you will have a place
Up above.[20]

For Montfort, the way of Mary is the Little Way of the childlike. Devotion to Mary is essential if we are to grow in true childlikeness. Our Lady is the definitive 'little one'. He refers to her lovingly as 'little Mary'. God came to us through little Mary, his lowly hand-maid; it is his will that we go to him the same way.

This devotion to the Most Holy Virgin is a *perfect* way to go to Our Lord, and to be united with him, for holy Mary is the most perfect and most pure of creatures, and Jesus, who came to us in a perfect manner, chose no other

road for his great and wonderful journey. The Most High, the Incomprehensible, the Inaccessible, He Who Is, deigned to come down to us, little
earthworms, who are nothing. How was this done? The Most High came
down to us perfectly and divinely through the humble Mary, without losing
any of his divinity or holiness; and it is through Mary that the very little must
ascend perfectly and divinely to the Most High without having anything to
fear. The Incomprehensible let himself be perfectly comprehended and
contained by little Mary, without losing any of his immensity; that is why
also through little Mary we must let ourselves be contained and perfectly led
without any reserve.[21]

Going to Jesus through Mary means we approach him as he wants us
to be, as little children dependent for everything on their Mother,
'without guile, without contradiction or criticism.' Montfort
perceives the subtle pride that can lurk behind the repudiation of
Mary's mediating role. While he is clear that Jesus Christ is the one
mediator between God and man and that we can come to the Father
only through him, he warns his readers against presumption in their
approach to Christ. There can be no personal relationship of faith
and trust in Jesus unless we remember that all grace comes to us as a
free gift of his divine love, and is to be received humbly as by a little
child. We must approach him as infants, and infants need mothers.
Mary is our Mother; Jesus on the cross confided us to her maternal
care and he did so for no other reason than that we should come to
him, as he came to us, as a baby in Mary's arms.

In St Louis-Marie's thought there is a strong theological connection between love of Mary and love of neighbour: Jesus is in
both; both are loved for Jesus's sake. Both are a test of the authenticity and generosity of our love of the Lord. Everything 'extreme'
Montfort says about Mary is matched by 'extreme' statements
about man, created as he is in the divine image and, in Christ,
restored to the full likeness of God; intense devotion to Our Lady is
similarly matched by an intense veneration of the neighbour, the
brother in Christ. Both the poor and Mary are loved because of
their relation to Jesus, because both Mary and the poor man are
shrines of Jesus Christ.

Montfort sings ardently of 'Jesus living and reigning in Mary':

Since the principal mystery celebrated and honoured in this devotion is
the mystery of the Incarnation where we find Jesus only in Mary, having
become incarnate in her womb, it is more appropriate for us to say 'the
slavery of Jesus in Mary', of Jesus dwelling enthroned in Mary, according to

that beautiful prayer of so many great souls, 'O Jesus living in Mary, come and dwell in us, in your spirit of holiness' etc. This way of speaking shows more clearly the intimate union existing between Jesus and Mary. They are united so closely that the one is in the other: Jesus is all in Mary and Mary is all in Jesus; or rather, it is no longer she who lives, but Jesus alone who lives in her. It would be easier to separate light from the sun than Mary from Jesus. So united are they that Our Lord may be called 'Jesus of Mary' and the Blessed Virgin 'Mary of Jesus'.[22]

Everything said here of Jesus in Mary, and of the need to love him in her, is paralleled in what Montfort says of the poor.

> What is a poor man? It is written
>   That he is the living image,
> The lieutenant, of Jesus Christ,
>   His most beautiful heritage.
> To speak even more truly,
>   The poor are Jesus Christ himself.
> This supreme Monarch
>   Is helped or refused in them.
>
> In one he suffers poverty,
>   In another vermin,
> In another captivity,
>   In another famine.
> In short, Jesus, in them suffering
>   Innumerable agonies,
> Reveals himself as the most needy
>   Of the destitute.[23]

One of his longest canticles is entitled 'The Endearments of Love of Neighbour', which describes fraternal charity as 'the essence of a Christian', 'the mark of the predestined'. Without mercy, he says, every sacrifice is useless, every prayer pernicious, every sacrament sacrilege, every good work an illusion. This is not rhetoric, for Montfort truly became one of the poor, lived with them and served them to the end.

Montfort is one of many examples of those whose high Mariology has been accompanied by an equally high anthropology, who have seen that the ineffable dignity bestowed upon our human nature by the Incarnation is the rationale of both devotion to Our Lady and love of neighbour. One thinks in our own century of the Polish Franciscan, Blessed Maximilian Kolbe (1894–1941), the apostle of both total consecration to the Immaculate and fervent love of neighbour, finally laying down his life for another man in Auschwitz.[24] The generous and foolish love of the Word made flesh, the love whose infinite depths he revealed when he 'loved them to the end' (John 13: 1), kindles within man a reciprocal love, which in its turn spreads out to others for the sake of Christ. This is the love given to Our Lady and to the poor, in the first case to a shrine fully perfect and transfigured, in the second to a shrine still unadorned and awaiting our reverent love and care; in both cases to the shrine of our humanity, containing Christ.

So, at the end of our long journey through the strange world of seventeenth-century French folly for Christ, we arrive at a truly evangelical perception of the foolishness of divine love. 'Oh, the folly of Eternal Wisdom!' exclaims St Louis-Marie:

How many times did he cry out when living on earth: 'Come to me, all of you, come to me; it is me, do not fear. Why are you afraid? I am like you; I love you. Is it because you are sinners? Well, they are the ones I am looking for; I am the friend of sinners. Is it because, through your own fault, you are wandering from the sheepfold? Well, I am the Good Shepherd. Is it because you are loaded down with sins, covered with filth, weighed down with misery? Well, that is just why you must come to me; for I will relieve you of your burden, I will purify you, I will console you.[25]

11

The Continuing Tradition

The study of Grignion de Montfort has brought us to the beginning
of the eighteenth century. It was suggested earlier that the tradition
of holy folly comes under new and yet more hostile pressure in the
age of the Enlightenment, but, as we shall see, it does not die out
altogether even in the following centuries of secularization; indeed,
the Holy Spirit continues to pour out his precious gift of apostolic
folly on Christians of our own time. In this chapter we shall survey
the continuing tradition of folly for Christ's sake, not in a fully
comprehensive study but in sketches of representative figures and
regions—a holy wanderer on the roads of eighteenth-century France
and Italy, a professor in nineteenth-century Oxford, the fools for
Christ's sake in modern Ireland.

St Benedict-Joseph Labre (1748–1783)

The life of St Benedict-Joseph is a classical instance of folly for
Christ's sake, and in that sense he is truly representative of the
tradition. But he could not be more unrepresentative of his times. If
the age of Voltaire, Rousseau, Diderot, and Hume had been one of
fiercely combative atheism rather than of elegant scepticism, it
might well have stirred the Church to renewal. As things were,
however, the religious temper of the eighteenth century was deistic
and latitudinarian. As Diderot put it in a famous letter to Voltaire,
'I believe in God but I get on very well with atheists . . . it is very
important not to mistake hemlock for parsley; but it makes no
difference at all whether you believe in God or not.'[1] God, in this
view, is the architect of the universe, who has bequeathed his *chef-
d'oeuvre* to its occupants but has little further interest in it or them.
A distinguished historian summarizes the spirit of the age thus:

It was the doctrine of divorce which won the day: in philosophy,
Cartesianism; in theology, deistic free-thinking; in ethics, rationalism and
the pursuit of happiness; in social thought, the self-seeking individual
combined with his fellows to construct the secular state, while remaining
separately a member of an invisible church concerned with a kingdom not of

this world. God remained on his throne, remote, majestic, reasonable, and disincarnate.[2]

Between 1751 and 1780 Diderot and his collaborators published the *Encyclopédie* in thirty-five volumes. Intended as a complete review of the arts and sciences of the day, its articles, while restrained to some extent by Church censorship, pointedly express the contempt felt by the apostles of reason for the extremism and fanaticism—as they saw it—of true Christianity. An example is de Jaucourt's contribution on the Sermon on the Mount:

It is agreed that if Christians tried to observe some of these commandments of Jesus Christ, society would soon be turned upside down: the honest a prey to the violence of the wicked, the faithful exposed to death by starvation because he had laid by nothing in his prosperity to feed and clothe himself in adversity: in a word, everybody admits that the precepts of Our Lord are not compatible with public security and peace. This is what has compelled interpreters to resort to restrictions, modifications . . . but none of this is necessary. . . . What leads the interpreters astray is that they believe that the precepts of the Lord in these three chapters concern all Christians. . . . As soon as one lays down the principle that the Sermon of Our Lord is addressed to his apostles, there is no longer any difficulty.[3]

Notwithstanding the eighteenth century's concern to spare its Christian citizens any difficulties in the matter of Christ's precepts, there still arose those who obeyed them to the letter: Benedict-Joseph Labre was such a one.

Benedict spent the greater part of his adult life as a poor wanderer for Christ's sake: he had no home and slept often out of doors; he wore only a ragged habit, which he never changed; he possessed nothing except his New Testament, an *Imitation*, Breviary, and rosary. He was never anxious about food or drink but was content with the scraps he found on rubbish heaps. He sought first the kingdom of God and his righteousness. In an age of enlightened self-interest, he lived voluntarily in abject poverty, rejoicing to be reviled and treated as a fool for Christ's sake. When the disincarnate god of the deists, the Master Watchmaker, was turning his back on the weakness and suffering of mankind, Benedict worshipped the incarnate God of Bethlehem and Calvary, Jesus enshrined in the poor, Jesus in the Blessed Sacrament of the altar. St Benedict-Joseph Labre was not a man of his time but, as Christ's holy pauper, a man for all times.[4]

He was born in 1748 at Amiettes, a village in the diocese of Boulogne-sur-mer, the eldest of fifteen children of the local shop-keeper. Even at the age of four or five, he was manifesting a fervent piety and asceticism and was soon regarded as a possible candidate for the priesthood. When he was twelve, he was sent to continue his studies with his uncle, François-Joseph Labre, the curé of Erin. During this period he began what was to be a lifetime's observance of the Forty Hours Devotion, practised all the Church fasts rigorously, and assisted his uncle in works of charity. So absorbed was he in his reading of Scripture and the lives of the saints that the good curé had to remind him of the importance of secular study. When after heroic work among the afflicted during an epidemic his uncle died of typhus, Benedict returned home, but soon made it clear to his family that he was resolved to serve God in total abandonment and solitude. His mother protested that he would have nothing to live on if he withdrew into the desert.

Benedict replied: 'I would live on grass and roots from the fields, like the hermits of old.' 'But those hermits were quite different from the men of today. And besides, then there used to be miracles, which do not happen nowadays!' 'They could, if we wanted them to', replied the saint, 'God is no less powerful today than he was at other times. If then he worked miracles to sustain his servants, do you not think he can still perform them today? Ah, my dear Mama, every day he does things nobody sees. Yes, with the help of God, you can do anything, if you really want to.'[5]

Benedict refused to narrow down the gospel, and thus the grace of God, to fit the straitjacket of the prevailing scepticism. Apostolic life and the life of the desert could be practised, with faith, as easily in modern France as in first-century Palestine or fourth-century Egypt.

Thus began a series of attempts to join a religious order. In mid-winter, at the age of eighteen, Benedict walked sixty miles to test his vocation at a Cistercian monastery, only to be told that he was too delicate and too young. The response was much the same in the other houses, Cistercian and Carthusian, to which he applied: he had zeal but he was immature; he was pious but eccentric. Having failed to enter the Cistercian community at Sept-Fons, he set out finally for Italy, where he hoped to find a more sympathetic response to his vocation. It was now, at the age of twenty-two, that Benedict came to see that he was already practising the life to which

God was calling him: a life of pilgrimage and poverty, of renunciation even of stability, of continual prayer on the road as well as in
church; a life in which his weakness, vulnerability, apparent folly,
could be consecrated to God's service. For the next thirteen years
Rome was his base, but from there he wandered all over Europe to
the major shrines—Loreto and Assisi in Italy, Einsiedeln in
Switzerland, Compostela in Spain. It has been estimated that
during this time he walked more than thirty thousand kilometres.
He carried with him neither purse nor scrip. He wore only his
ragged habit and a pair of broken shoes. His refectory was the
refuse heap. And yet whenever he was seen, whether in Rome or on
the road, he appeared to be rapt in prayer, joyful, and radiant.

In Lent 1783, when Benedict was thirty-five, he contracted a chill
with a violent cough. Quite undeterred, he persevered in his
customary devotions in the city of Rome—the Forty Hours, prayer
before the images of Our Lady, and all the others. At last, on the
Wednesday of Holy Week, having managed to attend Mass in his
favourite church of Santa Maria dei Monti, he was overcome by
faintness. Sympathizers gathered round him as he sat weak, helpless, and exhausted on the steps of the church. He was removed by a
local butcher to his home, where, having received the last sacraments, he died in peace. Almost immediately throughout the town
the children ran through the streets crying, '*E morto il santo!*
E morto il santo! The saint is dead! The saint is dead!'

The vocation of Benedict-Joseph which led him into a life totally
at odds with the dominant ideals of his age was also, from the
economic and political point of view, exceedingly inopportune.
Wanderers of other ages, such as the Irish *peregrini*, often had an
accepted place in society. But in these last years of the *ancien régime*
official intolerance of vagrancy and the itinerant life was growing.
The numbers of vagrants steadily increased in France from the
1740s onwards, and especially during the seventies and eighties, in
the wake of diminished grain harvests and textile slumps. In 1767
the government offered a reward for every beggar arrested, and in
the same year a special commission recommended new and harsher
laws against 'vagabonds'. Benedict, who chose to serve Christ as a
wandering beggar at precisely the time when in his own country that
class was enduring almost unprecedented harassment and persecution,[6] was forced to find his point of stability in the Eternal City, the
heart of Catholic Christendom.

Benedict-Joseph Labre closely conforms to our Eastern paradigm of folly for Christ's sake. Like the fools of Russia, he is a wanderer, moving restlessly from place to place, but like St Basil the Blessed he has a particular attachment to a holy city, to the eternal city of Rome, to which he returns each time at the end of his wanderings. Like most of the fools of East and West, he lives in abject poverty without shelter, regular nourishment or comfort of any kind. On the day of his death his provisions were found to be a scrap of stale bread and some orange peelings.[7] He would often be seen in the street 'using his teeth as weapons to overcome the toughness of a broccoli stalk . . . triumphing thus over the world and his own body'. On one occasion his devotions in Santa Maria dei Monti were disturbed by a pious woman who had come to invite him to dinner: 'Returning to himself with evident displeasure, as if disturbed in the enjoyment of something very agreeable, he quickly answered, "Dinner? dinner? I dine in the street!" '

Benedict manifested a sublime indifference to the world and to its judgement of him. His extreme asceticism inevitably brought upon him the accusation of madness, which he never sought to deny.

He was frequently the laughing-stock of impudent boys in the public streets, who vied with one another in throwing cabbage-stalks, orange peel, and similar rubbish at him, becoming bolder in consequence of his invincible patience. Benedict suffered all; he heard himself called a fool and a ragged fellow, without turning or giving the least mark of resentment; he went on his way as quietly as if he had not received insults.[8]

Benedict's folly for Christ's sake did not consist simply in an extravagant asceticism. His life was blessed with all the evangelical virtues, especially love of neighbour. As a vagabond for Christ's sake, he believed that he had been called to share the lot of the least of Christ's brethren. As the Rector of Fabriano, who knew the saint well, put it, 'To a great humility and a singular contempt of his own body, which he called his carcase, he joined an unbounded charity for his neighbour.'[9]

He several times denied himself the soup which he received at the convent doors, to give to others whom he thought more needy than himself . . . he always placed himself at the very end of the row of poor people, though he had arrived before them. And being asked why, he replied: 'Because I fear that it may fail before someone who came after me has received a portion.' . . . And as he sometimes noticed among the crowd some poor mother,

whose single portion was not sufficient for her large family, he compas-
sionately added his own share to hers.[10]

Perhaps the greatest blessing Benedict received from God was
the gift of unceasing prayer:

> The length of his prayers was well known in Rome, and many persons, in
> attesting to it, speak of them as prayers, while they were, in effect, contem-
> plations and divine favours. It was very common for him to spend the entire
> day on them. . . . All those who vouch for the length of his prayers, equally
> testify to his admirable manner of praying. Some call it ecstatic, others
> speak of him as an angel, immovable as a statue, a saint, as one absorbed in
> God. . . . Some placed themselves secretly behind a confessional, or in
> some hidden part of the church, particularly at the most solitary hours, on
> purpose to watch him: they saw him quiet, ecstatic, motionless, always the
> same.[11]

We are told that he continued his recollection and prayer even
when travelling on the high road when the beauties of nature led
him to even more fervent adoration of God in his omnipotence and
wisdom. His prayers seem to have been brief, repetitive acts of
praise or penitence, uttered with the impetuosity of a fool of love.
His confessor tells us:

> Reflecting on the infinite love of this Divine Majesty for men, he burned
> with a lively desire to receive him, breaking forth into expressions stronger
> . . . than those which are used by a foolish lover of the world: 'My Good,' he
> repeated, 'My Good . . . my All . . . sole subject of my love . . . O come
> . . . I desire thee . . . I sigh after thee . . . I wait for thee . . . every little
> delay seems a thousand years . . . Come, Lord Jesus, and delay not.'[12]

Like other holy fools we have mentioned, this tramp for Christ's
sake had a particularly strong devotion to Our Lady, God's lowly
handmaid, the queen of the poor. On one occasion, he was taken
for a drunkard when he was found at night prostrate before the
image of the Mother of God at Loreto.

Benedict-Joseph Labre practised a self-renunciation that rivals in
its intensity the asceticism of the first Christian monks. His was a
kenosis without reserve: he had so emptied himself to the greater
glory of God that at the end of his life there was literally very little
of him left. He founded no religious order, left no writings, was
rejected as unsuitable by monastic communities and had no
distinctive apostolate, apart from his wandering and his love of the
poor. He left nothing except a body worn out with excess of love of

God and neighbour. 'He had no form or comeliness that we should desire him', and yet many witnesses tell us that, whilst enraptured by the mystery of divine love, he was often transfigured by the uncreated light. For a few moments the wasted little figure was made radiant in the light of Tabor.

At other times, the face of Benedict, pale and emaciated by his mortifications, would all at once be illuminated and give off rays of fire. . . . One winter morning P. Biaggio Piccilli was saying Mass before daybreak, as was his custom, at the high altar of Santa Maria dei Monti. His few assistants could scarcely see one another in the darkness which was pierced only by the feeble glow of the candles. A gentlewoman, Maria Poeti, who had a charitable interest in the poor man, had not at first taken much notice of her protégé, who was kneeling in his accustomed place close to the balustrade. However, a few moments later, raising her eyes, she saw his figure irradiated by a brilliant light. Dazzled by the sight, she could no longer distinguish anything else in the shadows. [13]

Here, in a poor fool, clothed in rags, we see the only real enlightenment, which is the gift of God.

Dr Pusey and Père Surin

If Labre is at once both untypical of the century in which he lived and yet also faithfully representative of the folly tradition, Edward Bouverie Pusey (1800–1882), one of the leaders of the Oxford Movement, at first sight appears to be very much a man of his age and with no claim to be a fool for Christ's sake in the classical sense. The contrast, however, requires a certain qualification. There is an important sense in which the Catholic Revival was 'counter-cultural', in direct and conscious opposition to what its adherents regarded as the prevailing mood of their times, especially that of Liberalism. Their fidelity to the past was by no means a backward-looking conservatism but a positive expression of their desire for 'revolution by tradition', most clearly seen, perhaps, in the revival of the religious life. [14]

Common to all the Tractarians was an attitude of rebellion against the spirit of the age, and, while it would indeed be absurd to put Pusey among the 'fools', nevertheless it remains true that, at a moment of acute personal crisis, he was spiritually encouraged and sustained by the tradition of holy folly, and most especially by the example and writings of Jean-Joseph Surin.

The spring and summer of 1844 was a time of darkness for Dr Pusey. In the previous year the sermon 'The Holy Eucharist, a Comfort to the Penitent' had been condemned by the University and Pusey himself suspended. Newman had just resigned the living of St Mary's and in a letter in August revealed to his friend the direction in which his thoughts were moving. Pusey was profoundly distressed: 'I do not shut my eyes now', he said, 'I feel everything I do is hollow, and dread its cracking.'[15] In April 1844 his daughter Lucy died, and in May came the annual torment of the anniversary of his wife's death. Both deaths Pusey believed to be the punishment for his own sins, a conviction that imposed upon his life an almost incredible pattern of austerity and penitence.[16] In the midst of so much anguish of both a personal and ecclesiastical kind, Pusey was reading and translating Père Surin. The Preface to his translation of Surin's *Fondements de la vie spirituelle* is dated 'Vigil of St James 1844', that is, 17 July, the day on which his invalid son, Philip, was confirmed.[17] A bookseller's bill for 27 February 1845 gives us a list of his purchases for August and September 1844, included in which are Surin's *Lettres spirituelles, Catéchisme spirituel, Guide spirituel*, and *L'Homme de Dieu* (presumably Boudon's).[18] Pusey's Preface to the *Foundations* gives abundant proof of his admiration for Surin. In a fragment on 'The Inward Life', preserved at Pusey House, he mentions 'Books fitted to the formation of your inward life. The spiritual works of F. Guilloré, of F. Surin, of F. Huby' and other French divines. In reply to Dr Hook's description of the *Foundations* as 'Romish Methodism' Pusey replies: 'I do not Romanize; the great difference between us is, that you speak boldly and peremptorily, where I, knowing what holy men they were, dare say nothing.'[19]

Pusey, *in profundis*, became increasingly preoccupied with the spiritual writings of continental Roman Catholics, and of Surin in particular.[20] From what we have said already of Surin it is not hard to see the affinity Pusey felt with him. Indeed, so closely does Pusey identify with the Jesuit that the dividing line between hagiography and autobiography is not always discernible: 'The Author knew in its inmost depths, what is self-abnegation, and what "the abundance of the consolations" of Christ. This book, like so many others, was the direct fruit of the Cross.'[21]

Perhaps no one at that time was better qualified to evaluate Surin's twenty-year witness 'in chains' than Pusey, or to write, at least in English, more finely of it than he:

> So far must God's thoughts be from ours, that He broke, so to say, His
> own instrument in two, in the vigour of his age; and when, by destroying it,
> He had perfected it, employed it for nothing outwardly great in His
> Kingdom. For twenty years He tempered and polished and refined this
> sharp sword, and then laid him up in His everlasting armoury, for what ends
> in the world invisible we know not, but here chiefly, as a memorable
> specimen how His weapons of proof are formed and tried in the fire.[22]

As further evidence of Pusey's identification with Surin there are
remarkable parallels between one of Pusey's blackest letters and
certain passages in his introduction to Surin. In April 1844 he wrote
to Keble: 'I am indeed in earnest that all my sorrows are the fruits of
my own sins, and all my chastisements so many mercies. *Ut nos hic
urere et purgare, et in aeternum parcere digneris.'*[23] His agony was
made more intense by the fact that, while he absolved others, he
could not bring himself to go as a penitent to another priest. As his
biographer, Liddon, says: 'He was so overwhelmed with the consciousness of his sins that he shrank from making a confessor of one
of those friends with whom he was associated in common work, and
outside this circle there was no one whom he could choose as a
spiritual guide.'[24]

Until 1846, when he laid himself at the feet of Keble, who became
his confessor and whom thereafter he addressed, at his own insistence, not as 'friend' but as 'father', Pusey remained convinced that
the enormity of his sins was such that confession and absolution
were impossible. On St Cyprian's Day (26 September) 1844, he
wrote a letter, which to some has seemed pathological, but which, in
the light of the doctrine Pusey learnt from Surin, deserves a quite
different interpretation:

> I must pain you in return far more than what you say can pain me. I am
> quite unfit to think anything or express anything, one way or the other,
> about what you tell me, except that it seems a marvellous part of God's
> dealings with people in our Church, that He is giving them such quickened
> apprehensions of sin. But as you give me a hint that you might ask an
> opinion of me, I must speak, though it will very much pain you. My dear
> wife's illness first brought to me, what has since been deepened by the
> review of my past life, how, amid special mercies and guardianship of God, I
> am scarred all over and seamed with sin, so that I am a monster to myself; I
> loathe myself; I can feel of myself only like one covered with leprosy from
> head to foot; guarded as I have been, there is no one with whom I do not

compare myself, and find myself worse than they; and yet, thus wounded and full of sores, I am so shocked at myself, that I dare not lay my wounds bare to any one; since I have seen the benefit of confession to others, I have looked round whether I could unburthen myself to any one, but there is a reason against every one. I dare not so shock people; and so I go on having no such comfort as in good Bp. Andrewes' words, to confess myself 'an unclean worm, a dead dog, a putrid corpse,' and pray Him to heal my leprosy as He did on earth, and to raise me from the dead: to give me sight, and to forgive me the 10,000 talents; and I must guide myself as best I can, because, as things are, I dare not seek it elsewhere.

You will almost be surprised that, being such I should attempt, as I do, to guide any. I cannot help it. Those whom I in any way guide were brought to me, and by experience or reading, or watching God's guidance of them, I do what I can, and God Who loves them has blessed them through me, though unworthy. But I am trying to learn to wish to influence nothing on any great scale; to prefer, I mean, every one's judgment to my own, and only to act for myself as I best may, and for any souls whom He employs me any way to minister to. When I can, it is a comfort to use words classing myself with other sinners: it is a sort of disowning of what people make of me. I hope all this will not shock you too much, or do you harm; the real testimony to the life of the Church is not in such as me but in simple people, such as my own dear child. He is working marvels among such; it quite amazes me to see His work with individual souls. So then pray be not dismayed at what I write. I have not said so much to any one for fear of dismaying them. It seemed as if I had no right. But there is abundant, super-abundant proof of God's great grace with people's souls in our Church, though I am a poor miserable leper. . . .

I grieve thus to grieve you, but I cannot help it.

Ever your unworthy but still affectionate

E. B. P.[25]

Liddon points out that such extreme language in describing personal sin 'in all ages has been characteristic of those really advanced in holiness', and he mentions Paul, Augustine, Francis of Assisi, Vincent de Paul, and François de Sales, and, among Anglicans, Bishop Andrewes, John Wesley, and Charles Simeon. What he does not mention is Pusey's own discussion of this subject in his Preface to Surin written only two months before the St Cyprian Day letter. Reflecting on the depths of self-abasement plumbed by the saints (and here he anticipates what he is to say later of the ordeal of Surin), he speaks of 'that which has been the common maxim and first principle of all Saints, that they are to account themselves "the chief of sinners"'. Such self-abnegation, he insists, is not just professed with the lips: '. . . on each occasion acting instantaneously upon it, wishing others to believe it, bearing all reproach patiently, glad to be evil-spoken of untruly, acutely pained at any hint of praise, confounded at the mention of any good in them'.[26]

In a note on the same page he cites examples of those who have rejoiced in such self-abhorrence, including St Francis Borgia and St Ignatius Loyola. Commenting on the extreme sentiments of St Alphonsus Rodriguez, who 'compared himself to graves of dead, putrid carcasses, sewers, and sinks of vessels where all defilements collect', he says: 'Comp. our own Bp. Andrewes, Morning Devotions, "Despise me not, an unclean worm, a dead dog, a putrid corpse."' It is this latter quotation, of course, which appears in the St Cyprian's Day letter. Indeed, when we consider the main text of the *Foundations*, we find much that would have spoken to Pusey in his dereliction in the mid-1840s. For example, the Pusey who looked upon his suspension and humiliation in 1843 as a punishment for 'secret faults' will have drawn comfort from Surin's account of the Ignatian idea of wearing Christ's livery.[27]

What, then, is the significance of this correspondence between intimate self-revelation and (apparently) objective ascetical theology? It is not sufficiently appreciated, I believe, to what extent the Catholic Revival in the Church of England in the nineteenth century was undergirded by martyrdom, by faithful witness in the face of vilification and mockery, of legal harassment and discrimination, and, as we now see in the case of Pusey, in the face of deep psychological suffering, of a kind of madness. We are in a better position to make this judgement when we realize, as this brief study has shown, the influence upon the early Tractarians of seventeenth-century Catholic writers, who rejoiced to be 'fools for Christ's sake'. The word of Our Lord to Staretz Silouan in our own century, 'Keep thy mind in hell, and despair not', was conveyed to Dr Pusey in the reign of Victoria by a seventeenth-century Jesuit who for twenty years endured a dark night without ever abandoning his love of God. Surin was a medium of grace and healing for Pusey, leading him to a deeper understanding of the way of the Cross, and thus to a share in its reconciling power. When Pusey speaks of Surin, it is of a friend who has led him to a closer conformity to Christ crucified. 'Like Isaac, his one great office seems to have been to yield himself meekly to suffering, and therein to be a type of blessings, and transmit them. God employed chiefly not his active service, but himself.'[28]

The Holy Fools of Modern Ireland

Jokes about Irishmen as fools, dimwits or rogues have been common in England since Tudor times[29] and have, like all jokes based on racial stereotypes, a long and complicated history. Ever since the Tudors Ireland has known grinding poverty, economic and political subservience to its more powerful neighbour, and, as a consequence, the dispersal, by emigration, of large numbers of its sons and daughters. Like other cultural minorities living in diaspora, the Irish have inevitably been exposed to prejudice and mockery. 'Mick' or 'Paddy' has always been fair game for the satirist in America and England.

For the peace and reconciliation of the English and Irish, it is essential that those of us who have been brought up in an Anglo-Saxon culture should come to recognize the spiritual heritage of a nation we fail, too often, to take seriously. For the English Christian, who may be largely ignorant of Irish history, it is salutary to learn that Ireland has a rich, continuing tradition of spirituality, and that her people, so long regarded as a joke or a problem, have preserved an evangelical charism of holy folly for Christ's sake which flourishes today as it did in the days of Suibne, Moling, and the rest.

Perhaps the most striking modern Irish holy man is Matt Talbot, 'the Irish Worker's Glory', who was a fool for Christ's sake in the classical sense.[30] Born in 1856 into a poor Dublin family, he went, at the age of twelve, to work after only a year's schooling for a firm of wine merchants, and soon became a chronic alcoholic. He neglected his religion—although he never missed his Sunday Mass—and led a life of total squalor and degradation. At the age of twenty-eight, however, he was converted, signed the pledge, and embarked on a life of such heroism that it is difficult to believe we are describing a twentieth-century working man and not a fourth-century monk. For most of his life Matt worked faithfully and humbly as a manual labourer in a Dublin timber yard. He rose each day at four in the morning and prayed until five-thirty, when he heard Mass before going to work; he prayed again during the short lunch hour, and from six to ten-thirty, when he retired. He ate little more than was necessary for the preservation of life, and for fourteen years wore chains and ropes on his body. He slept on a wooden pillow; prayed and read on bare knees.

In spite of all this, Matt was a complete man. As with St Antony, his ascetical rigours did not destroy or warp his humanity but gave it a roundness and integrity. His devotions were completely unostentatious; most of them were not discovered until his death or, if during his lifetime, only by chance. His first biographer describes his lunch-break:

> During the time from 1 p.m. to 2 p.m. his duty was to open the gate to admit the lorries, and if necessary to load them with the man in charge of same. When not so employed, he retired to the little office or to the end of the yard, where Mrs M's children saw him praying. He did not mind the children but if a grown person came in view he rose from his knees and came out of the office, or from behind the timber.[31]

Matt loved children and gave them sixpences from his tiny wage every Christmas Eve. He was an 'enlightened illiterate'. While he had received only the barest elementary education, he regarded it as a duty to read—not only spiritual books such as those of Montfort, St François de Sales, Father Faber, Newman's *Apologia*, but also works relating to social and political problems, especially the Papal Encyclicals. His approach to political questions has all the marks of true spirituality. He supported the just cause of striking workers (he was a member of the Irish Transport and General Workers' Union), but he would not picket or draw strike pay. He strongly disapproved of his nephew wearing the uniform of the British army. Poor as he was he gave nearly everything away in alms, writing, on one occasion in December 1924, a pathetic note to the Maynooth Mission to China: 'Matt Talbot have done no work for past 18 months. I have Been Sick and Given over by Priest and Doctor. I dont think I will work any more there one Pound from me and ten shillings from my Sister.'[32] Finally, there is his teaching on folly for Christ's sake. Among the collection of tiny scraps of paper on which he wrote his thoughts and memorabilia, are the following:

> Oh King of Penitents who pass for fools in the opinion of the world but very dear to you oh Jesus Christ.
>
> O Blessed Mother obtain from Jesus a share of His Folly.
>
> The Kingdom of Heaven was promised not to the sensible and the educated but to such as have the spirit of little children.[33]

It is fitting that the body of Matt, the servant of God, should rest in a
tomb in a parish church in a poor area of central Dublin, awaiting
the verdict of the church.

In conclusion, I must mention a new community of men and
women living a most austere monastic life in the far west of Ireland,
entirely in the spirit of the Culdees and the fools for Christ's sake.
'Mary's Followers of the Cross', as they are called, were formed six
years ago as an off-shoot of the Legion of Mary, whose spirituality
has greatly influenced their own. They live in poverty and simplicity
in the outhouse of a cottage in an Irish-speaking seaside village in
Co. Galway, praying, eating and sleeping in one small room. They
have a rule of silence except during times of recreation and keep
seven hours of prayer, including two night offices, and, having only
laymen in the community, receive the sacraments in their parish
church. They have no apostolate except to visitors, who are
welcomed only if they wish to speak of the things of God; they read
nothing but the Bible and lives of the saints. There is no contact with
their families after admission to the community, and while solemn
vows are not yet taken since the community still awaits official
recognition from the diocesan bishop, they promise to observe
poverty, chastity and obedience.

The two modern sources of their spirituality are St Louis-Marie
Grignion de Montfort and St Thérèse of the Holy Child Jesus.
There is great stress on the Little Way, on simplicity, childlikeness,
smallness, and weakness. On their habits they wear a leather cross
with the inscription: 'My Greatest Treasure is My Weakness.' Their
leader explains that this is an attempt to take seriously the words
of Our Lord to St Paul at the end of the second letter to the
Corinthians.

I must realize that my weakness has been given to me by God
deliberately, and it has a specific purpose in my life, and according as I
understand this purpose and live according to it, will my life be pleasing to
God. Now the first reason for this weakness is that I may seek my strength in
God and not in myself, as St Paul said, 'It is in my weakness that I have my
strength'. According as I face up to my weakness will I turn away from
self-love and start to love God.[34]

Like the holy fools of Russia, Mary's Followers wander the streets
of nearby towns simulating madness, carrying bottles on the end of
a string and addressing them like little dogs; going into barbers'

shops and ordering a glass of Guinness; playing on children's amusements in department stores. In each case, like David, they say: 'I will make merry before the Lord, I will make myself yet more contemptible than this, and I will be abased in your eyes' (2 Sam. 6: 21f).

Ireland is indeed the Island of Saints, and her holy fools continue to reveal the power of the weak and little way. The prayer of the fool for Christ's sake—in Ireland as elsewhere, in our own century and at all times—is always the same; in the words of the Little Flower of Lisieux: 'Now I have no other desire than to love Jesus even unto folly.'[35]

12

Conclusion: Perfect Fools

In this book we have ranged from a discussion of undoubted fools for Christ's sake to a more general consideration of the motif of holy folly in authors and saints quite remote from the Eastern paradigm of folly. The intention of this chapter is to clarify the relationship between Christian perfection as such and the particular vocation of holy folly. It may be objected that to be perfect every Christian must be foolish *vis-à-vis* the world: as St Paul says, 'Be transformed by the renewal of your mind'—a precept which necessarily entails non-conformity to the world and thus to its wisdom (Rom. 12: 2). If perfection requires us to take up our cross and follow Christ, this will mean appearing foolish in the eyes of the world, for 'the word of the cross is folly to those who are perishing' (1 Cor. 1: 18). This primary, Pauline form of folly is incumbent upon all who seek perfection. There is, however, a second form of folly: some Christians are called a stage further, to be foolish in a particularly dramatic and symbolic way, not only in relation to the world but also, very often, in relation to the Church. This is the vocation of the fools for Christ's sake whose particular charism is to provoke and challenge their fellow Christians to remain faithful to folly in the first sense, the folly of the cross. We might, then, state this general rule: all saints are fools for Christ's sake, but some are called to be more foolish than others.

Perfection and Folly

Christians believe that, through the grace of God, man may be transfigured and that in such glorious change is the perfection, not the denial, of his humanity. The central affirmation of our faith is that God became man that man might become divine, that the perfect way to be human is to be divine, that the words of Jesus represent not an impossible dream but a pragmatic command: 'Be perfect, as your heavenly Father is perfect' (Matt. 5: 48).

In Christ, by the working of the Holy Spirit, we are changed: 'If anyone is in Christ, he is a new creation; the old has passed away, behold, the new has come' (2 Cor. 5: 17). In baptism we are reborn and remade and inherit a new birthright. We die out of the old world of sin and death and enter the glorious new life of the redeemed humanity. We are joined in the closest possible way to the risen Lord, becoming limbs of the Body of which he is the Head. Through the Spirit we are made coheirs with Christ of the unsearchable riches of divinity. Made in the image of God, in Christ we are restored to the full likeness: 'And we all, with unveiled face, beholding the glory of the Lord, are being changed into his likeness from one degree of glory to another; for this comes from the Lord who is the Spirit' (2 Cor. 3: 18).

Such change, a change wrought by sanctifying grace, is *real* change. But the end is not yet; we are still *in via*. 'Not that I have become perfect; I have not yet won, but I am still running, trying to capture the prize for which Christ Jesus captured me' (Phil. 3: 12). Christians are changed men, charged with becoming perfect men. The real change effected by baptism must, with our co-operation, extend and deepen itself within us until we 'become what we are'.

Christian perfection, then, is nothing less than the transformation of man by the Holy Spirit. It is the realization of baptism, the full revelation of our divine sonship. In the *Spiritual Canticle* St John of the Cross describes spiritual marriage, the nearest a soul may come to deification in this life:

It is a total transformation in the Beloved, wherein on either side there is made surrender by total possession of the one to the other with a certain consummation of union of love, wherein the soul is made divine and becomes God by participation, in so far as may be in this life.[1]

Such a state is a gift of God, but because of our sin and our failure to grow in holiness, it is rare. It must, however, be maintained that it is the definitive, the *normal* condition of the Christian, that which gives meaning to all his strivings. It is, as San Juan makes clear in an earlier passage, no more than the realization of the ineffable dignity and destiny given to man through the Incarnation.

And, looking upon them as he went, Left them, by his glance alone, clothed with beauty.

. . . And not only did He communicate to them their being and their natural graces when He beheld them, as we have said, but also in this image of His Son alone He left them clothed with beauty, communicating to them supernatural being. This was when He became man, and thus exalted man in the beauty of God, and consequently exalted all the creatures in Him, since in uniting Himself with man He united Himself with the nature of them all. Wherefore said the same Son of God: *Si ego exaltatus fuero a terra, omnia traham ad me ipsum.* That is: I, if I be lifted up from the earth, will draw all things unto Me. And thus, in this lifting up of the Incarnation of His Son, and in the glory of His resurrection according to the flesh, not only did the Father beautify the creatures in part, but we can say that He left them all clothed with beauty and dignity.[2]

In this book we have seen saints who were truly 'clothed in beauty and dignity' despite the poverty and weakness of their outward appearance; who, even in this life, were 'transformed in the Beloved', transfigured in the divine light: Columba, Louis-Marie, Benedict-Joseph, Seraphim. And there are many other examples of course, not all of whom, by any means, could be called holy fools. We can now see the significance of their transformation, the 'over-flowing of the soul's glory into the body', as St Thomas called it:[3] it is a foretaste of resurrection.

For Christians, normality, sanity, and wholeness are not ultimately determined by the criteria of psychiatry or sociology but by such configuration to Christ. He is the norm, and those most like him are the exemplars of his normality: 'It does not yet appear what we shall be, but we know that when he appears we shall be like him, for we shall see him as he is' (1 John 3: 2). The 'world', in the New Testament sense we have employed throughout this book of orga-nized opposition to God, cannot comprehend such eschatological normality and decries it as madness. To the world the saint is truly the odd man out, and the statement, 'it is no longer I who live, but Christ who lives in me' (Gal. 2: 20), seems sheer nonsense. In a word, if the world does not regard us as foolish it is probable that we are conformed to it.

Enthusiasm

If all authentic Christianity ought to seem mad to the world, why have only a relatively small number of saints been called to a life of folly? If eschatological folly is the vocation of all, what need is there for such a specific charism? This tension between the universal vocation of the Church and the particular vocation of individuals belongs to the mystery of sainthood and arises also in connection with the charism of prophecy. 'Would that *all* the Lord's people were prophets!' cried Moses (Num. 11: 29). But since they are not, and because of Israel's sin and failure to be true to the Covenant, God raises up and consecrates individual prophets to proclaim his word—while not, thereby, absolving Israel from her prophetic responsibility. On the contrary, the message of the individual concerns the kerygmatic vocation of the whole people to be a 'light to the nations' (cf. Isa. 49: 6). The multiplicity of offices, charisms, and forms of sanctity exists to enrich the whole Body: 'To each is given the manifestation of the Spirit for the common good' (1 Cor. 12: 7). Thus, while it is true that all saints are signs to the world of a transfigured humanity, the aim of the present book has been to draw out instances of that special vocation which emerges from time to time, especially when a certain harmony between Church and State encourages the Christian to hold back from a reckless following in the Way of the Cross, and to sink instead into a comfortable mediocrity.

The distinction between the universal Christian vocation to folly and the specific charism of folly for Christ's sake does not of itself do justice to the diversity and richness of the 'folly literature' presented in this book, but it allows a breadth to the terms of reference which have enabled us to include, for instance, the folly motif in the literature of monastic foundation or reform, the ideals of holy idiocy and spiritual infancy, the exponents of *iocunditas* and *hilaritas*—Christ's troubadours, jongleurs, and bards—and, above all, those who not only 'simulated' madness but who were 'really' mad. In regard to these last, we are not permitted by the tradition of holy folly any sentimentality about the horrors of insanity or the equation of 'breakdown' with 'breakthrough'—although on occasions the one may lead to the other. What the 'really' mad and the 'apparently' mad fools have in common is not so much the fact or nature of their madness as their consecration of suffering and humiliation to the service of Jesus Christ. In the case of Louise du Néant the two vocations were conjoined in one life: after her deliverance from 'real' madness, Louise chose to serve her Lord by feigning madness. In both parts of her life, however, she offered her weakness so that Christ's power might come to perfection in her.

These, then, are some of the kinds of holy folly we have examined, and we can see that all the categories of holy fool—the jesters and the 'really' mad as much as the classic *saloi*—fulfil the ministry we have outlined above, namely, that of a chosen part of the Body revealing the destiny of the whole. But, if we are to associate the various forms of folly, we must discover a common denominator other than the fact of folly itself—and that common denominator must surely be the fools' *enthusiasm* for God.

Thirty years ago Ronald Knox exposed the dangers of enthusiasm[4] so persuasively that we broach the subject with some diffidence. It is reassuring, therefore, that Hans Urs von Balthasar, perhaps the greatest living Catholic theologian, has himself vindicated the concept in his magisterial work, *Herrlichkeit*. To be transported or enraptured by the wondrous love of God Incarnate is, says Balthasar, the heart of Christianity.[5] Consequently, he explains, nearly all the great theologies in the history of the Catholic Church have been 'constructed amateurishly (when judged by the scientific norms of the present day), by "lovers" and "enthusiasts" of the Word of God'.[6] While arguing vigorously against any 'aestheticizing' of theology, he reminds us of the rhapsodic nature of so much Patristic theology: the Fathers composed not only polemical and dogmatic treatises but also personal confessions, meditations, richly imaginative and symbolically developed commentaries. They were truly enraptured by the truth and glory of God.

In theology, in prayer and in worship, as in every aspect of Christian existence, we are invited to be carried away, to go out of ourselves, by the Word of God who in his ecstasy leapt down from heaven and became man. Such enthusiasm is, of course, a 'serious game', as St Bernard said, a 'sober inebriation', according to St Gregory of Nyssa, not the dionysiac frenzy associated with certain sects. It takes us out of our *selves*, out of our fallen, finite egos; it does not gratify the instinct for excitement. Christian enthusiasm, folly, rapture, and delight have as their precise object the figure of the Word made flesh, and our joy in him is expressed and preserved by the dogma and discipline of Holy Church. Orthodoxy means right belief, right joy, and right glory. The enthusiasm of Christ's fools carries them away, out of the confines of the present age and into the heart of the Church and Holy Tradition.

The Folly of the Apostle

One last question remains: how far can the charism of holy folly be contained within the ordered structure of the Church? Could not the part end up by disrupting the whole instead of sustaining its life? Throughout this book it has been stressed that the fools for Christ have always, even when persecuted by ecclesiastical authority, remained faithful to the Bride of Christ. Our question, however, takes us further than mere consideration of the position of the fools in the Church; it raises the theological problem of the relationship between charism and institution.

In the last hundred years theologians have given this matter a great deal of attention. Newman's understanding of the 'idea' of the Church has been seminal,[7] and Eastern Orthodox theologians have made a vital contribution by their stress on the importance of the dogma of the Holy Trinity (especially the complementarity of the 'economy of the Son' and the 'economy of the Spirit') in achieving a right balance in ecclesiology between charism and institution.[8] Similarly, the Vatican II Dogmatic Constitution on the Church affirms that 'extraordinary gifts' must be tested and discerned by those in authority: 'Those who have charge over the Church should judge the genuineness and proper use of these gifts through their office, not indeed to extinguish the Spirit, but to test all things and hold fast to what is good.'[9] A Church without charism would be no more than an authoritarian organization; a Church without hierarchy would be an anarchic rabble. Charism and institution are necessarily interdependent.

In the case of the first man to call himself a fool for Christ's sake, the charism of holy folly and hierarchical office coincide: folly was an essential part of Paul's apostolic ministry to the Corinthians. From this we can legitimately infer that there is a kind of holy folly implicit in the apostolic office, a folly which the grace of ordination does not guarantee but, when the occasion arises, does empower. In virtue of his consecration the apostolic minister is delivered to exposure, to the painful manifestation of his weakness and his dependence on grace. The late Austin Farrer, preaching at a priest's first Mass, put it thus:

None of us can be let off being Christ in our place and station: we are all pigmies in giant's armour. We have to put up with it: it's the price (how small a price!) paid for the supreme mercy of God, that he does not wait for our dignity or our perfection, but just puts himself there in our midst; in this bread and wine; in this priest; in this Christian man, woman or child. . . . If Jesus is willing to be in us, and to let us show him to the world, it's a small thing that we should endure being fools for Christ's sake, and be shown up by the part we have to play.[10]

This apostolic, ministerial folly manifests itself supremely in the Petrine Office. What the Christian is to the world, what the individual fool is to his fellow Christians, what the bishop or priest may well have to be for their flocks, the Pope is called to be for the whole Church: the one in whose weakness Christ's power comes to perfection.

Peter is the chosen rock of Christ precisely because he is the weakest, the most foolish of the disciples. He is the one who always asks the questions, who always speaks first; the one who proclaims the faith of the Church but who sometimes misses the point. He is the leader of the apostolic choir, the one who voices the fears, as well as the faith, of the others. Peter is a kind of court jester, the representative fool who asks the question everyone else wants to ask but dares not: 'Lord, do you wash my feet?' (John 13: 6.) The Rock on which Christ builds his Church (Matt. 16: 18) is the stumbling-block who rebukes the Lord (Matt. 16: 22); the man with the keys of the kingdom (Matt. 16: 19) denies and disowns the Lord three times (Matt. 26: 69ff); Blessed Simon Bar-Jona, the man of faith (Matt. 16: 17), is also Satan, the tempter (Matt. 16: 23). In Peter, according to St Gregory Palamas, we see Adam, we see ourselves, our weak and foolish humanity transformed by the grace of God. Peter is truly a perfect fool, one who has been purified through penitence, brokenness, and tears. That is why he is the Rock; that is why he is the supreme pastor who feeds Christ's lambs.

Balthasar has used the Petrine paradoxes in the New Testament to illuminate the office of the papacy, the awesome charge laid upon St Peter's successors. The Pope has supreme jurisdiction, indeed, infallibility when he speaks *ex cathedra*, precisely because his role is one of humiliation, of being the servant of the servants of God. At moments of crisis, when prophetic leadership in the Church is required, the Pope stands alone, and, if need be, he is the scapegoat for the whole Church and the butt of the world's derision and misunderstanding. Then all eyes are upon him. He is a spectacle to angels and to men. And, true to form, the worldly wise laugh:

> They have all the laughs on their side. But Peter must have seemed fairly laughable too when he was crucified upside down; it was simply a good joke, simply an allusion to the Rabbi Yod, reducing the tragic opera to the level of a review, turning Bach into jazz, his own juice running down unremittingly

into his nostrils and, as a motto over his toes, the inscription in all languages of the world: *summus pontifex christianorum*. . . . Woe indeed to us if there is not a point where our common sins are concentrated and become visible, just as the poison circulating in an organism is concentrated at one point and breaks out as an abscess. And therefore blessed the office—whether it is the pope or the bishops or simple priests who stand firm, or anyone else who feels responsible when people start saying 'the Church should do this and that'—which offers itself to fulfil this function, to be the seat of the illness. There is no honour to be won in this role, but if the crowd is to have its fun, a face is needed which one can slap in order to try one's own strength.[11]

And they all condemned him as deserving death. And some began to spit on him, and to cover his face, and to strike him, saying to him, 'Prophesy!'

Notes

For the sake of brevity references have been given wherever possible to English translations, whether used or not. Exceptions to this rule give an English translation in brackets when there is some reason for quoting the original source or where I have been unable to check page numbers in the translation.

ABBREVIATIONS USED IN THE NOTES

AA.SS.	*Acta Sanctorum* (Antwerp, 1643ff)
Anal. Boll.	*Analecta Bollandiana* (Paris and Brussels, 1882ff)
ACW	Ancient Christian Writers. The Works of the Fathers in Translation (Westminster, Maryland-London, 1946ff)
ASOC	*Analecta Sacri Ordinis Cisterciensis* (Rome, 1945ff)
BHG	*Bibliotheca Hagiographica Graeca*, 3rd edn by F. Halkin (3 vols, Brussels, 1957)
BHO	*Bibliotheca Hagiographica Orientalis*, ediderunt Socii Bollandiani (Subsidia Hagiographica, x, Brussels, 1910)
BN	Bibliothèque Nationale, Paris
COCR	*Collectanea Ordinis Cisterciensium reformatorum* (Rome, 1934ff)
CP	Cistercian Publications (Spencer, Washington, Kalamazoo, 1970ff)
CSEL	*Corpus Scriptorum Ecclesiasticorum Latinorum* (Vienna, 1866ff)
DHGE	*Dictionnaire d'Histoire et de Géographie Ecclésiastiques*, ed. A. Baudrillart et al. (1912ff)
DS	*Dictionnaire de Spiritualité* (Paris 1932ff)
ET or tr.	English translation
HBS	Henry Bradshaw Society (1891ff)
ITS	Irish Texts Society (London, 1899ff)
JRS	*Journal of Roman Studies* (London 1911ff)
MGH	*Monumenta Germaniae Historica*
NPNF	Nicene and Post-Nicene Fathers (New York 1887–1892; Oxford 1890–1900)
PG	*Patrologia Graeca*, ed. J. P. Migne (162 vols, Paris, 1857–1866)
PL	*Patrologia Latina*, ed. J. P. Migne (221 vols, Paris, 1844–1864)
PO	*Patrologia Orientalis*, ed. R. Graffin and F. Nau (Paris 1907ff)

RAM   *Revue d'ascétique et de mystique* (Toulouse, 1920–1971)
RSR   *Recherches de Science Religieuse* (Paris, 1910ff)
SC   Sources Chrétiennes (Paris, 1940ff)
SSSOC   *Series Scriptorum Sacri Ordinis Cisterciensis*
TU   Texte und Untersuchungen zur Geschichte der altchrist-
             lichen Literatur, begründet von O. von Gebhardt und
             A. Harnack (Leipzig, 1882ff)

CHAPTER 1 (pp. 1–11)

1. In Islamic tradition there is, for example, the figure of the saintly buffoon, Nasr-ed-Din, whose mausoleum at Aqshehir is still venerated as a place of pilgrimage. See E. Welsford, *The Fool: His Social and Literary History* (London, 1935), pp. 29ff. See pp. 55ff on some fools in India and the Far East.
2. On 'symbolic actions', see J. Lindblom, *Prophecy in Ancient Israel* (Oxford, 1962), pp. 165ff.
3. M. Buber, *Tales of the Hasidim: The Early Masters* (New York, 1947), p. 26.
4. The primary theological source of the tradition is the person, work, and teaching of Our Lord himself. Moreover, as we shall see, his apostle St Peter should be regarded as a holy fool. Nevertheless, it was St Paul who coined the phrase 'fool for Christ's sake' and is therefore the original 'doctor of folly'.
5. ET, *The Homilies of St John Chrysostom on the First Epistle to the Corinthians*, viii (Oxford, 1839), p. 453.
6. See especially the study of A. Feuillet, *Le Christ, Sagesse de Dieu* (Paris, 1966).
7. On *sarx* see J. A. T. Robinson, *The Body: A Study in Pauline Theology* (London, 1952), pp. 15ff.
8. On the evolution of *mōros*, see the *Dictionnaire étymologique de la langue grècque*, ed. P. Chantraine, vol. iii (Paris, 1974), p. 731.
9. *Antigone*, 1. 469f, ed. R. Jebb, 3rd edn (Cambridge, 1900), p. 731.
10. St Gregory Nazianzen, 'We needed an incarnate God, a God put to death, that we might live', *Oration* xlv, 28; ET, *Select Orations*, tr. C. G. Browne and J. E. Swallow, NPNF vii (Oxford, 1894), p. 433.
11. *New Testament Theology*, ET (London, 1971), p. 180f.
12. Ibid., p. 182.
13. See J. Jeremias, *The Prayers of Jesus*, ET (London, 1967), pp. 11ff.
14. J. Galot, *La Conscience de Jésus* (Paris, 1971), p. 90f.
15. *Ad Autolycum* ii, 25; ed. and tr. R. M. Grant (Oxford, 1970), p. 66f.
16. ET, *The Writings of Irenaeus*, ii, 22, 4 and iv, 38, 3; tr. A. Roberts and W. H. Rambaut (Edinburgh, 1868), vols i and ii.
17. *On the Epiphany* ii, 3; ET, *Letters and Sermons of St Leo the Great*, tr. C. L. Feltoe, NPNF xii (Oxford, 1895).

CHAPTER 2 (pp. 12–30)

1. Op. cit., lxxii; ET, R. T. Meyer, ACW, x (Washington, 1950).
2. 'First Conference of Abbot Moses', i, 2,; ET, E. C. S. Gibson in NPNF xi (Oxford and New York, 1894).
3. *Sayings of the Desert Fathers*, Arsenius, 6; ET, Benedicta Ward (London, 1975), p. 8.
4. See his *De la Sainteté et des devoirs de la vie monastique*, vol. ii (Paris, 1683), pp. 290ff.
5. Op. cit., iv, 41; ET, E. C. S. Gibson, NPNF xi (see n. 2).
6. As a modern scholar has written, 'the individual traits and utterances characteristic of the holy fools are already found in the monasticism of the earliest period' (Ernst Benz, 'Heilige Narrheit', *Kyrios* iii (1938), 4).
7. Op. cit., xxxvii; ET, R. T. Meyer, ACW, xxxiv (London, 1965).
8. Ibid., xxxiv. See also the life of St Isidora, *AA.SS.*, May, p. 50.
9. *Sayings of the Desert Fathers*, op. cit. (see n. 3), Ammonas, 9, p. 24. See also the saying of St Antony on madness, ibid., 25, p. 5.
10. 'The Longer Rule of St Basil', viii, 3; ET, *The Ascetical Works*, tr. Sr M. M. Wagner (Washington, 1962).
11. *The Life of St Antony*, xiv, op. cit. (see n. 1).
12. *The God-Possessed*, ET, Roy Monkcom (London, 1961), p. 102.
13. Ed. M. Léon Chagnet in *Revue de l'orient chrétien*, v (1900), 60f.
14. *Lives of the Eastern Saints*, ed. and tr. E. W. Brooks, *PO* (Paris 1923), xix, 164.
15. Ibid., 166f.
16. Ibid., 169f.
17. For the Syriac life, see *BHO*, pp. 10ff, nn. 36ff; for the Greek, *BHG* i, pp. 15ff, nn. 51ff. See also F. M. Esteves Pereira, 'Légende grècque de l'homme de Dieu S. Alexis', *Anal. Boll.* xix (1900), 243ff. H.-M. Boudon, whom we shall study later, like other seventeenth-century writers, held up St Alexios as a model of renunciation. See 'La Vie cachée avec Jésus en Dieu', ii, 6, *Oeuvres complètes de Boudon* ed. J. P. Migne, vol. i (Paris, 1856), p. 590.
18. *Vita S. Symeonis Sali Confessoris* vi, ed. L. Rydén (Stockholm, Goteborg and Uppsala, 1963), p. 145f. On St Simeon and St Andrew see H. Urs von Balthasar, *Herrlichkeit. Eine theologische Ästhetik*, Band iii/1 (Einsiedeln, 1965), pp. 496ff.
19. Ibid., p. 149.
20. Nicephorus, *Vita S. Andreae Sali*, ed. S. Murray (Borna-Leipsig, 1910). It is presented as the work of Nicephorus, priest of the Greek Church in the reign of the Emperor Leo I (457–474), but in fact it was written in the tenth century in the reign of Leo VI (886–912).
21. Ibid., ccxlii.
22. Ibid.
23. 'The Life of St Andrew the Fool', TU cvii, *Studia Patristica* v (1970), p. 317.
24. For lives of the early monks, see *Paterik Kievo-Pecherskaion monastyria*, ed. D. I. Abramovich (St Petersburg, 1911). It should

perhaps be pointed out that St Isaac stands somewhat alone as a fool in Kievan Russia and has no obvious successor there.

25. Nestor, 'A Life of St Theodosius', in *A Treasury of Russian Spirituality*, ed. G. P. Fedotov (London, 1950), p. 20.

26. For details of the life of St Procopius, see I. Kovalevskii, *Iurodstvo o Khriste i khrista radi iurodivye rostochnoi i russkoi tserkvi* (Moscow, 1895), pp. 161ff.

27. See his *Of the Russe Common Wealth* (London, 1588), ed. E. A. Bond in *Russia at the Close of the Sixteenth Century* (London, 1856).

28. For details of the life of St Basil, see Kovalevskii, op. cit., (n. 26), pp. 212ff. For the incident at Novgorod, see G. P. Fedotov, *The Russian Religious Mind*, vol. ii (Cambridge, Mass., 1966), p. 338.

29. This should not be exaggerated. In September 1978 the Russian Orthodox Church Outside Russia canonized the eighteenth-century fool, Blessed Xenia of St Petersburg.

30. See H. Urs von Balthasar, 'Der Christ als Idiot. Dostojewskij', *Herrlichkeit*, op. cit. (n. 18), pp. 535ff.

31. For details of Bukharev's live, see N. Gorodetsky, *The Humiliated Christ in Modern Russian Thought* (London, 1938), pp. 115ff; and also E. Behr-Sigel, *Alexandre Boukharev*, Un théologien de l'Église orthodoxe russe en dialogue avec le monde moderne (Paris, 1977).

32. Cited in Gorodetsky, op. cit., p. 120f.

33. I. Kologrivoff, *Essai sur la sainteté en Russie* (Bruges, 1953), p. 261f.

34. 'Heilige Narrheit', op. cit. (n. 6), p. 12.

35. Ibid.

36. *The Creation of Man*, xi; ET, W. Moore and H. A. Wilson, in NPNF v (New York, 1893).

37. *St Augustine on the Psalms* xli, 13; ET, vol iii (Oxford, 1849).

38. Christos Yannaras, 'I "Kata Christon sali" kai i arnisi tis antikimenikis ithikis', *Christianikon simposion* iv (1970), p. 65.

39. 'The Rise and Function of the Holy Man in Late Antiquity', *JRS* lxi (1971), 83.

40. Ibid., p. 92. On the avoidance of women and bishops, see Cassian, *Inst.* xi, 18; op. cit. (n. 5).

41. 'Die "Narren um Christi Willen" in der Ostkirche', *Kirche im Osten* ii (1959), 36.

42. Op. cit. (n. 38), p. 65.

43. E. Behr-Sigel, 'Les Fous pour le Christ et la sainteté laïque dans l'ancien Russie', *Irénikon* xv (1936), p. 536.

44. G. P. Fedotov, *The Russian Religious Mind*, op. cit. (n. 28), p. 320. See also the important entry 'Fous pour le Christ', *DS* v, 757ff, by F. Vandenbroucke.

CHAPTER 3 (pp. 31–47)

1. Section 15; *Vatican Council II. The Conciliar and Post-Conciliar Documents*, ed. and tr. A. Flannery (Dublin, 1975), p. 465f.

2. N. K. Chadwick, *The Age of the Saints in the Early Celtic Church* (Oxford, 1961), p. 60.
3. The mission of Palladius is recorded by Prosper of Aquitaine, *Chron.* AD 431; *PL* 51.595B; *MGH, Auctores Antiquissimi* ix (1892), p. 473. One of the most venerated pre-Patrician saints is St Declan of Ardmore, whose twelfth-century Irish life has been edited and translated by P. Power, ITS xvi (London, 1914). On 'The Coming of the Faith' to Ireland, see J. F. Kenney, *The Sources for the Early History of Ireland: Ecclesiastical*. An Introduction and Guide (New York, 1929), pp. 157ff.
4. J. Ryan, *Irish Monasticism*. Origins and Early Development (Dublin and Cork, 1931), p. 189. See also K. Hughes, *The Church in Early Irish Society* (London, 1966), part 2, especially pp. 32–90.
5. *Serm.* xxiii, 1; *CSEL* 21.314.
6. E. Bishop, *Liturgia Historica.* Papers on the Liturgy and Religious Life of the Western Church (Oxford, 1918), p. 280; C. Beeson, *Isidor-Studien* (Munich, 1913), pp. 129ff. According to L. Bieler, it is conceivable that some of the works of Isidore arrived in Ireland before their author's death ('La transmission des Pères latins en Irlande et en Angleterre à l'époque préscolastique', *Sacris Erudiri* xxii (1974–1975), 80).
7. See especially his 'The East, Visigothic Spain and the Irish', TU lxxix, *Studia Patristica* iv (1961), 441ff; and 'Old Ireland and Visigothic Spain', *Old Ireland*, ed. R. McNally (Dublin, 1965), pp. 200ff.
8. Leontius of Neapolis, *The Life of St John the Almsgiver* ix; ET in *Three Byzantine Saints*, tr. Dawes and Baynes (Oxford, 1948).
9. St Isidore of Seville, *Etymologiae*, ix, 11.110; *PL* 82.339A.
10. See S. Ruiz, 'Britonia', *DHGE* 10.767ff.
11. M. Martins, *Correntes da filosofia religiosa em Braga* (Porto, 1950), pp. 23ff.
12. PL 74.381ff; See J. Madoz, 'Martin de Braga. En el xiv centenario de su advenimento a la Peninsula (550–1950)', *Estudios eclesiasticos* xxv (1951), 219ff. Mention should also be made of Paschasius of Dumium's translation of the Apophthegmata (ed. J. G. Freire (Coimbra, 1974)).
13. Of paramount significance in the stabilizing of Spain was the conversion of the Visigothic ruler, Recared, to Catholicism in 587. See F. Görres, 'Rekared der Katholiker', *Z. wiss. Theol.* xlii (1899), 270ff.
14. *The Irish Tradition* (Oxford, 1947), p. 63f.
15. Chadwick, op. cit. (n. 2), p. 109.
16. N. K. Chadwick, 'Geilt', *Scottish Gaelic Studies* v (1942), 106. See also P. L. Henry, *The Early English and Celtic Lyric* (London, 1966), pp. 198ff.
17. *Buile Shuibhne* (The Frenzy of Suibhne), being The Adventures of Suibhne Geilt. A Middle Irish Romance, ed. and tr. J. G. O'Keeffe, ITS xii (London, 1913).
18. P. Ó Riain, 'The Materials and Provenance of "Buile Shuibhne"', *Éigse* xv (1973–1974), 186f.
19. *Thesaurus Palaeohibernicus.* A Collection of Old-Irish Glosses, Scholia, Prose and Verse, ed. W. Stokes and J. Strachan, vol. ii (Cambridge,

1903), p. 294.

20. *Buile* (n. 17), sec. 11, p. 14.

21. Ibid., sec. 27, p. 40.

22. *Early Irish Lyrics. Eighth to Twelfth Century*, ed. and tr. G. Murphy (Oxford, 1956), p. 113.

23. Ibid., p. 129.

24. Ibid., p. 139f.

25. *Buile*, sec. 85, p. 156.

26. Ibid., p. xxxiv.

27. Ó Riain, op. cit. (n. 18).

28. *Buile*, sec. 80, p. 144.

29. For bibliography on the *céili dé*, see Kenney, op. cit. (n. 3), pp. 468ff. See also K. Hughes, op. cit. (n. 4), pp. 173ff; and P. O'Dwyer, *The Spirituality of the Céili Dé Reform Movement in Ireland 750–790* (Dublin, 1977).

30. According to the Irish text collated from two manuscripts by W. Stokes, 'The Birth and Life of St Moling', *Revue celtique* xxvii (1906), pp. 275ff.

31. *The Martyrology of Oengus*, ed. W. Stokes, HBS xxix (London, 1905), pp. 154ff.

32. Stokes, op. cit. (n. 30), p. 270.

33. J. Carney, '"Suibhne Geilt" and "The Children of Lir"', *Éigse* vi (1948–1952), 83. Carney's hypothesis has been challenged by K. Jackson, who has argued that the nucleus of the Suibhne legend originated in the Goidelic Kingdom of Dál Riada, whence it was developed independently by the Irish, who attached it to the battle of Moira, and by the Welsh of Strathclyde, who attached it to the battle of Arfderydd ('A further Note on Suibhne Geilt and Merlin', *Éigse* vii (1953–1955)). See also Professor A. O. H. Jarmon's inaugural lecture, *The Legend of Merlin* (Cardiff, 1960), *passim*; and R. P. Lehmann, 'A Study of the Buile Shuibhne', *Études celtiques* vii (1955–1956), 115ff.

34. RIA, MS D. iv. 1. All quotations that follow are taken from an unpublished translation by Professor Gearóid MacEoin of University College, Galway. Mac-dá-Cherda is never referred to as a *geilt* but as *óinmit* (modern Irish, *óinmhid*), which has been etymologized as *onment, 'lamb-witted'.

35. Sec. 17.

36. Sec. 30.

37. Sec. 59; poem 11.

38. *Lives of Saints from The Book of Lismore*, ed. W. Stokes (Oxford, 1890), p. 193.

39. Ó Riain, 'A Study of the Irish Legend of the Wild Men', *Éigse* xiv (1971–1972), 182f.

40. The Armagh text of Sulpicius Severus's *Life of St Martin* may well have come to Ireland from Gaul before 460 (see Kenney, op. cit. (n. 3), p. 668).

41. *The Life of St Martin*, i, 3, 2; ET, Alexander Roberts, in NPNF xi, p. 5.

42. *The Irish Liber Hymnorum*, ed. J. H. Barnard, vol. i, HBS xiii (London, 1890), pp. 62ff.

43. Adomnán's *Life of Columba*, lxxxiii A, ed. and tr. A. O. and M. O. Anderson (Edinburgh, 1961), p. 408.
44. D. J. Chitty, *The Desert a City*. An Introduction to the Study of Egyptian and Palestinian Monasticism under the Christian Empire (Oxford, 1966), p. 6.
45. Evagrius Ponticus, *Praktikos* xcii; ET, J. E. Bamberger in CP (Washington, 1970).
46. Chadwick, 'Geilt', op. cit. (n. 16), p. 136.
47. Chadwick, *Age* (n. 2), p. 82; also the important article by T. M. Charles-Edwards, 'The Social Background to Irish *Peregrinatio*', *Celtica* xi (1976), 43ff.
48. See *Navigatio Sancti Brendani Abbatis*, ed. C. Selmer (Notre Dame, 1959); ET, 'The Voyage of St Brendan', tr. J. F. Webb in *Lives of the Saints*, Penguin Classics, 1965.
49. *Two of the Saxon Chronicles, Parallel*, ed. C. Plummer, vol. i (Oxford, 1897) p. 82.
50. Adomnán, op. cit (n. 43), p. 186.
51. *V. Gal.*, i, 30; *PL* 114.1004; *MGH, Scriptores Rerum Merovingicarum* iv (1902), p. 308.
52. *Serm.* viii, 2; *Opera*, ed. and tr. G. S. M. Walker (Dublin, 1957), p. 96.
53. *Lives of Saints*, op. cit. (n. 38), p. 259f.
54. Cited in Chadwick, *Age* (n. 2), p. 83.
55. *Aux sources de la spiritualité occidentale*. Étapes et constantes (Paris, 1964), p. 51. The whole of ch. ii of this work is dedicated to the theme of 'Monachisme et Pérégrination'.
56. J. Raftery, 'Ex Oriente. . .', *J. Royal Society of Antiquaries of Ireland*, xcv (1965), 204.
57. 'Les Commencements du christianisme en Pologne et la mission irlandaise', *Annuaire de la société des sciences de Posen* (1902); summarized by L. Leger, *Revue celtique* xxvi (1905), 389.
58. M. L. Abraham, 'Mnisi irlandzcy w Kijowie', *Bulletin international de l'académie des sciences de Cracovie* vii (1901), 137; summarized in *Rev. Ben.* xix (1902), p. 294. See also B. Leib, *Rome, Kiev et Byzance à la fin du xie siècle*. Rapports religieux des Latins et des Greco-Russes sous le Pontificat d'Urbain II (1088–1099) (Paris, 1924), p. 90, and J. Hennig, 'Irish Monastic Activities in Eastern Europe', *Irish Ecclesiastical Record* lxv (1945), 394ff.
59. Abraham, op. cit. The Russian fool, Ivan the Hairy (d. 1581), seems to have been a Latin, perhaps a wandering monk. Until recently a Latin psalter lay on his sepulchre in Rostov. On one page there is an inscription dating from the beginning of the eighteenth century: 'Since the time of the death of blessed Ivan the Hairy and Merciful down to our days upon his sepulchre there was this book, a very old one, the Psalter of David, in Latin dialect, which the saint of God used to read in praying' (Fedotov, *The Russian Religious Mind*, vol. ii (Cambridge, Mass., 1966), p. 326).
60. *Martyrology of Oengus*, op. cit. (n. 31), p. 10f.
61. MS Rawlinson B.512, fo. 141B, 2; ed. and tr. K. Meyer, *The Gaelic*

Journal iv (1893), 229.
62. *Ep.* ii, 3; *Opera*, ed. and tr. G. S. M. Walker (n. 52), p. 14f.
63. *Thesaurus*, vol. ii. p. 246.
64. Op. cit. (n. 43) iv B, v A, p. 186.
65. Ibid., cxix Bff; pp. 504ff.

CHAPTER 4 (pp. 48–57)

1. 'Notes for a Philosophy of Solitude', *Disputed Questions* (London, 1961), p. 199.
2. *The Golden Epistle of Abbot William of St Thierry*, ET, W. Shewring (London, 1930), p. 10f.
3. Ibid., p. 9. 'In merriment of heart' translates *hilariter.*
4. See G. Tabacco, 'Romualdo di Ravenna e gli inizi dell'eremitismo camaldolese' in *L'eremitismo in occidente nei secoli XI e XII* (Rome, 1965), pp. 73ff.
5. St Peter Damian, *Vita Romualdi*, vii, ed. G. Tabacco (Rome, 1957), p. 41. Another important life is St Bruno of Querfurt's *Vita quinque fratrum*, ed. R Kade, *MGH, Scriptores*, xv, 709ff.
6. *St Pierre Damien.* Ermite et homme d'église (Rome, 1960), p. 96. I am also indebted to Dom Leclercq for another of the concepts in this book and chapter: the 'Gospel of Good Humour'. (See *Le défi de la vie contemplative* (Paris, 1970), especially pp. 360ff.)
7. St Peter Damian, op. cit. (n. 5), xxxvi, p. 77.
8. Ibid., xxxi, p. 68.
9. *The Divine Comedy* III, xxi; tr. J. D. Sinclair (London, 1946), p. 308.
10. *St Peter Damian*, Selected Writings, tr. P. McNulty (London, 1959), p. 80.
11. Leclercq, *Damien*, op. cit. (n. 6), p. 49f.
12. McNulty, op. cit. (n. 10), p. 54. See also J. Gonsette, *Pierre Damien et la culture profane* (Paris, 1956), *passim.*
13. *Ep. ad Greg. Thaum., PG* 11.89D. For a masterly discussion of 'spolia aegyptiorum', see von Balthasar, *Herrlichkeit*, op. cit. (ch. 2, n. 18), pp. 287ff.
14. *Op.* xxxii, 9; *PL* 145.560C.
15. 'The Prescriptions against the Heretics' vii, in *Early Latin Theology*, tr. S. L. Greenslade (London, 1956), p. 35f. On *simplicitas*, see J. Leclercq, 'Sancta simplicitas', *COCR* xxii (1960), 138ff; and *Etudes sur le vocabulaire monastique du Moyen Âge* (Rome, 1961), pp. 31ff.
16. *Hexaemeron*, i, 6, 22; ET, John J. Savage (New York, 1961), p. 20.
17. *Op.* xlv (*De sancta simplicitate scientiae inflanti anteponenda*), 3, *PL* 145. 697B.
18. *Serm.* lvii; *PL* 144.824B.
19. *Serm.* vi; *PL* 144.535Cf.
20. *Op.* lvii, 1, 4; *PL* 145.823B.
21. *Ep.* i; *PL* 144.205A, and *passim.*
22. *Op.* xv, l; *PL* 145.335C.
23. *Op.* xxiii; *PL* 145.471Dff.

24. Cited by Dom Yves Gourdel in his excellent article on Carthusian spirituality in *DS*, ii, p. 730.
25. *Ep. ad Raoul le Verd.* vi, in *Lettres des premiers Chartreux*, vol. i, ed. A Carthusian, SC (Paris, 1962), p. 70.
26. *Acta* xli; *PL* 152.418D.
27. G. K. Chesterton, *Orthodoxy* (London, 1969), p. 277.
28. *De fug. saec.* (Ep. i); *PL* 153.885C.

CHAPTER 5 (pp. 58–79)

(Unless an English translation is given, references to St Bernard are to the complete works in the Latin critical edition prepared by Jean Leclercq OSB, C. H. Talbot and Henri Rochais OSB, published in eight volumes by Editiones Cistercienses, Rome, and abbreviated here to show editors, year and page number.)

1. *The Letters of St Bernard of Clairvaux*, tr. B. Scott James (London, 1953), p. 130. In this collection Letter 87 appears as Letter 90.
2. Ibid., p. 130.
3. Ibid., p. 130.
4. See J. Leclercq, 'Le Thème de la jonglerie chez St Bernard et ses contemporains', *Rev. d'hist. de la spir.* xlviii (1972), pp. 393ff; and ' "Ioculator et saltator". St Bernard et l'image du jongleur dans les manuscrits', *Translatio Studii*. Manuscript and Literary Studies honoring O. L. Kapsner OSB, ed. J. G. Plante (Collegeville, 1973), pp. 124ff.
5. In all that I say here of 'marginality' I am indebted to the writing of Dom Jean Leclercq, especially an unpublished paper, 'Monasticism and One World', delivered at the 1973 Orthodox-Cistercian Symposium in Oxford.
6. Conrad of Eberbach, *Exordium magnum Cisterciense* i, 12; ed. B. Griesser (Rome, 1961), p. 64. (ET forthcoming in CP).
7. *The Mirror of Faith* liv, ed. M-M. Davy, SC (Paris, 1959), p. 71; ET, T. X. Davis, CP (Kalamazoo, 1969).
8. Ibid.
9. ET, *On the Nature and Dignity of Love*, tr. G. Webb and A. Walker (London, 1956).
10. *Serm. 3 in Nat.* ii; Leclercq and Rochais (1966), p. 259.
11. *Serm. 1 in Nat.* i; Leclercq and Rochais (1966), p. 245.
12. *On Conversion* ed. and tr. W. Williams (London, 1938), p. 1.
13. *Serm. 66 in Cant.* iv, 10; Leclercq, Talbot and Rochais (1958), p. 185; ET, *On the Song of Songs*, tr. K. Walsh and I. N. Edmonds, CP (Kalamazoo, 1979).
14. 'The First Sermon for Christmas' i; ET, *Liturgical Sermons* I, tr. Monks of St Bernard Abbey, CP (Shannon, 1970), p. 38.
15. Ibid., ii, p. 38.
16. Ibid., p. 39.

17. Ibid., p. 39.
18. Ibid., p. 41.
19. *Exord. Magn.* (n. 6) iv, 16, p. 242.
20. Ibid.
21. St Benedict himself speaks of the 'school of the Lord's service' in the Prologue to his Rule. On the *Schola caritatis* theme in Bernard, see E. Gilson, *The Mystical Theology of St Bernard*, ET (London, 1940), pp. 60ff.
22. *Serm. 121 de div.* i; Leclercq and Rochais (1970), p. 398.
23. *Serm. 40 de div.* i, p. 234.
24. *Serm. 3 in Pentec.* v; Leclercq and Rochais (1968), p. 173.
25. John Rylands Library Latin MS 196, fo. 10^v.
26. *The Enigma of Faith*, xi; tr. W. J. D. Anderson, CP (Washington, 1974), p. 43.
27. *Serm. 1 in sol. ap. Pet. et Paul* iii; Leclercq and Rochais (1968), p. 189.
28. Walter Daniel, *The Life of Ailred of Rievaulx* v; ed. and tr. F. M. Powicke (London, 1950), p. 11f.
29. Ibid., xv, p. 24.
30. *Metalogicon* ii, 10; ed. C. C. J. Webb (Oxford, 1909).
31. *Serm. 69 in Cant.* ii; Leclercq, Talbot and Rochais (1958), p. 203; ET, *Sermon on the Song of Songs*, tr. S. Eales (London, 1895).
32. *Vita Prima Bernardi* v, 25; Select ET, *St Bernard of Clairvaux*, tr. Geoffrey Webb and Adrian Walker (London, 1960).
33. 'Roger of Byland's Letter to a Young Scholar' ed. C. H. Talbot, *ASOC* vii (1951), 218f.
34. J. Leclercq, 'The Intentions of the Founders of the Cistercian Order', in *The Cistercian Spirit. A Symposium in Memory of Thomas Merton*, ed. M. Basil Pennington in CP (Spenser, 1970), p. 123. See also his 'Aux Origines bibliques du vocabulaire de la pauvreté and 'Les Controverses sur la pauvreté du Christ', in *Études sur l'histoire de la pauvreté. Moyen âge-XVIe siècle*, ed. M. Mollat, vol. i (Paris, 1974), pp. 36ff and 46ff.
35. *Serm. 9 in ps. Qui hab.* v; Leclercq and Rochais (1966), p. 439.
36. *Exord. magn.* (n. 6), iii, 22, p. 202f.
37. ET, *Exposition on the Song of Songs*, tr. Mother Columba Hart OSB, CP (Spencer, 1970), p. 54f.
38. *Life of Aelred* (n. 28), xxix; pp. 36ff (see n. 28).
39. D. Knowles, *The Monastic Order in England. A History of its Development from the Times of St Dunstan to the Fourth Lateran Council, 943–1216* (Cambridge, 1949), p. 259.
40. Jocelin of Furness on Aelred in his Life of St Waldef (*AA.SS.*, Aug., 1, p. 257).
41. *Sermones inediti B. Aelredi Abbatis Rievallensis*, ed. C. H. Talbot, *SSSOC* i (Rome, 1952), p. 134f.
42. This concept of 'substitution and exchange' is a central preoccupation of the novels and other writings of the Anglican lay theologian, Charles Williams (1886–1945). See especially his 'The Way of Exchange' in *The Image of the City* and Other Essays, selected by A. Ridler with a Critical Introduction (Oxford, 1958), pp. 147ff.

43. ET, *Sermons on the Final Verses of the Song of Songs*, tr. W. M. Beckett, CP (Kalamazoo, 1977).
44. Sermon 1, 17; ET, *Sermons on the Christian Year*, tr. Hugh McCaffery, CP (Kalamazoo, 1979), p. 7.
45. Ibid., *Serm.* ii, 1, p. 11.
46. Ibid., ii, 6, pp. 12f.
47. Ibid., ii, 7, p. 13. Cf. Juvenal, *Satires*, x, 22. Isaac himself spent the last years of his life in radical poverty and austerity on the island of Ré.
48. Ibid., ii, 12, p. 14.
49. Ibid., *Serm.* x, 4f, p. 85.
50. Ibid., x, 6, p. 85.
51. See J. Leclercq, *Études sur le vocabulaire monastique du Moyen Âge* (Rome, 1961), pp. 39ff.
52. Isaac of Stella, op. cit. (n. 49), x, 7, p. 85.
53. Ibid., x, 8, p. 86.
54. *Serm. 3 in Nat.* iv; Leclercq and Rochais (Rome, 1966), p. 260.
55. Cited in R. C. Zaehner, *Our Savage God* (London, 1974), p. 303f.
56. Knowles, op. cit. (n. 39), p. 252f.
57. See J. Leclercq, *Nouveau visage de Bernard de Clairvaux*. Approches psycho-historiques (Paris, 1976), *passim*.
58. Louis Bouyer, *The Cistercian Heritage*, ET, E. A. Livingstone (London, 1958), p. 29.

CHAPTER 6 (pp. 80–103)

1. See E. Welsford, op. cit. (ch. 1, n. 1), p. 115f. The most comprehensive study of the medieval fools remains Sir E. K. Chambers, *The Medieval Stage*, 2 vols (Oxford, 1903), especially, vol. i, pp. 274ff.
2. Welsford, op. cit., p. 114.
3. See Chambers, op. cit., vol. i, pp. 274ff.
4. Welsford, op. cit., p. 119.
5. *Summa theologiae*, iia iiae 46, 1, ad 2; ET, vol. xxv, tr. T. R. Heath (London, 1972), p. 182.
6. Ibid., p. 176.
7. Ibid., p. 194.
8. G. K. Chesterton, *St Thomas Aquinas* (London, 1933), p. 25.
9. *Summa*, ia, 1, 6, ad 2; ET, vol. i, tr. T. Gilby (London, 1964), p. 23.
10. *Processus canonizationis Neapoli*, lxxix; *Fontes Vitae S. Thomae Aquinatis*, ed. D. Prümmer (Toulouse, 1912ff), p. 376f. See J. A. Weisheipl, *Friar Thomas d'Aquino. His Life, Thought and Works* (Oxford, 1974), pp. 320ff.
11. See E. Colledge, 'The Legend of St Thomas Aquinas', *Commemorative Studies*, Pontifical Institute of Medieval Studies (Toronto, 1974).
12. J. Pieper, *The Silence of St Thomas*, ET (London, 1957), p. 45.
13. Bernard Guido, *Vita* xli; *Fontes* (n. 10), p. 206.
14. See J. R. H. Moorman, *The Sources for the Life of St Francis* (Manchester, 1940).

15. *Speculum perfectionis* xciii; ed. P. Sabatier, vol. i (Manchester, 1928), p. 270f; ET, L. Sherley-Price in *St Francis of Assisi, His Life and Writings* (London, 1959).
16. *Fioretti* viii; ET, S. Hughes, *The Little Flowers of St Francis* (New York, 1964), p. 63f.
17. The story of how the 'glorious wounds of the Blessed Christ came to St Francis' is told in the 'Five Considerations on the Stigmata of St Francis'. See Hughes, op. cit., pp. 149ff.
18. *Fioretti* xxx; p. 107f.
19. *Speculum perfectionis* lxviii; i, p. 196f.
20. Ibid., p. 197n.
21. See M. D. Lambert, *Franciscan Poverty*. The Doctrine of the Absolute Poverty of Christ and the Apostles in the Franciscan Order, 1210–1323 (London, 1961).
22. *Ep.* i; *Opuscula Sancti Patris Francisci Assisiensis*, ed. K. Esser (Grottaferrata, 1978), p. 121.
23. *Speculum perfectionis* xcv; p. 274f.
24. Ibid., c; p. 289f.
25. On *ioculator* see Chambers, op. cit. (n. 1), vol. ii, pp. 230ff; J. D. A. Ogilvy, 'Mimi, Scurrae, Histriones: Entertainers of the Early Middle Ages', *Speculum* xxxviii (1963), 603ff; J. Leclercq, '"Ioculator et Saltator". S. Bernard et l'image du jongleur dans les manuscrits', in *Translatio Studii*. Manuscript and Library Studies honoring O. L. Kapsner OSB, ed. J. G. Plante (Collegeville, 1973), pp. 124ff.
26. Cicero, *Letters to Atticus*, iv, 16, 3; ed. D. R. Shackleton Bailey, vol. ii (Cambridge, 1965), p. 110.
27. *Middle English Dictionary*, ed. H. Kurath and S. M. Kuhn, vol. ii (Ann Arbor, 1954ff), p. 388.
28. Cited in H. Waddell, *The Wandering Scholars*, 7th revd edn (London, 1934), p. 246. Appendix E (pp. 244ff) lists Councils relating to the *clericus vagus* or *ioculator*.
29. On the *Ordo vagorum* see Waddell, op. cit., pp. 161ff.
30. J. Leclercq, op. cit. (n. 25), p. 131.
31. For Innocent's statement, see Waddell, op. cit., p. 261. For St Thomas's views, see *Summa*, iia, iiae, 168, 2 and 3.
32. Iacopone da Todi, *Laudi*, ed. F. Ageno (Florence, 1953), p. 341f. See E. Underhill, *Jacopone da Todi*. Poet and Mystic (1228–1306). A Spiritual Biography (London, Toronto and New York, 1919).
33. See E. A. Peers, *Ramón Lull*. A Biography (London, 1929). See also J. N. Hillgarth, *Ramón Lull and Lullism in Fourteenth-Century France* (Oxford, 1971).
34. ET, E. A. Peers (London, 1926).
35. *Blanquerna*, lxxix, 3.
36. Ibid., lxxxii, 6.
37. *The Book of the Lover and the Beloved*, liv; ET, E. A. Peers (London, 1945), p. 28.
38. Ibid., xii, p. 21.
39. E. A. Peers, *Fool of Love*. The Life of Ramón Lull (London, 1946),

p. 114.
40. F. Belcari, *The Life of Blessed Giovanni Colombini*, ET from the editions of 1541 and 1832 (London, 1874), p. 11.
41. Ibid., p. 14.
42. Ibid., p. 24.
43. Ibid., p. 67.
44. *The Vision of William concerning Piers the Plowman*, modern ET, J. F. Goodridge, Penguin Classics, 1966, p. 164f.
45. Ed. and tr. C. Kirchberger under the title *The Goad of Love* (London, 1952), p. 212f. See D. Knowles, *The English Mystical Tradition* (London, 1961), pp. 100ff.
46. Op. cit., ET, Betty Radice, Penguin Classics, 1971, p. 61.
47. 'To the English Martyrs', *Poetical Works* (London, 1913), p. 284f.
48. T. Stapleton, *The Life and Illustrious Martyrdom of St Thomas More*. In the translation of P. E. Hallett, ed. E. E. Reynolds (London, 1966), p. 121.
49. Ibid., p. 128.
50. Cited in R. W. Chambers, *Thomas More* (London, 1938), p. 311.
51. *The Correspondence of St Thomas More*, ed. E. F. Rogers (Princeton, 1947), p. 564.
52. *The Mirror of Vertue in Worldly Greatness or the Life of Sir Thomas More Knight by William Roper*, revd edn of Singer's modernized text (London, 1903), p. 176.
53. Ibid., p. 99.
54. For the details of St Philip's life, see the excellent modern study by L. Ponnelle and L. Bordet, *St Philip Neri and the Roman Society of His Time*, ET (London, 1932).
55. Ibid., p. 59f.
56. F. W. Faber, *Hymns*, revd edn (London, 1867), p. 237.
57. Cited in D. Knowles, *The Religious Orders in England*, vol. iii, The Tudor Age (Cambridge, 1959), p. 327.
58. *A Dialogue against light lewde and lasciuious dauncing: Wherin are refuted all those reasons which the common people use to bring in defence thereof* (London, 1582): no pagination.
59. Welsford, op. cit. (ch. 1, n. 1), p. 193.
60. 'L'énonciation mystique', *RSR* lxiv (1976), 189f.
61. *Herrlichkeit*, op. cit. (ch. 2, n. 18), p. 519.
62. Cervantes, *Don Quijote de la Mancha*, ET, J. M. Cohen, Penguin Classics, 1950, p. 939.

CHAPTER 7 (pp. 104–117)

1. *De sublimitate perfectionis religiosae* xxiv; *Opera omnia ascetica* (Ingolstadt, 1732), p. 537.
2. For details of St Ignatius's early life, see his *Autobiografia*, ET, J. F. O'Callaghan (New York, 1974). On Jesuit spirituality in general, see

J. de Guibert, *La Spiritualité de la compagnie de Jésus.* Esquisse historique (Rome, 1953); ET (Chicago, 1964). On *caritas discreta* see H. Rahner, *St Ignace de Loyola et la genèse des Exercices* (Toulouse, 1948), *passim.*

3. St Ignatius Loyola, *The Constitutions of the Society of Jesus*, ET, G. E. Ganss (St Louis, 1970), p. 107.
4. *Spiritual Exercises* 167; ET, T. Corbishley (London, 1963), pp. 59ff.
5. H. Bremond, *Histoire littéraire du sentiment religieux en France.* Depuis la fin des guerres de religion jusqu'à nos jours, vol. v (Paris, 1923), p. 4. See the important article on Lallemant by G. Bottereau in *DS* ix, 125ff.
6. *La Vie et la doctrine spirituelle du Père Louis Lallemant*, ed. F. Courel (Paris, 1959), p. 99; ET, *The Spiritual Teaching of Father Louis Lallemant*, ed. and tr. A. G. McDougall (London, 1928).
7. See A. Pottier, *Le Père Pierre Champion.* L'évangéliste du Père Louis Lallemant et de son école au xviie siècle (Paris, 1938).
8. Courel, op. cit. (n. 6), p. 41.
9. Ibid., p. 70f.
10. Ibid., p. 59.
11. Bremond, op. cit. (n. 5), p. 10.
12. Courel, op. cit., p. 61.
13. On Álvarez's doctrine and practice of prayer, see the *Life* by Luís de la Puente, ET, vol. i (London, 1868), pp. 141ff.
14. Courel, op. cit., Introduction, p. 17.
15. A. Pottier, *Le P. Louis Lallemant et les grands spirituels de son temps*, vol. i (Paris, 1927), pp. 298ff.
16. Op. cit. (n. 4), 254, p. 84.
17. See K. Ware, *The Power of the Name.* The Jesus Prayer in Orthodox Spirituality (Fairacres Publication, Oxford, 1974), p. 15.
18. ET, *Complete Works*, ed. and tr. E. A. Peers vol. ii (London, 1946), p. 128.
19. Ibid., p. 130.
20. Ibid., xxv, 1, p. 104.
21. V. Larrañaga, *San Ignacio de Loyola.* Estudios sobre su vida, sus obras, su espiritualidad (Zaragoza, 1959), p. 313f.
22. ET, *Complete Works*, ed. and tr. E. A. Peers, vol. i (London, 1934), p. 92f.
23. Op. cit. (n. 18), pp. 72ff.
24. *Interior Castle*, op. cit. (n. 18), p. 301.
25. *Spiritual Canticle*, op. cit. (n. 22), vol. ii, p. 333.
26. See *Constitutions*, op. cit. (n. 3), p. 233f.
27. Courel, op. cit., p. 126.
28. Ibid., p. 110.
29. Ibid., p. 90.
30. Ibid., p. 177.
31. V. Zander, *St Seraphim of Sarov*, ET (London, 1975), p. 85.
32. Courel, op. cit., p. 197.
33. Ibid., p. 198 (my italics).
34. Ibid., p. 99.

CHAPTER 8 (pp. 118–146)

1. The onset of schizophrenia is usually in adolescence 'but occasionally in the fourth decade or later' and is characterized by 'extreme alterations in behaviour, varying from stupor to excitement' (W. L. Linford Rees, *A Short Textbook of Psychiatry* (London, 1976), p. 170). See also Abbé Penido's penetrating study, 'Grâce et Folie, à propos du P. Surin', *Études Carmélitaines* i (1939), 172ff; and E. Costa, 'La Tromperie, ou le problème de la communication chez Surin. Notes sur quelques textes de la "Science expérimentale"', *RAM* xliv (1968), 413ff.

2. *L'Homme de Dieu en la personne du R. P. Jean-Joseph Surin, de la Compagnie de Jésus*, H.-M. Boudon, *Oeuvres complètes*, ed. J. P. Migne, vol. iii (Paris, 1856), p. 59.

3. Letter of mid-March 1661 to Mère Jeanne des Anges (Letter 356); *Correspondance*, ed. M. de Certeau (Paris, 1966), p. 1084.

4. *La Science expérimentale des choses de l'autre vie* iii, 6; ed. L. Michel and F. Cavallera in *Lettres spirituelles du P. Jean-Joseph Surin*, vol. ii (Toulouse, 1928), p. 101.

5. On the trial of Grandier, see J. Texier, 'Les procès d'Urbain Grandier', unpublished thesis (Poitiers, 1953).

6. Surin, *Science expérimentale*, i, 1; cited by de Certeau, op. cit. (n. 3), p. 243.

7. *Correspondance*, p. 8244f.

8. 'Triomphe de l'amour divin sur les puissances de l'enfer en la possession de la Mère Supérieure des Ursulines de Loudun exorcisée par le R. P. Jean-Joseph Surin', iii; Archives SJ, Chantilly, MS 231a, fos 20ff; cited, *Correspondance*, p. 251.

9. Letter 52; *Correspondance*, pp. 263ff.

10. R. D. Laing has described this as a 'false-self system' (*The Divided Self. An Existential Study in Sanity and Madness* (Harmondsworth, 1965), p. 75f).

11. On the understanding of mind and body in early seventeenth-century France, see R. Mandrous, *Introduction à la France moderne (1500–1640)*. Essai de Psychologie historique (Paris, 1961), pp. 68ff.

12. 'Triomphe de l'amour divin', ii; fos 267ff; cited, *Correspondance*, p. 423f.

13. *Science expérimentale* ii, 4; op. cit. (n. 4), p. 14f.

14. Ibid., 12, pp. 51ff.

15. On the controversy between P. Bastide and Surin, see Michel and Cavellera, ibid., vol. i, pp. 437ff.

16. *Science expérimentale* ii, 15, p. 67.

17. M. de Certeau, 'Jean-Joseph Surin', in *Spirituality Through the Centuries*, ed. J. Walsh (London, 1964), p. 295. See also Père de Certeau's important article on 'Les Oeuvres de J.-J. Surin. Histoire des textes', *RAM* xi (1964), 444ff.

18. Archimandrite Sophrony, *The Monk of Mount Athos. Staretz Silouan 1886–1938* (London and Oxford, 1973), p. 117f.

19. See for example, T. S. Szasz, *The Myth of Mental Illness. Foundations of a Theory of Personal Conduct*, revd. edn. (New York, 1974).

20. Toulouse, Archives SJ, MS; cited in *Correspondance*, pp. 481ff.
21. Ibid., p. 483.
22. Ibid., p. 481.
23. Letter 321; *Correspondance*, p. 1001f.
24. Letter 320; ibid., p. 996.
25. See M. de Certeau, 'Jean-Joseph Surin, interprète de Saint Jean de la Croix', *RAM* xlvi (1970), 45ff.
26. Letter 483, to M. du Sault; *Correspondance*, p. 1423.
27. A. Vermeylen, *Sainte Thérèse en France au xviie siècle, 1600–1660* (Louvain, 1958), pp. 280ff.
28. Letter 484 to Mère Madeleine du Saint Sacrement, carmelite; *Correspondance*, p. 1425f.
29. *L'Homme de Dieu*, op. cit. (n. 2), p. 72.
30. *The Life of St Teresa*, ed. and tr. J. M. Cohen, Penguin Classics, 1957, p. 115.
31. Ibid., pp. 112, 114.
32. Ibid., p. 115f.
33. Letter 426; *Correspondance*, p. 1266f.
34. Ibid., p. 1269.
35. The definitive study of this letter is M. de Certeau, 'L'illettré éclairé dans l'histoire de la lettre de Surin sur le Jeune Homme du Coche (1630)', *RAM* xliv (1968). See also Bremond, *Histoire littéraire*, vol. v, p. 118f. Here the episode is directly linked with the revival of lay spirituality in Brittany.
36. Letter 18; *Correspondance*, p. 140.
37. Ibid., p. 142.
38. De Certeau, op. cit. (n. 35), p. 405.
39. Letter 184; *Oeuvres complètes*, vol. iii, op. cit. (n. 2), p. 1024f.
40. De Certeau, op. cit. (n. 35), p. 411.
41. Letter 49; *Correspondance*, p. 257.
42. Letter 131; ibid., p. 403.
43. Letter 172; ibid., p. 600.
44. *Catéchisme spirituel, contenant les principaux moyens d'arriver à la perfection* (Paris, 1683), p. 575.
45. Letter 336; *Correspondance*, p. 1039.
46. Letter 341; ibid., p. 1048.
47. Letter 443; ibid., p. 1314f.
48. *Cantiques spirituels* (Paris, 1660), p. 26.
49. Letter 50; *Correspondance*, p. 258.
50. Letter 20, to Père Achille Doni d'Attichy, 7 June 1631; ibid., p. 152.
51. Cf. P. Caraman, *The Lost Paradise. An account of the Jesuits in Paraguay 1607–1768* (London, 1975), *passim*.
52. 'L'Amour enivrant', *Poésies spirituelles suivies des Contrats spirituels*, ed. E. Catta (Paris, 1957), p. 118.
53. Letter 45, to Père Achille Doni d'Attichy; *Correspondance*, p. 235.
54. Letter 207; ibid., p. 700.
55. Ibid., p. 702.
56. Letter 530, of 7 April 1664; ibid., p. 1532.

57. Letter 363; ibid., p. 1103.
58. Letter 319, to Père Antoine Blanchard, October 160; ibid., p. 994f.
59. G. K. Chesterton, *The Catholic Church and Conversion*, new edn (London, 1960), p. 103.
60. Letter 380, to Mère Jeanne de la Conception, June 1661; *Correspondance*, p. 1139.
61. Letter 427; ibid., p. 1279.
62. Letter 428; ibid., p. 1281f.
63. *Cantiques spirituels* op. cit. (n. 48), p. 20; *Correspondance*, p. 1279.
64. Letter 206, New Year 1659; ibid., p. 696f. It would seem that Surin's irony was misinterpreted; Mère Françoise assumed the Father was commending her style (Letter 256; ibid., p. 841). By the end of the year there was some improvement (Letter 274; ibid., p. 880). But, by April 1660, Surin is again speaking of *ce style de roman qui paraît dans vos lettres* (Letter 298; ibid., p. 942).
65. Letter 455, to Madame de Barrière, 26 May 1662; ibid., p. 1355.
66. Letter 520, to Mère Jeanne; ibid., p. 1507.
67. Letter 573, to Mère Jeanne; ibid., p. 1641.
68. Letter 380, to Mère Jeanne de la Conception; ibid., p. 1139f.

CHAPTER 9 (pp. 147–184)

1. Bremond, *Histoire Littéraire*, vol. v, p. 70.
2. Ibid., p. 120.
3. For details of his life, see P. Champion, *La Vie du P. Jean Rigoleuc de la Compagnie de Jésus*. Avec ses traités de dévotion, et ses lettres spirituelles (Paris, 1686); mod. edn. P. Hamon (Paris, 1931). See also Bremond, op. cit., pp. 66ff.
4. Champion, op. cit., p. 409f.
5. Ibid., p. 98.
6. Ibid., p. 457f.
7. For details of Huby's life, see P. Champion, *La Vie des fondateurs des Maisons de la Retraite*. Monsieur de Kerlivio, Le Père Vincent Huby de la Compagnie de Jésus, et Mademoiselle de Francheville (Nantes, 1698); mod. edn. J. Bainvel (Paris, 1929). See also the excellent article in *DS* vii, 842ff.
8. See Champion, ibid., *passim*; and J. Héduit, *Catherine de Francheville, initiatrice et fondatrice des retraites de femmes*. Sa vie (1620–1689), son oeuvre: la retraite de Vannes, 2 vols (Tours, 1957).
9. Champion, ibid., p. 180.
10. *Motifs journaliers d'aimer Dieu* (Vannes, 1693), p. 117.
11. Ibid., p. 121.
12. Ibid., p. 165f.
13. *Apologie des Images*. Ou Peintures morales autrement dit des Tableaux; Bibl. Maz. MS, H 1752; ed. H. Watrigant (Paris, 1911), p. 27f.
14. *Les Images morales et leur explication* (Paris, 1675), *passim*. See H. Hosten, *Le P. Huby aux Indes* (Paris, 1911). On the 'enigmatic

tableaux', see J. Montagu, 'The Painted Enigma and French 17th Century Art', *Journal of the Warburg and Courtauld Institute* xxxi (1968), 307ff.

15. *Apologie des Images*, p. 31.
16. *Pratique de l'Amour de Dieu et de Notre-Seigneur Jésus Christ* (Paris, 1672); ed. J. Bainvel, vol. ii (Paris, 1931), p. 12.
17. *Méditations sur l'amour de Dieu* (Vannes, 1696), p. 260.
18. *Motifs journaliers*, p. 199.
19. *Oeuvres spirituelles*, ed. J. Lenoir-Duparc (Paris, 1864), p. 136f.
20. Ibid., p. 143.
21. Ibid., p. 141.
22. Op. cit. (n. 19), p. 238.
23. *Retraite*, p. 148.
24. Ibid., pp. 148ff.
25. 'Exercice de Piété sur le crucifix', *Oeuvres spirituelles*, p. 225.
26. Cited by Champion, op. cit. (n. 7), p. 146.
27. *Maximes spirituelles*; ed. J. Bainvel, vol. i (Paris, 1931), p. 119f.
28. Cited in L. Kerbirou, *Les Missions bretonnes*. L'oeuvre de Dom Michel Le Nobletz et du P. Maunoir (Brest, 1935), p. 36.
29. For an introduction to the history of Brittany, see J. Delumeau, *Histoire de la Bretagne* (Paris, 1969).
30. Kerbirou, op. cit., p. 15f.
31. P. Boschet, *Le parfait missionnaire,* ou La vie du R. P. Julien Maunoir de la Compagnie de Jésus, Missionnaire en Bretagne (Paris, 1697), p. 43.
32. For details of his life, see J. Maunoir, *La Vie du Vénérable Dom Michel Le Nobletz*; ed. H. Perennes (Saint-Brieuc, 1934); and A. Verjus, *La Vie de M. Le Nobletz,* Prestre et Missionnaire de Bretagne (Paris, 1666).
33. Cited in H. Le Gouvello, *Le Vénérable Michel Le Nobletz* (1577–1652) (Paris, 1898), p. 23.
34. Maunoir, op. cit. (n. 32), p. 87.
35. J. Sainsaulieu, *Études sur la vie érémitique en France de la Contre—Réforme à la restauration* (Paris thesis, 1973), p. 15.
36. Verjus, op. cit. (n. 32, second part).
37. Ibid., p. 406.
38. Ibid., p. 408f.
39. Maunoir, 'Vie de Michel Le Nobletz' (Kerdanet MS), i, 13.
40. Ibid., 17.
41. D. Gwenallt Jones, 'Pantycelyn', tr. R. Gerallt Jones in *Poetry of Wales (1930–1970)*, ed. R. Gerallt Jones (Llandysul, 1974), p. 111.
42. MS, Quimper diocesan archives; cited in Le Gouvello (n. 33), p. 213f.
43. Maunoir, *Vie*, ed. Perennes, pp. 255ff.
44. F. Renard, *Michel Le Nobletz et les missions bretonnes* (Paris, 1954), p. 331.
45. For a lively account of Le Nobletz's commissioning of Maunoir, see R. M. de la Chevasnerie, *Le 'Mad Tad'*. Vie du Bx. Julien Maunoir SJ (Paris, 1957), pp. 46ff. Other lives include P. Boschet, *Le parfait missionnaire* (n. 31); X.-A. Séjourné, *Histoire du vénérable serviteur de*

Dieu, Julien Maunoir de lat Compagnie de Jésus (Paris and Poitiers, 1895); P. d'Hérouville, *Le Vincent Ferrier du xviie siècle.* Le Vénérable Julien Maunoir (Paris, 1932).

46. This is the judgement of Renard, who thus interprets what Bremond calls a 'mysterious manuscript' passed on from the senior missionary to his successor (*Histoire littéraire*, vol. v, p. 88).

47. As an example of his conservatism is the part played in quelling the insurrection in Brittany in 1675. Père Boschet tells us that 'M. le duc . . . was very pleased with Père Maunoir and the other missionaries. He testified to the zeal they had shown on that occasion for the glory of God, the service of the King and the well-being of all Brittany' (*Le parfait missionnaire*, p. 306).

48. De la Chevasnerie, op. cit. (n. 45), p. 27.

49. The title of a book about Maunoir by an Anglican author, Canon G. H. Doble (Truro, 1926).

50. Séjourné, op. cit. (n. 45), p. 85f.

51. *Le Sacré Collège de Jésus divisé en cinq classes, où l'on enseigne en langue Armorique les leçons Chrétiennes avec les trois clefs pour y entrer, un Dictionnaire, une Grammaire et Syntaxe en même langue* (Quimper, 1659).

52. Maunoir follows the common Patristic view that there are as many languages in the world as there are generations descended from the children of Noah (*Le Sacré Collège de Jésus*, ibid., p. 10).

53. Ibid., p. 4.

54. Cited in Bremond, op. cit. (n. 1), p. 123f.

55. Ibid., p. 125f.

56. Une religieuse du monastère de Sainte-Ursule de Vannes (= Jeanne de la Nativité), *Le Triomphe de l'amour divin dans la vie d'une grande servante de Dieu nommée ARMELLE NICOLAS, décédée l'an de N.-S. 1671* (Vannes, 1676), p. 74f.

57. Bremond, op. cit., p. 127f.

58. Jeanne de la Nativité, op. cit., p. 172f.

59. Ibid., p. 177.

60. Jeanne de la Nativité, op. cit., 2nd edn (Vannes, 1707), p. 517.

61. Op. cit. (Bristol, 1772).

62. J.-F. de la Marche, *Abrégé des vies de Marie Dias, Marie-Amice Picard, et d'Armelle Nicolas dite la Bonne Armelle* (Nantes, 1761), pp. 115ff.

63. *Histoire de Catherine Daniélou. Morte en odeur de sainteté et inhumée dans l'église de Saint-Guen au diocèse de Saint-Brieuc d'après le Père Maunoir SJ*, ed. Abbé Perrot (Saint-Brieuc, 1913). The tradition of women mystics and holy idiots continued in Brittany into the eighteenth century. See P. Nicol, *Madeleine Morice. Une mystique bretonne au xviiie siècle* (Paris, 1922).

63. See J. Buléon and E. Le Garrec, *Yves Nicolazic. Le paysan, le voyant, le bâtisseur* (Abbéville, 1936). Yves, surprisingly for his day, was a weekly communicant.

64. Champion, *La Vie des fondateurs*, op. cit. (n. 7), p. 35.

65. C. Parcheminou, *Monsieur de Trémaria 1619–1674. En mission avec le*

Père Maunoir (Paris, 1937).

66. Père Dominique de Sainte Catherine, *Le grand pécheur converty*, représenté dans les deux estats de la Vie de Monsieur De Queriolet, Prestre, Conseiller au Parlement de Rennes (Lyon, 1690), preface.
67. Ibid., p. 284.
68. Ibid., p. 172f.
69. Our scanty knowledge of Guilloré's life comes from the Jesuit catalogues and archives. In the provincial archives in Paris there is a manuscript Life written by a Jesuit contemporary. The most reliable modern study of Guilloré's life and letters is by A. Klaas, 'Un grand spirituel du 17e siècle, Le Père François Guilloré SJ', *RAM* xviii (1937), 359ff. See also the article in *DS* vi, cols 1278ff.
70. See Klaas, op. cit. (previous note), p. 374.
71. See J. Maillard, *Le Triomphe de la pauvreté et des humiliations*. La vie de Mademoiselle de Bellère du Tronchay appellée communément Soeur Louise. Avec ses lettres (Paris, 1732).
72. Ibid., p. 70.
73. Bremond, op. cit. (n. 1), p. 353.
74. Maillard, op. cit. (n. 71), p. 97f.
75. Ibid., p. 98.
76. Ibid., p. 89.
77. Ibid., p. 105f.
78. See R. D. Laing, *The Divided Self* (Harmondsworth, 1965), p. 163.
79. Guilloré, op. cit. (Paris, 1673).
80. Ibid., dedication, ii.
81. Ibid., p. 5.
82. 'La manière de conduire les âmes dans la vie spirituelle', iii; *Oeuvres spirituelles* (Paris, 1684), p. 819.
83. Cf. *Conférences spirituelles*, vol. i (*pour bien mourir à soi-même*) (Paris, 1683), pp. 201ff.
84. Ibid., vol. ii (*pour bien aimer Jésus*), 2nd. edn. (Paris, 1689), p. 473.
85. Ibid., p. 482f.

EXCURSUS TO CHAPTER 9

1. See the article on Boudon in *DS* i, 1887ff; and L. d'Appilly, *H. M. Boudon, ou La folie de la croix* (Paris, 1863).
2. Letter 4, *Oeuvres complètes*, ed. J. P. Migne, vol. iii (Paris, 1856), p. 794.
3. Letter 36; ibid., p. 834f.
4. *Oeuvres complètes* i, 4, vol. ii, p. 386.
5. BN, MS Fr. 25174, fo. 132.
6. *La Règne de Dieu en l'oraison mentale*, ii, 10, *Oeuvres complètes*, vol. i, p. 741f.
7. Letter 296; ibid., vol. iii, col. 1240. St John of God (1495–1550) was converted to a life of great sanctity by St John of Avila (1500–1569), the 'Apostle of Andalusia'. Immediately after his conversion he ran round

Granada tearing his hair, beating his chest and pleading for mercy, behaviour which caused him to be admitted to a lunatic asylum. After a further interview with St John of Avila, however, he decided to channel his enthusiasm into the service of the sick and poor and founded the Brothers Hospitallers for that purpose (*AA.SS*, Mar. i (1668), pp. 814ff).

8. Letter 327; ibid., 1291.

CHAPTER 10 (pp. 185–196)

1. J. Delumeau, *Catholicism between Luther and Voltaire*. A New View of the Counter-Reformation, ET (London, 1977), p. 38.
2. H. H. Martin, *Livre, pouvoirs et société en Paris au xviie siècle*, vol. i (Paris 1969), pp. 76ff.
3. See, among recent works, S. Mours, *Le Protestantisme en France au XVIIe siècle* (1598–1685) (Paris, 1967); and A. Adam, *Du Mysticisme à la révolte*. Les Jansénistes du xviie siècle (Paris, 1968).
4. Cited in E. Welsford, *The Fool*. His Social and Literary History (London, 1935), p. 192.
5. The verdict of Father Faber in the preface to his translation of Montfort's *Treatise on The True Devotion to the Blessed Virgin*, ET (London, 1863), p. vi.
6. Cited by A Secular Priest, *Life and Select Writings of the Venerable Servant of God, Louis-Marie Grignion de Montfort* (London, 1870), p. cvii.
7. Canticle 1, 10, *Oeuvres complètes*, ed. M. Gendrot et al. (Paris, 1966), p. 1243.
8. Canticle lv, 18, ibid., p. 1253.
9. *L'Amour de la sagesse éternelle* i, 11f, ibid., p. 98.
10. Ibid., xiv, 174, p. 185.
11. Canticle xvii; *Oeuvres complètes*, pp. 1452–5.
12. *Règles des missionnaires de la compagnie de Marie*, xxxviif; ibid., p. 699f.
13. Canticle xxiv, 7; ibid., p. 1165.
14. Canticle clxii, 2ff, ibid., pp. 1663ff.
15. A Secular Priest, op. cit. (n. 6), p. 275f.
16. *Traité de la vraie dévotion à la sainte Vierge* lxi; *Oeuvres complètes*, op. cit., p. 527.
17. *L'Amour de la sagesse éternelle* xiv, 174; ibid., p. 185f.
18. Canticle lvii, 1, p. 1256.
19. Canticle xcvii, 1, p. 1392.
20. Ibid., pp. 1392–3.
21. *Traité* clvii, ibid., p. 586.
22. Ibid., ccvlvif, p. 652.
23. Canticle xvii 17, 14f, p. 1004f.
24. See my article 'Maximilian—The Fool of Love', *Christian* iii (1976), pp. 123ff.
25. *L'Amour de la sagesse éternelle* vi, 70; *Oeuvres complètes*, p. 128.

CHAPTER 11 (pp. 197–211)

1. A. M. Wilson, 'Une partie inédite de la lettre de Diderot à Voltaire, le 11 juin 1749', *Rev. d'hist. litt. de la France* li (1951), 259.
2. C. Vereker, *Eighteenth-Century Optimism*. A Study of the Inter-relations of Moral and Social Theory in English Thought between 1689 and 1789 (Liverpool, 1967), p. 19.
3. *Encyclopédie*, ou Dictionnaire raisonné des sciences, des arts et des métiers par une société des gens des lettres, mis en ordre et publié par Mr. ***, vol. xv (Neuchâtel, 1765), p. 105f.
4. The earliest life is by Labre's confessor, G. L. Marconi, *Ragguaglio della vita del servo di Dio, Benedetto Labre Francese* (Rome, 1783). An abridged edition was published in ET in Wigan in 1786. Reference will also be made below to A. M. Coltrato's *Life of the Venerable Servant of God, Benedict-Joseph Labre*, ET (London, 1850); and F. Gaquère, *Le Saint Pauvre de Jésus-Christ, Benoît-Joseph Labre* (Avignon, 1936).
5. Gaquère, op. cit. (previous note), p. 18.
6. See the chapter on 'Begging, Vagrancy and the Law' in O. H. Hufton, *The Poor of Eighteenth-Century France* (Oxford, 1974), pp. 219ff.
7. Coltrato, op. cit. (n. 4), p. 105.
8. Ibid., p. 262.
9. Marconi, op. cit. (n. 4), p. 67.
10. Coltrato, op. cit., p. 228f.
11. Ibid., p. 161f.
12. Ibid., p. 210.
13. Gaquère, op. cit. (n. 4), p. 69f.
14. See M. Hill, *The Religious Order*. A study of virtuoso religion and its legitimation in the nineteenth-century Church of England (London, 1973), pp. 85ff and *passim*. See also A. M. Allchin, *The Silent Rebellion*. Anglican Religious Communities 1845–1900 (London, 1958).
15. Letter of 30 August 1844; Liddon Bound Volume (LBV), ETP to JHN, iv.
16. The effects of his wife's death on Pusey's spiritual and mental state have been insensitively discussed by G. Faber, *Oxford Apostles*. A Character Study of the Oxford Movement (London, 1933), p. 399f.
17. According to a letter from Ilfracombe of that date; LBV, EBP to JHN, iv.
18. Pusey House MS; without number.
19. Letter of 7 February 1845; Pusey House MS, LBV, EBP to Dr Hook.
20. Particularly after the death of Lucy. See H. P. Liddon, *Life of Edward Bouverie Pusey*, vol. ii (1836–1846) (London, 1893), p. 388f.
21. *Foundations*, preface, p. cl.
22. Ibid., p. li.
23. Pusey House MS, LBV, EBP to JK, i.
24. Liddon, op. cit. (n. 20), vol. ii (London, 1894), p. 96.
25. Pusey House MS; LBV, EBP to JK, i; cited in Liddon, op. cit., p. 96f.
26. *Foundations*, preface, p. xx.
27. Ibid., p. 176.

28. Ibid., preface, p. li.
29. See Keith Thomas, 'The Place of Laughter in Tudor and Stuart England', *Times Literary Supplement*, 21 January 1977, 77f.
30. J. F. Cassidy, *Matt Talbot. The Irish Workers' Glory* (Dublin, 1934). See also M. Purcell, *Matt Talbot and His Times*. A new edn (Alcester and Dublin, 1976).
31. J. A. Glynn, *Life of Matt Talbot* (Dublin, 1928), p. 45.
32. Purcell, op. cit., p. 213.
33. Ibid., pp. 145ff.
34. Unpublished manuscript.
35. Sainte Thérèse de l'Enfant Jésus, *Manuscrits autobiographiques* (Lisieux, 1956), MS, A, fo. 82.

CONCLUSION: *Perfect Fools*

1. *Complete Works*, ed. and tr. E. A. Peers, vol. ii (London, 1934), p. 308.
2. Ibid., p. 50.
3. *Summa theologiae* iiia, 7, 4, ad 2; ET, vol. xlix, tr. L. Walsh.
4. R. A. Knox, *Enthusiasm. A Chapter in the History of Religion with Special Reference to the 17th and 18th Centuries* (Oxford, 1950), *passim*.
5. Hans Urs von Balthasar, *Herrlichkeit. Eine theologische Ästhetik*, Band i (Einsiedeln, 1961), p. 30.
6. Ibid., p. 72.
7. See J. Coulson, *Newman and the Common Tradition. A Study in the Language of Church and Society* (Oxford, 1970), pp. 58ff.
8. See, for example, V. Lossky, *The Mystical Theology of the Eastern Church*, ET (London, 1957), chs. vii and viii.
9. 'Dogmatic Constitution on the Church', 12; *Vatican Council II. The Conciliar and Post-Conciliar Documents*, ed. and tr. A. Flannery (Dublin, 1975), p. 363f.
10. A. Farrer, 'Walking Sacraments', *A Celebration of Faith* (London, 1970), p. 111.
11. Von Balthasar, *Elucidations*, ET (London, 1975), p. 103. See also his *Der antirömische Affekt. Wie lässt sich das Papsttum in der Gesamtkirche integrieren* (Freiburg-im-Breisgau, 1974), *passim*.

Index

Guerric of Igny, 63–5
Guibert, J. de, 233 n. 2
Guilcher, François [Le Su], 165
Guilloré, François, S.J., 174–82, 186, 204, 239 nn. 69, 70, 79–81

Hall, Edward, 96
Hauptmann, P., 28
Hayneufve, Julien, S.J., 174
hermits 12–16, ch. 4 *passim*, 157–9
Hérouville, P. d', 238 n. 45
Hesychasm, 111
hilaritas, 48, 50, 86, 101, 215
Hill, M., 241 n. 14
Hillgarth, J. N., 33, 231 n. 33
Hilton, Walter, 95, 100
Hook, W. F., 204
Huby, Vincent, S.J., 108, 109, 141, 148–54, 164, 170, 174, 204, 236 nn. 7, 14
Hughes, K., 224 n. 4, 225 n. 29
Hume, David, 197

Iacopone da Todi, 88–9
idiocy, holy, 12–13, 53, 65–8, 135–6, 167–73
Ignatius Loyola, St, 104, 105–7, 112, 140–1, 179, 207, 232 n. 2, 233 nn. 3, 4
Innocent IV, Pope, 88
ioculator, jester, 58–60, 87–9, 231 n. 25
iocunditas, 48, 86, 215
Ireland, ch. 3 *passim*, 161, 197, 208–11
Irenaeus, St, 10, 63, 221 n. 16
Isaac of Stella, Blessed, 74–6, 230 nn. 47–50, 52, 53
Isaac Zatvornik, St, 22
Isabelle des Anges, Mère, 119, 131
Isidora, St, 15–16, 222 n. 8
Isidore of Seville, St, 33, 110, 224 n. 6
Ivan the Hairy, 226 n. 59
Ivan the Terrible, Tsar, 23

Jackson, K., 225 n. 33
Jansenism, 185
Jarmon, A. O. H., 225 n. 33
Jeanne des Anges, Mère, 120–4, 143, 234 nn. 3, 8, 236 nn. 66, 67
Jeanne de la Conception, Mère, 138, 236 nn. 60–2, 68
Jeanne de la Croix, Mère, 131
Jeanne de la Nativité, 168–9, 238 nn. 56, 58–60
Jeremias, J., 221 n. 13
Jerome, St, 110, 161

Jesuits (Society of Jesus), 6, chs. 7, 8, 9 *passim*
Jogues, St Isaac, S.J., 164
John of the Cross, St, 110, 112–14, 126, 131, 213–14
John of Ephesus, 18
John of Ford, 74
John of God, St, 184, 239–40, n. 7
John of Salisbury, 67
Joseph, St (Husband of Our Lady), 135
Joseph of Copertino, St, 93

Keble, John, 205
Kenney, J. F., 224 n. 3, 225 n. 21
Kerbirou, L., 237 nn. 28, 30
Kerlivio, Louis Eudo de, 149, 173, 236 n. 7
Kiev, 21, 22, 45
Kilian, St, 43
Knowles, David, 78, 229 n. 39, 232 n. 45
Knox, Ronald, 216, 242 n. 4
Kolbe, Blessed Maximilian, 195–6, 240 n. 24
Kologrivoff, I., 223 n. 33
Kovalevskii, I., 223 n. 26

Labre, St Benedict-Joseph, 186, 197–203, 214, 241 n. 4
Lacarrière, Jacques, 17
Lallemant, Louis, S.J., ch. 7 *passim*, 130–1, 138, 140–3, 145, 147, 149, 151, 168, 182, 185, 186, 233 nn. 5–10, 12, 14–16, 27–30, 32–4
Lambert, M. D., 231 n. 21
Landévennec, 155
Langland, William, 94–5, 99
Larrañaga, V., 112
Laurence Justinian, St, 110, 139
Leclercq, Jean, 44, 50, 52, 227 nn. 6, 11 15, 228 nn. 4, 5, 10, 11, 13, 229, nn. 22–4, 27, 31, 34, 35, 230 nn. 51, 57, 231 nn. 25, 30
Leo, Brother, 85
Leo the Great, Pope, St, 221 n. 17
Leontius of Neapolis, 19, 224 n. 8
Lérins, Island of, 32
'Livery of Christ', The, 6, 106–7, 112–13, 116–17, 140–3, 152–3, 168, 180–1
Loreto, 200
Lossky, V., 242 n. 8
Loudun, 118, 120–4